WITHDRAWN

THE JOHNS HOPKINS HISTORICAL PUBLICATIONS

LONDON: HUMPHREY MILFORD
OXFORD UNIVERSITY PRESS

TREATIES DEFEATED BY THE SENATE

A STUDY OF THE STRUGGLE BETWEEN PRESIDENT AND SENATE OVER THE CONDUCT OF FOREIGN RELATIONS

BY

W. STULL HOLT

Department of History
The Johns Hopkins University

BALTIMORE
THE JOHNS HOPKINS PRESS
1933

PRINTED IN THE UNITED STATES OF AMERICA
BY J. H. FURST COMPANY, BALTIMORE, MARYLAND

PREFACE

The charm of guessing ancient motives from the records of ancient deeds fascinated me—there is much in the pursuit to appeal to a gambler.
D. G. HOGARTH.[1]

Whipping a dead horse was ever a waste of effort, yet not more so, many people would maintain, than proving that senators are influenced by considerations alien to the merits of the questions on which they vote. Everyone knows that the Senate has sometimes rejected treaties for reasons that have nothing to do with the wisdom of the foreign policy presented. Everyone knows that these extraneous reasons can usually be traced either to the struggle between the President and Senate for the control of foreign policy or to the warfare of the President's political opponents who hope to secure some partisan advantage. Students have often noted that these considerations have been present and have contributed to the defeat of various treaties. But no attempt has hitherto been made to examine the circumstances attending the defeat of every treaty that failed of completion through the action of the Senate, in the hope of ascertaining which were lost either because of domestic politics or because of the contest between President and Senate.

Such an inquiry presents the problem of determining human motives which are always elusive even under the most favorable conditions of search. It is obvious that a senator whose vote is really cast as political considerations dictate would not say so publicly, but would find more creditable reasons for his action. In private letters to his friends and probably in his own thoughts he would not admit that anything but the merits of the question decided his vote. Conclusions must, therefore, be based either on deductions from his actions or on the evidence supplied by political opponents, who are often too ready to impute wrong

[1] *Accidents of an Antiquary's Life*, p. 2.

motives. Yet, if care is exercised, the use of such a method and of such material is permissible. Certainly, when all the senators of one party vote one way, and all the senators of the opposing party vote the other way, it is reasonable to attribute their action to politics.

No such guage is available to identify and measure the desire of senators to maintain or extend their share of the treaty-making power. Members of the Senate have frequently admitted that this motive determined their attitude towards a treaty, but it is not safe to accept their assertions without a careful examination of all the circumstances. Political opponents of the President desiring to defeat a treaty for political ends have often waged the fight under the guise of defending the constitutional prerogatives of the Senate. On the other hand, senators belonging to the same party as the President and not wishing to attack his policies have commonly left the defense of the Senate's treaty-making powers to the senators of the other party.

The situation is further obscured because the secret sessions of the Senate have prevented even the alleged reasons from being known in most instances. In short, the light available is little better than that of "a damn dim candle over a damn dark abyss."

TABLE OF CONTENTS

CHAPTER I

THE ORIGIN OF THE CONFLICT

Has not the famous political fable of the snake, with two heads and one body, some useful instruction contained in it? She was going to a brook to drink, and in her way was to pass through a hedge, a twig of which opposed her direct course; one head chose to go on the right side of the twig, the other on the left; so that time was spent in the contest, and before the decision was completed, the poor snake died with thirst.

BENJAMIN FRANKLIN.[1]

Is is possible that imperfect men can make a perfect constitution?

REV. MR. WEST in the Massachusetts convention.[2]

The fathers had intended to neutralize the energy of government and had succeeded, but their machine was never meant to do the work of a twenty-million horse-power society in the twentieth century, where much work needed to be quickly and efficiently done . . . bad machinery merely added to friction.

HENRY ADAMS.[3]

The struggle for the control of foreign policy, to which the President and the Senate of the United States are apparently condemned by the constitutional arrangement of the treaty-making power, has repeatedly caused dismayed witnesses to ponder the question of why the framers of the Constitution devised such a plan. The answer is not difficult to discover from the history of the provision of the Constitution saying that the President " shall have Power, by and with the Advice and Consent of the Senate, to make Treaties, provided two-thirds of the Senators present concur." [4] It was not one of the points

[1] John Bigelow, ed., *The Complete Works of Benjamin Franklin,* X, 188.

[2] Jonathan Elliott, ed., *The Debates in the Several State Conventions on the Adoption of the Federal Constitution,* II, 33.

[3] Henry Adams, *The Education of Henry Adams,* p. 375.

[4] The history of this provision in the convention has often been told but usually with little or no consideration of the reasons leading to those results. See especially, Samuel B. Crandall, *Treaties Their Making and Enforcement,* pp. 43-63; Charles H. Butler, *The Treaty-Making Power of the United States,* I, 285-392.

about which the struggle centered in those memorable debates and, consequently, it received little attention. The record, so faithfully kept by Madison, shows that the question of who was to make treaties for the new or reformed government was discussed on only three days.[5] These relatively short debates, for they occupied only a small part of each day, and an occasional remark made when discussing other matters constitute all that was said on the subject. But the little that was said in the convention, amplified by the statements of members of the convention in their respective state conventions and in their writings, is enough to make clear the reasons which led them to give the power of making treaties concurrently to the President and the Senate and to require a two-thirds majority of the Senate in exercising that power. Fully as interesting are some of the problems which they did not discuss or only barely mentioned, and yet which seem both important and inevitable in a distribution of the treaty-making power such as they were arranging, at least to those enjoying a retrospective view.

Of all branches of governmental activity the conduct of foreign relations was the one in which the Americans of 1787 had the least experience to guide them. Prior to 1776 it had been one of the burdens, or privileges, which Great Britain had assumed for them, and since that year the precariousness of their existence as an independent state or states and the brevity of the period both tended to prevent them from accumulating much experience in the making of treaties. They had not been bothered by the question of whether the treaty-making power was executive or legislative or by contests between the two departments over the control of that power, for under the Articles of Confederation Congress was both legislature and executive. One thing in respect to treaties which their brief experience had shown them needed correction was that treaties could be violated too easily under the Confederation, and this, as Madison stated, "must involve us in the calamities of foreign wars."[6]

[5] August 23, September 7 and 8.

[6] He goes on to say "The files of Congs. contain complaints already, from

Thus it was natural that, at first, no one contemplated changes from the existing arrangements in regard to treaties except to secure their better observance. The resolutions embodying what has come to be known as the "Virginia plan" say nothing as to how treaties should be made. Nevertheless it is apparent from the subsequent proceedings that the men who drafted this plan expected that the practice under the Confederation would be continued and that this power would be exercised by Congress or by one of the two houses Congress would now have.[7] Certainly this was the intent of the men who prepared the "New Jersey plan."[8] A radically different method was proposed in the plan which Hamilton submitted to the convention. Under it treaties would be made by the supreme executive authority "with the advice and approbation of the Senate."[9] But Hamilton's plan was not seriously considered and its details were not discussed at all. The result was that when the first draft of the Constitution was reported to the convention on August 6 by the Committee of Detail, the original views of the convention on the proper way to make treaties were faithfully expressed in the first section of the ninth article which read "The Senate of the United States shall have power to make treaties, and to appoint Ambassadors, and Judges of the Supreme Court."[10]

By this time the members of the convention had effected the great compromise which made the Constitution possible by giving the states equal representation in the Senate and representation according to population in the House of Representatives. All subsequent decisions were reached in the

almost every nation with which treaties have been formed. Hitherto indulgence has been shewn to us. This cannot be the permanent disposition of foreign nations." Max Farrand, ed., *The Records of the Federal Convention of 1787,* I, 316.

[7] *Ibid.*, pp. 20-22.

[8] The second of the resolutions introduced by Patterson read, "Resd. that in addition to the powers vested in the U. States in Congress, by the present existing articles of Confederation, they be authorized. . . . *Ibid.*, p. 243.

[9] *Ibid.*, p. 292.

[10] *Ibid.*, II, 183.

light of this settlement and its influence on the location of the treaty-making power can be easily seen. When, on August 23, the ninth article came before the convention for discussion it was immediately attacked. The first comment was by Madison who "observed that the Senate represented the States alone, and that for this as well as other obvious reasons it was proper that the President should be an agent in treaties." [11] He was immediately followed by Gouverneur Morris, a representative from a large state and a leader in the fights for a strong executive and a national government, who "did not know that he should agree to refer the making of Treaties to the Senate at all, but for the present wd. move to add as an amendment to the section, after 'Treaties'—'but no Treaty shall be binding on the U. S. which is not ratified by a law.'" [12] Both these remarks show the desire to reduce the special powers of the Senate, as the representative of the states as states, in favor of the more national House of Representatives and President, both of whom would be more under the influence of the large states.[13] Others joined in the discussion, expressing their views chiefly on the question of whether a ratified treaty is of its own force the law of the land. After the amendment put forward by Morris was defeated by a vote of eight to one no other action was taken and the provision was referred back to a committee because, as Randolph remarked, nearly every speaker made some objection to it.[14]

The subject next came before the convention in a report on September 4 from the Committee of Eleven which had been created to consider all unfinished business. On that date, after

[11] *Ibid.*, p. 392. Even before the article came before the convention an expression of dissatisfaction with it was made by Mercer who remarked incidentally that "the Senate ought not to have the power of Treaties. This power belonged to the Executive department." *Ibid.*, p. 297.

[12] *Ibid.*, p. 392.

[13] Charles C. Thach, "The Creation of the Presidency, 1775-1789," in *Johns Hopkins University Studies,* XL, No. 4, p. 128.

[14] Ferrand, *Records,* II, 393-394.

the convention had been in session over three months and within two weeks of its close, the executive was for the first time made a participant in the treaty-making power. Their report said, "The President by and with the advice and Consent of the Senate, shall have power to make Treaties; . . . But no Treaty shall be made without the consent of two-thirds of the members present." [15] This solution was discussed in the convention on September 7 and 8. Although several amendments were offered, none was finally accepted and the provision appeared in the final draft of the Constitution with only a slight change in style.[16]

If, on the one hand, the large state men, the strong executive men, and the nationalists did not want the Senate alone to have the treaty-making power, on the other hand the insistence of the men from the small states and the prevailing distrust of executives precluded the possibility of giving it to the President alone. Charles Cotesworth Pinckney, in expounding to the South Carolina convention the decisions of the Federal Convention on the subject, said that a few members had desired to give this power to the President, but "political caution and republican jealousy rendered it improper for us to vest it in the President alone." [17] In the North Carolina convention Davie, who had also been a member of the Federal Convention, explained why the power of making treaties, which was in the executive department in all countries, had not been given to the President. He stated that the extreme jealousy of the little states and between the commercial states and the non-importing states "made it indispensable to give to the senators, as representatives of states, the power of making, or rather ratifying, treaties. Although it militates against every idea of

[15] *Ibid.*, pp. 498-499.

[16] "It was evident that the convention was growing tired. The committee had recommended that the power of appointment and the making of treaties be taken from the senate and vested in the president 'by and with the advice and consent of the senate.' With surprising unanimity and surprisingly little debate, these important changes were agreed to." Max Farrand, *The Framing of the Constitution of the United States*, p. 171.

[17] Elliot, *Debates*, IV, 265.

just proportion that the little state of Rhode Island should have the same suffrage with Virginia, or the great commonwealth of Massachusetts, yet the small states would not consent to confederate without an equal voice in the formation of treaties. . . . Every man was convinced of the inflexibility of the little states in this point." [18]

The possibility of permitting the House of Representatives to share in the treaty-making power was also considered. No proposal to give the power to the House of Representatives alone is recorded, and almost certainly none was made; but there were two attempts in the convention to include the House with the Senate. On the first occasion, when Morris moved that no treaty should be binding until ratified by a law, several members pointed out that such a legal ratification would involve great inconvenience and the proposal was voted down by eight to one.[19] Several weeks later Wilson moved the addition of the words "and House of Representatives" after the words "advice and consent of the Senate." He explained the arguments in support of this proposal. "As treaties . . . are to have the operation of laws, they ought to have the sanction of laws also. The circumstance of secrecy in the business of treaties formed the only objection; but this he thought, so far as it was inconsistent with obtaining the Legislative sanction, was outweighed by the necessity of the latter." [20] The only answer recorded to this reasonable statement was that of Sherman who thought that the power could be safely trusted to the Senate and that the necessity of secrecy forbade the reference of treaties to the whole legislature. The amendment was then voted down by ten to one, Pennsylvania again casting the only favorable vote.

Though little was said in the convention on the treaty-making clauses, they received much more attention in the state conventions and in the pamphlets of the period. The part of the Constitution relating to treaties which was most severely at-

[18] *Ibid.*, IV, 120.

[19] Farrand, *Records,* II, 392-394.

[20] *Ibid.*, p. 538.

tacked by the anti-federalists in the state conventions was the provision saying that treaties shall be the supreme law of the land.[21] Through this clause, it was asserted, all the rights of the states could be taken away until, as Patrick Henry said, " if anything should be left us, it would be because the President and senators were pleased to admit it." [22] The objections were that treaties should not be made the law of the land or, if so, the process of making treaties should be more carefully guarded by requiring the consent of the House of Representatives or a larger majority than two-thirds of the senators present. To the first point the federalists answered that treaties were in all countries the law of the land of their own force. To meet the second, they devoted much energy to establish the proposition that the House of Representatives was not a fit body to participate in the treaty-making power. The necessity for secrecy and the absurdity of expecting it from the House, the necessity for quick action, the fact that the House would be in session only for several months of the year, the short terms of the members of the House which would prevent them from mastering the intricacies of foreign relations, and the fluctuating membership of the House were the arguments stressed as reasons for eliminating the House from a participation in the treaty-making power.[23]

Obviously the treaty-making power had to be lodged somewhere. With the House of Representatives disqualified for what seemed, at least to the vast majority of the members of the convention, to be sufficient reasons, with one group opposed to putting the power solely in the hands of the Senate, and another group insisting that it should not be given to the President

[21] The most interesting debate was in the Virginia convention with Patrick Henry and Mason attacking and Madison defending. Elliot, *Debates,* III, 499-516. See also *Ibid.,* IV, 115-135, 263-271.

[22] *Ibid.,* III, 500.

[23] " Can secrecy be expected in sixty-five members? The idea is absurd." C. C. Pinckney in the South Carolina convention. *Ibid.,* IV, 280. The reasons against the House are martialed by Jay in *The Federalist,* No. 64 (Lodge edition), pp. 400-406, and by Hamilton in No. 75, pp. 468-469.

alone, the compromise giving it jointly to the President and Senate was almost inevitable. Such a settlement was particularly satisfying to the members as it exemplified so well their dominant political belief that liberties and good government could only be preserved if each branch of the government could be checked by the others.[24]

Very little was said of the reasons which induced them to require a majority of two-thirds of the Senators present, probably because the necessity for an extraordinary majority seemed obvious to most of the members of the convention. Experience seemed to confirm the wisdom of such a requirement. Although under the Articles of Confederation the consent of nine of the thirteen states was necessary in making treaties, Congress by a bare majority of seven to five had changed its instructions to Jay in his negotiations with Gardoqui in 1786, so that he could offer to forego the " right " to the navigation of the Mississippi River for a period of years. One of the most bitter fights in the Confederation Congress centered around this action. It may well have convinced contemporary Americans, especially those in the sections of the country which were economically dependent upon the Mississippi River as an outlet, that the interests of a minority could be protected only by continuing the restriction of requiring a two-thirds vote when making treaties. Nevertheless, an attempt was made in the convention to free the treaty-making power from that restriction. On September 7, Wilson said he considered it objectionable to require concurrence of two-thirds as that would enable a minority to control the will of a majority. In this he was supported by King who remarked that the executive would serve as a check, thereby making unnecessary the two-thirds majority required in the Congress of the Confederation.[25]

[24] However, Hamilton claimed in *The Federalist* that the power of making treaties belonged neither to the executive nor legislative department but formed a distinct department. *Ibid.*, pp. 466-467. Although he rejected this idea a few years later in the famous Pacificus-Helvidius correspondence, he has at least one modern follower. See Quincy Wright, *The Control of American Foreign Relations*, pp. 140-150.

[25] Farrand, *Records*, II, 540.

No other comments were then made, but the next day Wilson returned to the subject and moved that the clause requiring the consent of two-thirds of the Senate present be stricken out. He pointed out that if two-thirds are necessary to make peace a minority may perpetuate war against the wish of the majority and said that " if the majority cannot be trusted, it was a proof, as observed by Mr. Ghorum, that we were not fit for one Society." This time he received aid from his usual ally, Gouverneur Morris, who maintained that the prospect of having to secure two-thirds of the Senate in making peace treaties might deter the legislature from declaring war " on account of the Fisheries or the Mississippi, the two great objects of the Union." He also suggested that if the majority of the Senate were prevented from making peace when they desired it, they might achieve their purpose " in the more disagreeable mode, of negativing the supplies for the war." In answer to them the opposition, speaking through Williamson and Gerry, said that eight men might be a majority of the quorum of the Senate, that these might represent less than one-fifth of the people, that it was not safe to put the great treaty-making power in the hands of so small a number, and that they might be corrupted by foreign influence. The vote on the question showed only Delaware in favor of Wilson's amendment. Indeed, the convention was rather inclined to make the process of making treaties even more difficult as three states voted for an amendment to require the consent of two-thirds of all the members of the Senate.[26]

When the Constitution was being debated in the states, one of the most frequent complaints about its treaty-making provisions was that two-thirds of the members of the Senate present was too small a number to prevent abuse of the great power involved.[27] Much was made of the fact that ten members might

[26] *Ibid.*, pp. 548-549.

[27] This was especially true in the Virginia convention where the two groups were struggling for the votes of the delegates from Kentucky to whom the Mississippi question was so vital and the Jay-Gardoqui negotiations of 1786 so instructive. Elliot, *Debates*, III, 331-365, 499-516. The " scuffle for Kentucky

be two-thirds of a quorum of the Senate and in several states the conventions suggested amendments to the Constitution which would have required larger majorities for certain kinds of treaties.[28] The federalists devoted their energies to proving that the treaty-making power was as well protected as under the Confederation and that treaties could not be made too easily. The few who, like Wilson, would have preferred an arrangement by which an ordinary majority of the Senate could approve treaties, were strenuously defending the Constitution. Naturally they said nothing of their misgivings because five members of the Senate, with only a quorum present, could defeat all treaties.

The prospect of having one more than one-third of the members of the Senate defeat a treaty was not one to excite apprehension in the minds of the framers of the Constitution.[29] There can be no doubt that they neither desired nor expected to make many treaties. Even Gouverneur Morris said that " in general he was not solicitous to multiply and facilitate Treaties. He wished none to be made with G. Britain, till she should be at war. Then a good bargain might be made with her. So with

votes," as one member referred to it, was of such importance that more than one writer has maintained that the Jay-Gardoqui negotiations nearly prevented the ratification of the Constitution. See for example, Samuel F. Bemis, *Pinckney's Treaty,* p. 179. On the other hand evidence has been submitted by another student to support the view that these men of the " Western waters " opposed the treaty-making power not because they feared the use of the Mississippi River might be bartered away but because they feared Indian treaties that would interfere with their operations in western lands. Arthur P. Whitaker, *The Spanish-American Frontier, 1783-1795,* pp. 123-126. For instances of similar complaints in other state conventions see John B. McMaster and Frederick D. Stone, eds., *Pennsylvania and the Federal Convention,* p. 476; and Elliot, *Debates,* II, 287, IV, 119, 124, 265, 271.

[28] *Ibid.,* III, 660; IV, 245.

[29] In referring to this provision Duc de Broglie said in 1870, " Pour poser un pareil principe dans la constitution de son pays, il fait bon n'avoir pas de voisins; il fait bon n'etre vulnérable sur aucun point de son territoire; il fait bon ne courir aucun risque d'aucune espèce, et n'avoir jamais de parti à prendre dans des circonstances difficiles." *Vues sur le Gouvernement de la France,* p. 286.

other foreign powers. The more difficulty in making treaties, the more value will be set on them." [30] Madison thought that it had been too easy for Congress to make treaties under the Articles of Confederation, although the consent of nine of the thirteen states was required.[31] And yet at the time he said this, treaties had been made with only six foreign powers.[32]

It is clear that in joining the Senate with the President in the treaty-making power the framers of the Constitution did not intend or think that the Senate was to be an instrument for the democratic control of foreign relations. In the course of time the Senate became such, but the framers had no idea that they were creating what proved to be the first treaty-making system subject to democratic control, at least among modern nations. If the idea had occurred, it would undoubtedly have frightened most of them because democracy was not in high favor among the members of the convention whose temper was expressed by Randolph when he said, " our chief danger arises from the democratic parts of our constitutions." [33] The Senate, which they admitted to the treaty-making power, represented the states, as had the Congress under the Articles of Confederation. If there had been any desire to give even an appearance of democratic control over foreign relations the House of Representatives and not the Senate would have shared this power with the President, although under the electoral restrictions that then prevailed it would be inaccurate to call the House a democratic body.

Another aspect of the problem which the convention did not consider was that the country might be reduced to impotence in the conduct of its foreign relations by a struggle between the President and the Senate for control. The few allusions made in

[30] Farrand, *Records,* II, 393.

[31] *Ibid.*, II, 548.

[32] There is a chronological list of all treaties to which the United States has been a party in W. M. Malloy, comp., *Treaties, Conventions, International Acts, Protocols, and Agreements between the United States of America and Other Powers,* III, ix-xxiv.

[33] Farrand, *Records,* I, 26.

the convention and in the state conventions to the possibility of such a contest show that great benefits were expected from it. Implicity believing in the doctrine of checks and balances, the Americans of 1787 saw in the reciprocal veto power of the President and the Senate in foreign relations their strongest protection against abuse.[34] The reverse side of the picture was not examined. The fear of abuse of power was so overwhelming that no consideration was given to the question of whether the defenses raised against it might not prevent a proper use of the power. That the Senate and President might check each other so effectively that the foreign policy of neither would prevail, thus leaving the country with no policy even during a crisis; that the motives in the struggles between President and Senate might not be to defend the liberties of the people but merely to extend the power of one at the expense of the other; and that treaties might be sometimes defeated not because of their merits or demerits, but because they would serve as a battleground in the struggle for control of foreign policy, were contingencies the convention did not foresee.

Another dangerous possibility, which was not mentioned in the convention, was that treaties might be defeated for reasons of domestic politics. The failure of the framers of the Constitution to anticipate the rise in political parties in the United States had serious consequences. Within a few years the presence of political parties made a dead letter of the elaborate system of electing the President that the convention had devised at the cost of so much time and effort. The appearance of political parties also profoundly affected the treaty-making arrangements provided in the Constitution. If the framers of the Constitution had realized that the members of the Senate would be divided into political parties to one of which the President would also belong, and that two-thirds of the members of the Senate would very seldom belong to the same party

[34] "Neither the President nor the Senate, solely, can complete a treaty; they are checks upon each other, and are so balanced as to produce security to the people." James Wilson, in the Pennsylvania convention. Elliot, *Debates,* II, 507.

as the President, they would hardly have put the power of defeating treaties in the hands of one more than one-third of the members of the Senate present. From the time political parties first appeared senators in voting on treaties have inevitably felt the pressure of political motives. The temptation to defeat a treaty made by a President belonging to another political party was certain to be present. Either the treaty, if completed, might redound to his and his party's political advantage or the defeat of his foreign policy would produce an impression of ineffectiveness and thus be of advantage politically.

CHAPTER II

EARLY CONTESTS AND PRECEDENTS, 1789-1815

They debated it and proposed alterations, so that when Washington left the Senate-chamber he said he would be damned if he ever went there again. And ever since that time treaties have been negotiated by by the Executive before submitting them to the consideration of the Senate.

JOHN QUINCY ADAMS.[1]

I can not now be mistaken. The President wishes to tread on the necks of the Senate. . . . He wishes us to see with the eyes and hear with the ears of his Secretary only . . . Form only will be left to us.

WILLIAM MACLAY.[2]

The importance of the foreign relations of the United States during the period from 1789 to 1815 cannot be easily exaggerated. The new government had scarcely been established when its relations with the countries of Europe assumed an acute form which was destined to last for approximately a quarter of a century. During most of that time foreign relations dominated domestic politics and influenced the economic and social life of the people more than during any other period in the history of the United States. Foreign policy was the outstanding issue between the two political parties which, indeed, originated to a considerable extent on that issue.[3] A large proportion of the time and thought of Congress and of the political leaders of both parties was devoted to foreign affairs. Most of

[1] Charles F. Adams, ed., *Memoirs of John Quincy Adams,* VI, 427.

[2] Edgar S. Maclay, ed., *Journal of William Maclay,* p. 131.

[3] Contrary to the widespread belief there is no fundamental reason why foreign policy should not be a political issue. Conflicting ideas on questions of foreign policy can be properly expressed through the medium of political parties, and perhaps can be expressed in no other way. But insofar as possible the questions should be settled on their merits, and the machinery for deciding foreign policy should be so arranged as to reduce to a minimum the opportunity and temptation for purely political motives or for contests between two branches of the government over their relative powers in reaching the decision.

the many partisan debates during this period, when political warfare was waged with a bitterness that has seldom been duplicated, were on the subject of foreign relations. Thus, within a few years the machinery designed by the framers of the Constitution for deciding foreign policy had to operate under an unforeseen system of party politics and with foreign relations as the dominant issue.

Under these conditions it would be natural to expect that many treaties would be lost through partisan votes in the Senate. Yet during the period not a single treaty was absolutely rejected by the Senate and only one, which was of minor importance, was lost because of amendments made by the Senate.[4] At first glance this result would seem to justify high praise for the treaty-making process established by the framers of the Constitution, but a closer examination of the facts shows that it was possible only as the result of extraordinary circumstances.

In the first place, only a few treaties were submitted to the Senate during the twenty-six years in question. With very few exceptions the questions of foreign policy which formed the basis for the long and bitter political battles were not presented to the country in the shape of treaties to be ratified. Only eighteen agreements with foreign powers were submitted to the Senate for its advice and consent from 1789 until December 1815. Even this number is deceptive. The cession of Louisiana by France, the payment of sixty million francs by the United States for Louisiana, and the payment of claims of citizens of the United States against France were each the subject of a separate convention.[5] Essentially, however, they constituted a single transaction, each containing a portion of the agreement. This fact was recognized in the Senate where they were considered together and approved in one resolution.[6] Three of the

[4] Strictly speaking the Senate does not make amendments but proposes them. Unless they are accepted by the President and by the other party to the treaty, ratifications will not be exchanged.

[5] Malloy, *Treaties,* I, 508, 511, 513.

[6] *Journal of the Executive Proceedings of the Senate of the United States,* I, 450; hereinafter cited as *Sen. Ex. Jour.*

other agreements submitted to the Senate were merely in explanation of and supplementary to the Jay Treaty, and were of minor significance, so that once that treaty was ratified they followed as a matter of course.[7] Consequently, it is more accurate to say that thirteen and not eighteen treaties were considered by the Senate prior to December 1815. From December 1805 until February 1815 not a single treaty was submitted to the Senate.[8]

The small number of treaties made and the fact that so few of them involved the major questions of policy in dispute explain in part the apparent lack of friction in the exercise of the treaty-making power. But this explanation is not sufficient because among the treaties submitted to the Senate were the important Jay's treaty, the treaties for the purchase of Louisiana and the Treaty of Ghent. If the joint possession of the treaty-making power by the President and the Senate tends to precipitate a contest for control between the two or to cause the President's political opponents in the Senate to defeat any treaties of political consequence, was such a tendency evident in the action of the Senate on these treaties and, if so, how is their successful completion to be explained?

That the treaty which Jay negotiated with Great Britain became the subject of one of the most famous political contests in the history of the United States is well known. But attention has been centered on the spectacular and heated public meetings which took place after the Senate had given its consent to ratification, and after the treaty had been made public despite the Senate's order for secrecy. These and the debates in the House of Representatives on the question of whether it would pass the legislation necessary to execute the treaty contained highly

[7] Malloy, *Treaties,* I, 607, 609, 610.

[8] Writing to Mazzei on July 18, 1804, Jefferson said, "On the subject of treaties, our system is to have none with any nation, as far as can be avoided." *The Writings of Thomas Jefferson,* XI, 38-39. Treaties with Indian tribes have not been counted nor will they be studied, because of their peculiar status. They were, however, submitted to the Senate for its advice and consent until 1871.

dramatic features which attracted contemporaneous and historical attention. The stoning of Hamilton when he tried to speak in favor of the treaty and the tumultuous demonstrations in which the British flag was insulted and Jay was burnt in effigy invite description. So, too, does the much more serious contest in the House of Representatives, which was won by the narrowest of margins and then only after reaching an intensely dramatic climax in the oration deliverd by Fisher Ames.[9] These stirring events have caused the action of the Senate on the treaty to be dismissed with only the statement that the treaty was approved, and yet the contest in the Senate was as desperately fought as in the House. The advice and consent of the Senate was given by a party vote of twenty to ten.[10] The defeat

[9] John B. McMaster, *A History of the People of the United States,* II, tells of the party vote in the Senate in a portion of one paragraph on page 215, while he devotes pp. 216-230, 245-256, 263-284 to the other phases. The proportions are about the same in the other standard histories. In a stimulating chapter in Charles A. Beard, *Economic Origins of Jeffersonian Democracy,* pp. 268-298, the economic motives underlying the political struggle are emphasized, but, again, little is said of the Senate's part. The political features of the contest over the treaty are described vividly and with an unorthodox bias by Claude G. Bowers, *Jefferson and Hamilton,* pp. 269-307, yet he, too, gives only a little more attention to the Senate than the others have given. No mention of the reception of the treaty is made in S. F. Bemis's, *Jay's Treaty,* which is solely concerned with the negotiation of it. The reason for the apparent neglect of the Senate's part in the transaction is that the dramatic features were lacking and no one knew what was said. Even now practically nothing is known of what was said in the Senate for an examination of the writings of participants, now available, shows that they contain almost no information on the subject. Yet from the personnel involved and from the closeness and importance of the contest there must have been interesting debates during the two weeks the treaty was being considered in the Senate. *The Executive Journal of the Senate,* of course, does not include what was said but merely gives a record of what was done.

[10] *Sen. Ex. Jour.,* I, 186. The determination of the political faith of members of the Senate is an astonishingly difficult problem, especially during these early years and during other periods when parties were being formed. John Langdon of New Hampshire had been a Federalist at least until 1794 and was still considered one by some when he voted against the treaty, but he has been counted here as a Democrat as he remained permanently with that party from this time

of the treaty was only prevented by the fact that it happened to be one of those rare occasions when two-thirds of the members of the Senate were of the same party as the President. The tendency to vote on treaties according to party lines operated as completely as conditions permitted.

There was a factious rather than a great political contest over the treaties for the purchase of Louisiana. The vote in the Senate shows that again the treaties were saved from defeat only because the President and two-thirds of the Senate were of the same political faith. This time it was the Democrats who were in control and their margin of safety was larger than the Federalists had enjoyed when Jay's treaty secured the exact constitutional majority necessary. The resolution giving the advice and consent of the Senate to the Louisiana treaties was passed by a vote of twenty-four to seven.[11] With one exception the Federalists in the Senate did what they could to defeat the treaties, while every Democrat voted in favor of them.[12] In telling Livingtson of the favorable reception of the treaty Jefferson correctly reported the situation: " the federalists spoke and

and was one of its ardent members. Beard, pp. 47-48; Bowers, p. 282. Pierce Butler is another who had been a Federalist, or at least had been thought one, and who voted against the treaty. But before the treaty reached the Senate he had drifted to the opposition when Hamilton's tariff was proposed, and must be counted with the Democrats. Beard, p. 38; Ulrich B. Phillips, " The South Carolina Federalists," *American Historical Review,* XIV, 731 ff. Although some of the other senators are equally hard to place a careful examination substantiates the statement that the vote on the treaty represents the strengh of the two parties. For a discussion of the methods used to determine the political affiliations of members of the Senate see Bibliography p. 313.

[11] *Sen. Ex. Jour.,* I, 450. This one member absent was John Quincy Adams, at this time a Federalist, who entered the Senate for the first time on the following day.

[12] One of the Federalist members wrote in his notes of that day, " General Dayton with twenty-three democrats voted in favor of the resolution, & the seven federal senators against it." Everett S. Brown, ed., *William Plumer's Memorandum of Proceedings in the United States Senate, 1803-1807,* p. 14. Dayton was a Federalist whose loyalty to his country was as doubtful as that to his party, for he later played a prominent part in the Burr conspiracy.

voted against it, but they are now so reduced in their numbers as to be nothing.[13]

The action of the Senate on the Treaty of Ghent shows no trace of political motives. The treaty was accepted unanimously the day after it was received from the President.[14] But in this case there was no temptation for the political opponents of the President to vote against the treaty. The Federalists had gone to great lengths in opposing the war with Great Britain and, therefore, were not in a position to obstruct a treaty restoring peace even if it had been politically advantageous to do so. Moreover, the terms of the treaty were not such as would be likely to prove of great political benefit to the administration. And dominating the situation was the great and obvious necessity for making peace as quickly as possible.[15]

The one treaty which was defeated during this period because of the action of the Senate upon it was the treaty of May 12, 1803, with Great Britain, known from the names of the two negotiators as the King-Hawkesbury treaty.[16] It was a treaty of minor importance, but is of interest as the first treaty to be lost through the refusal of the other signatory to accept a change made by the Senate. The object of the treaty was to settle more precisely both the northeastern and northwestern boundaries between the United States and British territory. In 1783 the northwestern boundary had been fixed as a line drawn due west from the northwesternmost point of the Lake of the Woods to the Mississippi River. It later was learned that the Mississippi River did not extend north far enough to intersect this line, so by the fifth article of the new treaty the boundary

[13] *Writings,* X, 425. In a letter to Captain Meriwether Lewis, Jefferson said, "The votes of both Houses on ratifying and carrying the treaties into execution, have been precisely party votes, except that General Dayton has separated from his friends on these questions, and voted for the treaties. *Ibid.,* p. 434.

[14] *Sen. Ex. Jour.,* II, 620.

[15] Henry Adams, *History of the United States of America,* IX, 58-59; Frank A. Updyke, *The Diplomacy of the War of 1812,* pp. 361-368.

[16] The treaty and some papers relating to it are in *American State Papers, Foreign Relations,* II, 584-591.

was "declared to be the shortest line that can be drawn between the northwest point of the Lake of the Woods and the nearest source of the river Mississippi." Upon the request of either party commissioners were to be appointed to ascertain the northwest point of the Lake, and the nearest source of the river and to mark the line.

These provisions would have been readily accepted had it not been for the treaties for the purchase of Louisiana, which had been approved by the Senate four days before the King-Hawkesbury treaty was received from the President.[17] Fears were now expressed that the fifth article of the latter treaty might operate as a limitation to the claims of territory acquired by the Louisiana treaties, and some of the Democratic members thought the treaty should not be ratified at all.[18] The treaty was referred to a committee which corresponded with King through the Secretary of State to see if any information he could give would remove the possible danger.[19] King stated that the terms of the treaty had been settled on April 11, and that when he signed the treaty on May 12, he had no knowledge of the treaty with France.[20] This statement the committee reported to the Senate with the further observation that, as they had no means of ascertaining the northern limits of Louisiana they could not say whether the line provided in the treaty with Great Britain would interfere or not.[21] When a vote was reached in the Senate the fifth article was rejected by twenty-two to nine and then the treaty with that article omitted was approved unanimously.[22]

[17] *Sen. Ex. Jour.*, I, 451.

[18] *Memoirs of John Quincy Adams,* I, 269, 271.

[19] The correspondence is given in *Am. State Papers, For. Rels.*, II, 590-591, and in Charles R. King, ed., *The Life and Correspondence of Rufus King,* IV, 330-332.

[20] This was technically true, but he knew the cession of Louisiana was likely, for in his notes under the date of May 12, after mentioning the signature of the treaty he records that he spoke to Lord Hawkesbury of the probable cession of Louisiana, *ibid.*, p. 256.

[21] *Am. State Papers, For. Rels.*, II, 590.

[22] *Sen. Ex. Jour.*, I, 463.

The votes of the senators when refusing to give their advice and consent to the fifth article shows the influence of party, since all the Democrats except two were against the article while the Federalists saw no danger in it.[23] In this case it was the members of the Senate belonging to the President's party who insisted on the alteration of the treaty. Apparently this was done contrary to his wishes, for in his annual message delivered on October 17, 1803, he had referred to the treaty approvingly as providing "for a practicable demarcation of those limits to the satisfaction of both parties." [24] The Secretary of State informed one of the senators that he did not approve of the resolution for conditional ratification. But the fifth article was rejected either because the Democratic majority did not want to run the risk of endangering the smallest part of the vast empire they had secured for the country, or, as Senator Pickering wrote to King, because the President changed his mind and instructed the Democratic senators to do so.[25]

Madison evidently anticipated that Great Britain would offer no objections to the alteration in the treaty proposed by the Senate. Nevertheless, in his instructions to Monroe, who had succeeded King at London, he outlined the reasons to be used in case Great Britain should be reluctant to exchange ratifications.[26] The strongest argument was the last, in which he pointed out that there was no pressing need for the northwest boundary line to be marked out for a long time to come, so new negotiations could easily settle the problem, and the rest of the treaty providing for the northeastern boundary could be saved.

But before Monroe could test the persuasiveness of these arguments on the British Secretary of State for Foreign Affairs the situation had changed radically. There had been a change in

[23] Plumer, p. 141.

[24] James D. Richardson, comp., *Messages and Papers of the Presidents,* I, 347.

[25] King, IV, 363. Little reliance can be placed on this statement of Pickering who, in his fanatical opposition, saw the hand of Jefferson in all that was wrong.

[26] *Am. State Papers, For. Rels.,* III, 89-90.

the British ministry and, what was much more serious, a decided change for the worse in Anglo-American relations. The extreme cordiality with Great Britain, which had prevailed for some time, had been largely due to the assiduous efforts of Jefferson when the fear of having the French as neighbors in Louisiana was driving him into the arms of Great Britain. Suddenly the cession of Louisiana and the renewal of the war in Europe reversed the situation. Jefferson no longer needed British aid and could assume a stronger tone than ever in stating the American views on neutral rights.[27] The evidence of the change soon reached London and produced a corresponding alteration there in the former spirit of accommodation.[28]

The result was that when Monroe brought up the question of exchanging ratifications in accordance with the Senate's modification Lord Harrowby, the new Foreign Minister, read him a lecture on the proper conduct of foreign relations. "He censured, in strong terms," so Monroe reported to Madison, "the practice into which we had fallen of ratifying treaties, with exceptions to parts of them, a practice which he termed new, unauthorized, and not to be sanctioned." [29] It did Monroe no good to point out that Great Britain had already sanctioned the practice by accepting the alteration in the Jay Treaty, or to plead the reasonableness of the present change. The only answer Monroe received consisted of some remarks delivered "with some degree of severity" to the effect that we "seemed desirous of getting rid of an article on finding that it did not suit us," and a refusal to accept the conditional ratification.

The action of Great Britain was due not merely to irritation

[27] The whole situation and the sudden change is brilliantly described by Henry Adams, II, 344-388. Even the outraged feelings of Merry, British Minister in Washington, at what he thought were studied insults, when Jefferson received him in slippers, and when he was pushed aside by a member of the House of Representatives in the pell mell to Jefferson's dinner table, contributed in a small way to the change in sentiment.

[28] An interesting illustration of the effect of the news from America can be seen in a letter to King from his friend Gore in London. King, IV, 341-343.

[29] *Am. State Papers, For. Rels.,* III, 93.

at the changed tone of the administration in Washington, or to the supposed insults to Merry, or even to arrogance on the part of Lord Harrowby. The practice of the United States in ratifying parts of treaties was, as will be pointed out below, a "new" and "unauthorized" procedure and one well calculated to arouse the suspicions and anger of the more orthodox powers. Then too, Harrowby had reason to suspect the motives of the United States in amending the treaty, for Merry had reported to him that "notwithstanding Mr. Madison's assurances to the contrary, I have some reason to suspect that ideas of encroachment on his Majesty's just rights are entertained by some persons who have a voice in deciding upon the question of the ratification of this convention."[30] The reason for the British refusal to accept the altered treaty may have been the hope that the failure to settle the northeastern boundary question would further arouse the New England states against their government and might hasten their separation from the rest of the states. Certainly Merry reported that some of the members from Massachusetts assured him that would be the effect of defeating the treaty.[31]

Whatever its motives, the British government proved determined not to accept the treaty in altered form, as it had Jay's treaty. It offered to reopen the whole subject but stated it could

> never acquiesce in the precedent which in this as well as in a former instance the American government has endeavored to establish, of agreeing to ratify such parts of a convention as they may select, and of rejecting other stipulations of it, formally agreed upon by a minister invested with full powers for the purpose.[32]

---

[30] Henry Adams, II, 384. Merry probably got the idea from his very close friend Senator Pickering, for Pickering in a letter to King expressed the same idea saying, "Mr. Jefferson is not contented with the immense extent of Louisiana as held by the French. Its northern boundary not having been explicitly defined . . . he wants to carry it to the parallel of the 49 of North Latitude. To effect this end, he certainly supposes the suppression of the 5th Article will contribute. For this object your *entirely satisfactory* convention is put in jeopardy. He thinks, however, or pretends to think, that G. Britain will readily agree to the other articles." King, IV, 363.

[31] Henry Adams, II, 392.

[32] *Ibid.*, p. 424.

Monroe made several more attempts to secure ratification, particularly after a new ministry came into office in February 1806, but with no success.[33] All hope of saving the treaty was now abandoned. Although negotiations for a new convention were soon opened, neither the northwestern nor the northeastern boundary was fixed until many years later and until the friction, which the question subsequently developed, threatened to bring on a war.[34]

The Senate only narrowly escaped responsibility for the loss of another treaty during this early period. The story of this case is of interest because of the votes on party lines, because the Senate again furnished the excuse to the other signatory for attempting to avoid ratification, and because in this instance the United States took the position that a government was obligated to ratify without change a treaty made by a minister with full powers. On the 11th of August, 1802, Charles Pinckney concluded a treaty with Spain which provided for the payment of claims arising from the depredations of Spanish citizens on American commerce.[35] The further claims based upon the condemnation of American vessels and merchandise in Spanish ports were expressly excluded from the treaty and reserved without prejudice for future negotiation. The success of the United States in securing this partial recognition of their claims was due to the political situation in Europe, from which American diplomacy has so often benefited.[36] The last article of the treaty provided that ratifications should be exchanged "as soon as possible."

Unfortunately for the treaty, it was received by the Senate during the excitement caused by Morales' withdrawal of the right of deposit in New Orleans.[37] Irritated by this action and by the failure to include all claims in the treaty, the Senate postponed its decision until the end of the session and then, on

[33] *Am. State Papers, For. Rels.*, III, 95-98, 113-114.

[34] Jesse S. Reeves, *American Diplomacy under Tyler and Polk,* p. 1-57, 190-223.

[35] Malloy, *Treaties,* II, 1650. *Am. State Papers, For. Rels.*, II, 475-483.

[36] Henry Adams, II, 21.

[37] *Sen. Ex. Jour.*, I, 435.

March 3, 1803, refused its advice and consent by a vote of thirteen to nine in favor of the resolution.[38] The result shows that, in this instance too, party considerations were a major factor, as the nine votes against giving the Senate's advice and consent came from the nine Federalists while all the Democrats who voted were in favor of the treaty, but enough of the latter refrained from voting to prevent the treaty from receiving the necessary two-thirds majority.[39] The majority immediately voted voted to reconsider the vote and postponed the consideration of the treaty to the next session.[40]

In the interim a new attempt was made to persuade Spain to admit her responsibility for all the claims, but without success. The correspondence resulting from this fruitless effort was submitted to the Senate in the following December with a message from the President in which he said the Senate could "judge whether the prospect it offers will justify a longer suspension of that portion of indemnities conceded by Spain."[41] The judgment of the Senate now was to accept what could be gained, for on January 9, 1804, almost exactly a year after the treaty had been received and some eighteen months after it had been signed, the Senate gave its advice and consent.[42] The vote was twenty-one to seven, all of the seven being Federalist senators and nineteen of the majority being Democrats.[43]

But now Spain was irritated. The purchase of Louisiana, which had occurred in the meantime, had been accomplished over her indignant protest, while the Mobile Act seemed to her an invasion of her territory in West Florida, so that she was

[38] *Ibid.*, p. 447.

[39] Plumer, p. 93; Henry Adams, II, 250. Adams goes on to say, "Thus, owing to the action of Federalist senators, when Jefferson in the following summer, after buying Louisiana, looked about for the means of buying Florida, he found these classes of claims, aggregating as he supposed between five and ten million dollars, ready to his hand."

[40] *Sen. Ex. Jour.*, I, 448.

[41] *Am. State Papers, For. Rels.*, II, 596-606.

[42] *Sen. Ex. Jour.*, I, 462.

[43] Henry Adams says the "least factious of the Federalists" joined the majority. II, 259. One of the two was John Quincy Adams.

glad of an excuse to escape from the necessity of settling any claims. The long delay of the Senate supplied the desired excuse and Spain offered to exchange ratifications only upon certain conditions, among which were the surrender of the additional claims of the Americans and the revocation of the Mobile Act.[44] These, of course, were unacceptable to the United States. The result was a long and acrimonious exchange of notes in all of which the United States laid down the doctrine that, by the law of nations, " a monarch cannot, in honor, refuse to ratify a convention made by a minister with full powers, unless it can be proved that the minister had remarkably and openly deviated from his instructions, or the monarch has some other very strong reasons for so doing, but they must be very strong," such as deception.[45] Appeals to this well-established principle of international law were as futile as the threats of war which were made. Spain rested her case on the length of time the United States took to ratify and maintained that an offer must be accepted within a reasonable time or it lapsed.

Eventually the United States gained its point, for Spain exchanged ratifications of the treaty on December 21, 1818. The victory was an empty one, however, as no action was taken before a new treaty provided that the claims convention of 1802 should be annulled.[46]

The rule which the United States urged Spain to observe undoubtedly had the sanction of international law, and Lord Harrowby was correct in calling the practice of the United States of ratifying treaties with exceptions to parts of them "new" and "unauthorized."[47] The claim of the United

[44] *Am. State Papers, For. Rels.,* II, 619-620.

[45] *Ibid.,* p. 623, 613-695.

[46] Malloy, *Treaties,* II, 1651. Spain then refused to ratify this treaty for about two years, undoubtedly because she wished to delay American recognition of the Latin American republics, and the United States continued to insist upon the obligation under international law to ratify properly negotiated treaties. *Am. State Papers, For. Rels.,* IV, 657, 673, 686-687.

[47] John Bassett Moore, *A Digest of International Law,* V, 184-193; Henry Wheaton, *Elements of International Law,* pp. 319-329; Wright, pp. 42-45.

States to exemption from the prevailing rule was based on its Constitution. This prevented its representatives, even with full powers, from engaging the honor of the country to ratify the treaties they made, since all treaties must be submitted to the Senate for constitutional action. It is clear, and was then recognized, that if the advice and consent of the Senate should be given prior to the negotiations, the United States would be morally obligated to ratify any treaty made under instructions to which the Senate had given its approval.

The usual practice, however, has been to request the advice and consent of the Senate after the treaties have been negotiated.[48] Under these circumstances, unless the Senate could reject or amend treaties submitted to it the constitutional requirement would be an empty form. Accordingly the United States has considered itself justified in altering properly negotiated treaties before ratifying them, and the principle has come to be accepted by the other governments of the world. Nevertheless, although the principle has been accepted, the amended treaties frequently have not. The insistence of the Senate upon modifications in treaties before giving the advice and consent required by the Constitution has caused the defeat of many of them. It is, therefore, necessary to describe, at least in outline, the establishment of the practice of requesting the advice and consent of the Senate after the negotiation of treaties, which led to the "new" and "unauthorized" procedure of partial ratifications.[49]

The framers of the Constitution had no idea that the joint possession of the treaty-making power which they were giving to the President and the Senate would affect the procedure for ratifying treaties. The evidence shows that they expected the Senate would be consulted in advance, as was natural, for they were accustomed to seeing the instructions to diplomatic rep-

[48] For the principal occasions when the advice and consent of the Senate was requested in advance, see Crandall, pp. 67-75.

[49] The development of the new practice is admirably traced by Ralston Hayden, *The Senate and Treaties, 1789-1817*.

resentatives passed upon by the Congress of the Confederation. In speaking of the disadvantages that would result from requiring the consent of the House of Representatives to treaties, Gorham stated in the convention that instructions to ministers abroad must be given by the same authority that was to ratify their acts or else they would not know how to proceed.[50] This caused Johnson to remark that he "thought there was something of solecism in saying that the acts of a Minister with plenipotentiary powers from one Body, should depend for ratification on another Body."[51] Absurd or not, that is the practice of the United States.

The framers of the Constitution were not the only ones who expected that the Senate would participate with the President in formulating the instructions to be followed in making treaties and thus give its advice and consent prior to the signing of the treaties. The same idea was also held by the persons who were first called upon to use the treaty-making power of the new government. The provisions of the Senate for personal conferences with the President, which were adopted after consultation with him, clearly indicate the expectation that the Senate would participate equally with the President in the negotiation of treaties.[52] The procedure adopted in the case of the first few treaties considered affords conclusive proof that this view prevailed. Several Indian treaties and a consular convention with France had been signed but not ratified before the new government began to function. These were accordingly submitted to the Senate for its advice and consent. The convention with France was the first to receive the sanction of the Senate. In considering it the Senate did not enter into the merits of the treaty, but determined its action upon the question of whether or not the faith of the United States was engaged to ratify the treaty. The question was answered by Jay, the Secretary of Foreign Affairs under the old government who had temporarily remained in office under the new. Jay appeared in person before

[50] Farrand, *Records,* II, 392.

[51] *Ibid.,* p. 393.

[52] *Sen. Ex. Jour.,* I, 19; Hayden, pp. 17-20.

the Senate to explain and also submitted a written opinion in which he said that the treaty conformed to the instructions given and that the United States ought to ratify. The Senate then gave its advice and consent unanimously, thereby showing that it recognized the rule of international law on the subject.[53]

The intention of Washington to consult the Senate prior to the negotiation of treaties was carried into practice at first, but the inevitable contest between the two, which began immediately, caused this procedure to be abandoned. On August 21, 1789, the President sent a message announcing that he would meet the Senate on the following day "to advise with them on the terms of the treaty to be negotiated with the southern Indians." [54] The *Journal of the Executive Proceedings of the Senate* records the decisions taken at the conference which followed, but supplies no further information. In this instance the skeleton of the official records is furnished with flesh and the warm blood of life by the *Journal* of William Maclay, in which the Senator from Pennsylvania daily wrote an account of those parts of the day's transactions which impressed him, and reported the determined resistance which he constantly offered to the "monarchical" tendencies and designs of the other officials of the government. Maclay's vivid and much-quoted description of what took place when Washington for the first time consulted the Senate about a contemplated negotiation explains why Washington gave up the idea of using the Senate as a council to assist him in the conduct of foreign relations.[55]

Maclay described the entry of the President and the Secretary of War and the brief statement of the former that he had come for the advice and consent of the Senate, and then stated that the Vice-President hurriedly read the paper given to him, but the noise of passing carriages prevented the senators from hear-

[53] *Sen. Ex. Jour.*, I, 5-9; Hayden, pp. 4-9.

[54] *Sen. Ex. Jour.*, I, 20.

[55] Maclay, pp. 128-132; Hayden, pp. 23-28; Edward S. Corwin, *The President's Control of Foreign Relations*, pp. 85-88.

ing much of it. Another paper was read and then the Vice-President read the first proposition to which the advice and consent of the Senate was requested. The first paper was read again because of the noise of the carriages and immediately the Vice-President put the question on the first article. A pause followed during which a colleague whispered to Maclay, "We will see who will venture to break silence first," and then, just as the Vice-President started to call for the ayes and nays, Maclay arose because it appeared to him that no one else would, and that "we should have these advices and consents ravished, in a degree, from us." He pointed out the importance of the business, the duty of the senators to inform themselves as well as possible, and called for the reading of the treaties and documents which had been alluded to in the papers read. In spite of the fact that the President "wore an aspect of stern displeasure," the reading of the documents continued. Others then asked for particular documents they wanted to have read.

The first proposition which related to the Cherokees was again taken up and was postponed so that the latest information could be obtained from an agent who had just returned from their country. The second question which concerned the Chickasaws and Choctaws was likewise postponed. A motion to postpone the third brought on a debate, some of it entirely irrelevant, but the motion was carried. Maclay, because he "saw no chance of a fair investigation of subjects while the President of the United States sat there, with his Secretary of War, to support his opinions and overawe the timid and neutral part of the Senate," had whispered to Senator Morris that all papers and proposals should be referred to a committee. Morris made such a motion. Some others objected and Butler made a lengthy speech against commitment saying the Senate was acting as a council. Maclay rose to the defence of having a committee report on the proposals, speaking, he says, in such a way that "peevishness itself could not have taken offense at anything I said."

As I sat down, the President of the United States started up in a violent fret. "This defeats every purpose of my coming here," were the first words that he said. He then went on that he had brought his Secretary of War with him to give every necessary information; that the Secretary knew all about the business, and yet he was delayed and could not go on with the matter. He cooled, however, by degrees. Said he had no objection to putting off this matter until Monday, but declared he did not understand the matter of commitment. He might be delayed; he could not tell how long. He rose a second time, and said he had no objection to postponement until Monday at ten o'clock. By the looks of the Senate this seemed agreed to. A pause for some time ensued. We waited for him to withdraw. He did so with a discontented air. Had it been any other man than the man whom I wish to regard as the first character in the world, I would have said, with sullen dignity.

I can not now be mistaken. The President wishes to tread on the necks of the Senate. Commitment will bring the matter to discussion, at least in the committee, where he is not present. He wishes us to see with the eyes and hear with the ears of his Secretary only. The Secretary to advance the premises, the President to draw the conclusions, and to bear down our deliberations with his personal authority and presence. Form only will be left to us. This will not do with Americans. But let the matter work; it will cure itself.

Maclay's heated but picturesque words reveal the instinctive and inevitable attitude of the Senate toward the President in their joint exercise of the treaty-making power, an attitude which has been characteristic of the Senate ever since. Maclay felt the constant senatorial fear that its constitutional prerogatives were being invaded and voiced the equally constant senatorial insistence that not merely form but complete independence of action should be secured to it. Like Maclay the Senate has jealously suspected the motives of any President who has attempted to hasten its action and has often asserted its duty to see with its own eyes and hear with its own ears. Also like Maclay the Senate has repeatedly shown itself greatly concerned about these things but interested not at all in the merits of the particular treaty under consideration. In still another way the resistance of Maclay foreshadowed the senatorial opposition to be met by many treaties submitted by Presidents, for, although political parties had not been formed in 1789, Maclay was in spirit already a member of Jefferson's party. Senators belonging to the party opposed to the President have been on most occasions the staunchest defenders of the powers of the Senate.

Apparently Washington's first experience convinced him of the inadvisability of personal consultations with the Senate. Although he returned to the Senate on the following Monday, when, according to Maclay, "he was placid and serene, and manifested a spirit of accommodation," and when the business relating to the treaty with the southern Indians was completed, he never repeated his visit for a similar purpose. Nevertheless, he at first continued to ask for the advice and consent of the Senate on the instructions to be given negotiators,[56] except in the case of several Indian treaties that were made without consulting the Senate before or during negotiations.[57] The first important treaty to be made without the previous advice of the Senate and the treaty which definitely established the precedent that has been seldom disregarded was the Jay Treaty.[58]

While the negotiations which ultimately led to that treaty were first being considered, Washington still regarded the Senate as a council to advise him on the conduct of foreign relations and he requested their opinion on the method to be

[56] *Sen. Ex. Jour.*, I, 60-61. That the Senate felt obligated to give its consent to the resulting treaty is further illustrated by its action on the treaty of October 26, 1791, with the Cherokee Indians. A committee reported "That they have examined the said treaty and find it strictly conformable to the instructions given by the President of the United States.

That these instructions were founded on the advice and consent of the Senate, of the 11th of August, 1790.

* * * * * * * *

The Committee are therefore of opinion, that the Senate advise and consent to the ratification of said treaty." Immediately the Senate unanimously passed a resolution giving its advice and consent. *Ibid.*, pp. 88-89. This procedure would, undoubtedly have been followed if it had become the rule to secure the advice and consent of the Senate prior to negotiations.

[57] *Ibid.*, pp. 193, 219.

[58] The significance of the Jay Treaty in the development of the procedure on treaties, the part played by certain members of the Senate, and the action of the Senate is traced with his usual skill by Hayden, pp. 58-94.

adopted in settling the dispute with Great Britain.[59] Four years later, however, when he submitted the name of John Jay as Envoy Extraordinary to His Britannic Majesty nothing was said in his message of the instructions that were to bind Jay's actions.[60] The omission was undoubtedly due to " the Difficulty of passing particular instructions in the Senate," as Senator King recorded in his diary.[61] Those opposed to the contemplated negotiations also realized it would be unlikely that the Senate would approve instructions which would permit Jay to make a treaty, and accordingly moved

> That previous to going into the consideration of the nomination of a special Envoy to the Court of Great Britain, the President of the United States be requested to inform the Senate of the whole business with which the proposed Envoy is to be charged.[62]

This motion was defeated by the Federalist majority and the President was committed to the policy of requesting the constitutional sanction of the Senate to treaties after they had been signed.

The policy was not yet established, however, for another attack was made on it when the Jay Treaty was being considered by the Senate. The main object of the attack was not to defend the right of the Senate to participate in the negotiation of treaties but to defeat that particular treaty. Burr moved that the consideration of the Jay Treaty be postponed and " that it be recommended to the President of the United States, to proceed without delay to further friendly negotiations with his Britannic Majesty, in order to effect alterations in the said treaty, in the following particulars." [63] The particulars specified would have made any treaty with Great Britain impossible. The motion was defeated by a vote of twenty to ten, the same majority and alignment that subsequently gave the advice and consent of the Senate to the treaty. The defeat of the resolution, like its introduction, was due to political motives and not to considerations

[59] *Sen Ex. Jour.*, I, 36-37.
[60] *Ibid.*, p. 150.
[61] King, I, 521.
[62] *Sen. Ex. Jour.*, I, 151.
[63] *Ibid.*, pp. 183-184.

of the Senate's rights in the conduct of foreign affairs. Yet the action of the Senate was of great consequence, for, as Hayden says, "It is probable that the passage of this resolution would have modified the subsequent development and exercise of the treaty-making powers of the Senate. Washington might well have considered such an act as notice that, in the future, the Senate would expect to participate in the determination of the conditions under which a proposed treaty would be signed; at the very least it would have suggested forcibly the expediency of always consulting them before opening negotiations. It might also have led the Senate to expect such consultation and thus have made it easier for Senators or groups of Senators to demand it."[64]

If the Senate was not to be consulted beforehand, it must have the power to reject or amend the treaties submitted to it despite the well-established rules of diplomatic practice, or else its constitutional power over treaties would be meaningless. This was recognized by the leading Federalist senators and when they met with Hamilton and Jay after the latter's confirmation, they all agreed "that as the Pr. might give the instructions without consulting the Senate, it would be most advisable so to conduct the business, and that the Treaty, if any shd. be formed, should be signed subject to the approbation of the Senate."[65] Accordingly they felt justified in the action they took when they refused their advice and consent to the twelfth article of the treaty while granting it to the rest.[66]

In this fashion the right of the United States to ratify parts of treaties and its practice of having the Senate consent after the negotiations was admitted, at least tacitly. That the right was later denied on at least one occasion has already been pointed

[64] Hayden, p. 79. In the bitter political fight after the treaty was made public the impeachment of Washington was urged, one of the alleged grounds being that "he had violated the constitution in negotiating a treaty without the previous advice of the senate." John Marshall, *The Life of General Washington*, V, 637.

[65] King, I, 523.

[66] *Sen. Ex. Jour.*, I, 186.

out. It is interesting to note that the next treaty made with Great Britain, the Treaty of Ghent, provided in its final article that it would become binding " when the same shall have been ratified on both sides, without alteration by either of the contracting parties. . . ." [67] If the foreign powers had always insisted or had been able to insist upon such a provision, the power of the Senate would have been restricted to rejection or approval without modifications. As it was, they acquiesced with remarkably little protest in the partial ratifications of the United States. At first the United States was careful to explain its peculiar constitutional position when seeking to exchange a partial ratification, although the assumption is that every government contracting with the United States has a knowledge of its constitution and understands that treaties must be considered inchoate until sanctioned by the Senate.[68]

Whether the right of the Senate to alter or reject treaties has given the United States an advantage over other powers, which do not require a similar review of treaties they have signed, is a tempting field for speculation. Lord Harrowby evidently thought it did and in his protest, noted above, asserted that the practice might do " an injury to the other party of a very serious kind." On the other hand, when objecting in the Senate to an amendment to a treaty, John Quincy Adams said, " Indeed I think amendments to treaties imprudent. By making them you agree to all the treaty except the particular you amend—& at the same time you leave it optional with the other party to reject the whole. This is unequal."[69]

[67] Malloy, *Treaties,* I, 618.

[68] It is apparent, however, that even the leading statesmen of Europe have not always understood the situation. Henry Cabot Lodge's essay on " The Treaty-making Powers of the Senate " in *A Fighting Frigate and Other Essays,* first published in *Scribner's Magazine,* January 1902, was an answer to such a misunderstanding on the part of Lord Landsdowne in 1901. And the defeat of the Treaty of Versailles occasioned a large literature in Europe on this point. See especially, Paul Vexler, *De L'Obligation de Ratifier les Traites.*

[69] Plumer, p. 262. Since the World War there has been marked tendency among European countries to follow the American practice of securing the

Two other developments of this early period must be mentioned. On January 6, 1801, the Senate adopted a standing rule governing the procedure to be followed when considering treaties.[70] This rule stated that the treaty would be read a first time for information only, when no motion to act on it in any way could be received. On a subsequent day the treaty would be read a second time with the Senate sitting as in a committee of the whole. It could then be debated and motions could be made to act on all or part of it. Any article could be voted on separately by moving the question, "Will the Senate advise and consent to the ratification of this article?"; or amendments could be proposed either by inserting or leaving out words, in which case the question would be "Shall the words stand as part of the article?" In both cases a majority of two-thirds of the senators present was required for an affirmative decision. After going through the whole treaty the proceedings would be reported to the Senate and confirmed by a two-thirds vote for whatever was retained or inserted. These decisions would then be embodied by the Senate, or a committee, into a resolution of ratification which would be proposed on a subsequent day. Again amendments could be moved and would be adopted if they received a majority of two-thirds of the votes. The final question to advise and consent to the resolution of ratification in the form agreed to would then be taken and, of course, it required an affirmative majority of two-thirds of the senators present to pass it.

Although, under this rule, nothing could be added or inserted in the treaty except by a two-thirds vote, any part of the treaty could be struck out by one more than one-third of

approval of the legislature before ratifying treaties. If this continues, as seems likely, all advantages or disadvantages arising from this source will be ended.

[70] *Sen. Ex. Jour.,* I, 365. Two weeks earlier the Senate adopted a rule providing that all confidential communications from the President should be kept inviolably secret and that all treaties received should be kept secret until the Senate should remove the injunction of secrecy by resolution. Prior to this time secrecy had been ordered in the individual cases. *Ibid.,* p. 361.

the senators present. This has increased the powers of the opposition, as a minority of one-third or less desiring to defeat a treaty may attract a few votes from the majority favoring the treaty on a motion to strike out one or more of the concessions made by the United States. It has frequently been easy for the opposition to secure additional votes against points yielded by the United States. Yet these concessions may be the very ones which induced the other party to enter into the bargain and without which no agreement would have been made. The result is that the altered treaty is not accepted and the minority of less than one-third has attained its end. Killing a treaty by striking out the advantages to the other party has also been the method used even when there were enough votes in the Senate to reject it immediately, because, in addition to the obvious advantages, this method relieves the senators from the possible odium that the direct method might bring. The power of inserting amendments by a simple majority was not given to the opposition until 1868.

The other development of this period which profoundly influenced the use of the treaty-making power was the establishment of the Committee on Foreign Relations. On some occasions during these early years, the Senate considered treaties without referring them to any committee. More frequently a special committee would be appointed to study the treaty and report to the Senate, after which it would cease to exist. By the force of circumstance the same men were usually appointed to most of these select committees and gradually a permanent committee emerged.[71] A similar process in other fields was producing the other great standing committees of Congress, which have exercised so much power without being controlled by the publicity which Congress receives. The Senate Committee on Foreign Relations has proved an especially effective agency for the Senate in its struggles with the President for the control of

[71] It was not made a standing committee until December 1816, but had been so in everything except name prior to that time. The origin and growth of the committee are carefully traced by Hayden, pp. 168-195.

foreign relations. With a semi-permanent personnel, composed of the most prominent senators, very conscious of its position and jealous of its powers, the committee has often shown itself more concerned with defending or extending the prerogatives of the Senate than with the merits of the treaty before it. The committee undoubtedly increases the already great opportunities for the opposition to a treaty. This is particularly true when, as is very frequently the case, the chairman and majority of the committee are political enemies of the President. Under the guise of protecting the constitutonal powers of the Senate the committee can delay action on a treaty until a hostile public opinion can be aroused. The committee can also kill a treaty by not reporting it to the Senate, a method which has the advantage of not fixing responsibility as it would be if the members of the Senate voted on the treaty.

CHAPTER III

A PERIOD OF QUIESCENCE, 1815-1841

I mentioned this to Colonel [Senator] Taylor, who had told me that the opposition to the Convention in the Senate was entirely a Presidential electioneering manoeuvre. Van Buren and Holmes, of Maine, were its prime instigators, and almost all its supporters are dead-set Crawford men.

JOHN QUINCY ADAMS.[1]

The arrival of the Convention had scarcely been announced before the opponents of Mr. Adams began to sound the alarm on his concession to Great Britain of the right of search, and this point they are evidently resolved to make a lever for discrediting him with the nation, and thereby crushing his hopes of attaining the Presidential Chair.

HENRY U. ADDINGTON.[2]

The knowledge that the Constitution of the United States renders all their diplomatic compacts liable to this sort of revision undoubtedly precludes the possibility of taking exception at any particular instance in which that revision is exercised; but the repetition of such instances does not serve to reconcile to the practice the feelings of the other contracting party whose solemn ratification is thus rendered of no avail, and whose concessions in negotiation having been made (as all such concessions must be understood to be made) conditionally, are thus accepted as positive and absolute, while what may have been the stipulated price of those concessions is withdrawn.

GEORGE CANNING.[3]

After peace had been established in 1815 the United States turned its back on the old world and for the next twenty-five years gave its almost undivided attention to domestic problems. Occasionally a glance might be thrown over one shoulder when relations with some foreign power would claim public attention with a development that disturbed the prevailing calm; but such occasions were rare and the interest of the people was only

[1] *Memoirs,* VI, 345.

[2] Addington to Canning, May 21, 1824. *Public Record Office, Foreign Office* 5, vol. 185. Library of Congress Photostats.

[3] Canning to Rush, August 27, 1824, *Am. State Papers, For. Rels.,* V, 365.

temporarily diverted from internal affairs. With public interest elsewhere it was natural that questions of foreign policy no longer served as the battlefield for political struggles. The influence of such questions in elections during this period was negligible. Foreign policy was not one of the issues between the factions that struggled for political power during the early part of the period nor between the regularly defined political parties of the latter part.

The number of treaties made would, perhaps, have seemed dangerously large to the members of the federal convention. From December 6, 1815, when the first treaties after the Treaty of Ghent were submitted to the Senate, until Tyler became President in 1841 the Senate passed upon fifty-nine treaties.[4] Among these were few that could be considered important or that did more than establish the formal relations which, by that time, even the United States had accepted as a necessary part of international intercourse. The treaties that stand out are the treaty of 1819 with Spain for the cession of Florida, the Rush-Bagot exchange of notes in 1817 limiting naval forces on the Great Lakes, the treaty of 1818 with Great Britain, that of 1826 with Denmark regarding the Sound dues, and the claims convention of 1831 with France.[5] Practically all the rest concerned the routine establishment of formal contact with Euro-

[4] This number was obtained by going through the *Executive Journal of the Senate*. Several treaties were submitted to the Senate twice as the exchange of ratifications did not take place within the prescribed time, but have only been counted once here. The list in Malloy, *Treaties,* III, ix-xi, does not include the treaties which were not ratified by both parties and does include several decisions of commissioners which were provided for by treaty, and which were not submitted to the Senate.

[5] The Rush-Bagot agreement did not appear as important to contemporaries as it has to those enjoying a retrospective view. The importance of the claims convention with France is chiefly due to the dispute which occurred after ratifications had been exchanged, and therefore it was not deemed important when the Senate acted upon it. In the subsequent dispute, when the possibility of war was evident, the political opponents of the President, particularly in the Senate, attempted to get what partisan advantage they could from the situation. Their attempts are described by Claude G. Bowers, *The Party Battles of the Jackson Period,* pp. 386-422.

pean powers and with the newly independent governments of Latin-America.

Of the four treaties lost during this period through the action of the Senate, the first and most important was that which had been signed with Great Britain on March 13, 1824, for the suppression of the slave trade. In the early years of the century laws against the slave trade had been passed by many countries, including the United States, but it was soon apparent that the traffic could not be effectively stopped unless an international right of search was permitted.[6] Great Britain assumed the initiative in seeking treaties granting a mutual right of search in times of peace, and succeeded in concluding them with several European powers. There can be no doubt of the influence of humanitarian motives on the action of Great Britain, yet in this instance interest coincided with ideals. Great Britain as the supreme naval power would become the policeman of the seas and thus secure many advantages, including the chance of much prize money. The controversies that the United States had recently had with Great Britain over rights at sea caused the failure of the first attempts to obtain a reciprocal extension of the right of search for the suppression of the slave trade.[7] The negotiations were resumed, however, when the solicitations of Great Britain were supplemented by the pressure from the humanitarian movement within the United States. On May 15, 1820, a law declaring the slave trade piracy was enacted.[8] The House of Representatives was particularly active in the agitation against the trade and a number of reports on the subject were made by various committees.[9] In several of these it was stated that a mutual right of search was indispensable for the suppression of the trade.[10] By a vote of one hundred and thirty-one to nine the

[6] W. E. Burghardt Du Bois, *The Suppression of the African Slave Trade to the United States of America*, pp. 131-141.

[7] *Am. State Papers, For. Rels.*, V, 69-76.

[8] *U. S. Statutes at Large*, III, 600.

[9] The reports are all noted by De Bois, pp. 137-138.

[10] See especially *Annals of Congress*, Feb. 29, 1861, p. 1069, also *17th Cong., 1st sess., H. Rept.*, No. 92.

House adopted a resolution on February 28, 1823, requesting the President to negotiate with the powers of Europe and America for the suppression of the slave trade and for its denunciation as piracy under international law.[11]

Spurred on by these expressions of opinion, Adams, who had been opposed to the slightest extension of the right of search, gave instructions to Rush which permitted him to sign a treaty in London on March 13, 1824.[12] It included all the provisions which Adams had insisted upon as necessary to prevent abuse of the mutual right of search granted by the treaty. Slavers were to be brought to their own country for trial; no persons were to be taken from the captured vessels; the boarding officer and commanding officer of the searching warship were to be personally liable "for every vexatious and abusive exercise" of the right, to the amount fixed by the court of admiralty hearing the case; and Great Britain was to make the slave trade piracy by law. From the point of view of the British plenipotentiaries, the treaty "exhibited a preponderance of concession on the side of Great Britain in accommodation to the principles and views of the United States." [13]

The treaty was submitted to the Senate with a brief message of transmittal on April 30, 1824.[14] It was a year for a presidential election, always a particularly unhealthy season for treaties of possible political effiect. This treaty suffered severely. The official record of the Senate, as usual, sheds no light on

[11] *Annals of Congress,* Feb. 28, 1823, pp. 1147-1155.

[12] The treaty, with correspondence relating to it, is given in *Am. State Papers, For. Rels.,* V, 315-341.

[13] *Ibid.,* p. 318. Adams truthfully stated in his diary that the treaty "differs only in a very few unimportant particulars from the draft which I sent to R. Rush last June." *Memoirs,* VI, 311. Eighteen years later, when Lord Ashburton came to the United States on his famous mission, Adams reviewed the history of this treaty in a speech in the House of Representatives. He then stated the case more forcibly saying Canning signed the treaty which Rush presented to him "without varying the dot of an i or the crossing of a t—thus assenting to our own terms, in our own language." *Congressional Globe,* April 14, 1842, p. 424.

[14] *Sen. Ex. Jour.,* III, 373.

the proceedings until votes were taken; but again the diary of one of the interested persons has illuminated the dark corners and has saved the opinions of some of the actors as to why things were done as they were. This time it was John Quincy Adams, Secretary of State and heir-presumptive to the presidency, who watched over the treaty with the solicitude of a father and wrote down his fears and suspicions with a heavy heart. Somehow the treaty had become entangled with his political future, for his rivals were going to use it as one means to discredit him and to prevent him from succeeding to the presidency. There were, at this time, no regularly defined political parties, but in their place were several political factions, each supporting its leader for the presidency. Adams, as Secretary of State, enjoyed the advantage of holding the position from which his immediate predecessors had been promoted to the White House. His most formidable rival in the eyes of officialdom was Crawford, the Secretary of the Treasury, for the great support which Jackson, a rank outsider, was to receive at the ballot boxes in November was not anticipated in Washington.

At first there was no expectation of opposition in the Senate and Adams even drafted a form of ratification to be given to the British representative. On May 7 came the first signs of hostility, due, wrote Adams, to two causes.[15] The first was that Canning, when asking Parliament to pass a bill declaring slave traders pirates, stated that the right of search was mutually conceded and the reports of his speech reaching America said nothing of the great restrictions on the right of search as granted. Perhaps Canning did not stress the restrictions unduly, as he wished to have the bill passed and they had politics in England, too. As this report was all that the public in the United States knew of the treaty it was perhaps natural that uneasiness should be felt and a meeting should be called in Baltimore to memorialize the Senate against the ratification of the treaty. The second cause of opposition, said Adams, " is

[15] *Memoirs*, VI, 321.

the keen and eager look-out of my political opponents at this moment for anything that may serve as a missle weapon against me. They have thus snatched at this jesuitical statement of Canning, and, without seeing the Convention, endeavor to raise a popular clamor against me for conceding the right of search."

The subsequent proceedings justify the suspicions of Adams which were sometimes aroused on slight provocation. The same boat which brought news of Canning's speech also brought a copy of the law which he had persuaded Parliament to approve. This was communicated to the Senate on May 8, so that the Senate throughout the discussion was fully informed that Canning had acted in good faith and had fulfilled his pledges to the American government.[16] From then until the final action of the Senate two weeks later the daily fluctuations in the prospects of the treaty were noted by Adams, together with the substance of his conversations on the subject with many of the senators. The reports from the Senate became less and less sanguine until hope for the treaty was almost gone.[17] As a last resort the President decided to send a special message to the Senate concerning the treaty and requested Adams to prepare one for him, a task Adams immediately performed.[18]

The message, which was sent to the Senate on May 21, contained a strong appeal.[19] After referring to the act of Congress and the resolutions of the House of Representatives on the subject, and calling attention to the strict provisions in the treaty to prevent abuse of the right of search the President based his appeal on the broader grounds of protecting his foreign policy. He said

> Other considerations of high importance urge the adoption of this convention. We have, at this moment, pending with Great Britain, sundry other negotiations, intimately connected with the welfare, and even the peace of our Union. In one of them, nearly a third part of the territory of the State of Maine is in contestation . . . and in the

[16] *Am. State Papers, For. Rels.*, V, 341-343.

[17] *Memoirs*, VI, 329, 330, 336, 338, 341.

[18] *Ibid.*, p. 344.

[19] *Sen. Ex. Jour.*, III, 380-383.

fifth, the whole system of South American concerns, connected with a general recognition of South American independence, may again, from hour to hour, become, as it has already been, an object of concerted operations of the highest interest to both nations, and to the peace of the world.

It cannot be disguised, that the rejection of this convention cannot fail to have a very injurious influence on the good understanding between the two governments on all these points. That it would place the Executive administration under embarassment, and subject it, the Congress, and the nation, to the charge of insincerity . . . must be obvious. To invite all nations with the statute of piracy in our hands, to adopt its principles as the law of nations, and yet to deny to all the common right of search for the pirate, whom it would be impossible to detect without entering and searching the vessel, would expose us, not simply, to the charge of inconsistency.

Although all this had already been said in the Senate, according to Senator Rufus King, the message of the President saved the treaty from an almost certain rejection.[20] On the following day the Senate gave its advice and consent to the treaty by a vote of twenty-nine to thirteen, but in such a mutilated form that both friends and opponents did not expect Great Britain to accept the remnants.[21] Among the changes required by the Senate for its consent to the treaty the most important was the omission of the words " of America " in the first article. This article had provided that vessels of the two powers could cruise on the coasts of Africa, of America, and of the West Indies, and seize slave traders. By striking out the words " of America " and leaving only the neutral coast of Africa and the coast of the British territory in the West Indies as the area for operations the reciprocal nature of the treaty was lost. Great Britain would be permitting the United States to capture vessels off her

[20] Adams, *Memoirs,* VI, 350, 356.

[21] *Sen. Ex. Jour.,* III, 386. Senator King who favored the treaty said in a letter written that day, " in other words they have rejected it." King, VI, 571. Senator Van Buren who voted against the treaty also considered the amendments as equivalent to rejection as he says in his *Autobiography,* p. 203, " We opposed the treaty and defeated it by a decided vote." But Adams hoped Great Britain would accept. *Memoirs,* VI, 350.

slave territory while she was denied a similar right off the coasts of the United States. This was a concession too great to be granted by any government in Great Britain. In urging this vital amendment the opponents of the treaty hoped to cause the ultimate defeat of the entire treaty by attracting to their side enough votes to remove from the treaty the concessions made by the United States. In this they were successful, as the vote on the question of retaining the words "of America" was twenty-three to twenty, all of the thirteen opponents of the treaty being among the twenty who refused to give their consent to the words.[22]

The reasons for the opposition, as given by the senators leading it, were that the pretext of searching for slaves might be used as an excuse when the real object was to impress seamen, and that the treaty was not necessary as the slave trade was already forbidden by law.[23] These reasons lacked substance since the treaty expressly forbade the taking of anyone off a captured boat, besides containing other restrictions which would have prevented impressment. Furthermore, the necessity of supplementing the legal prohibition of the slave trade had been amply demonstrated. No satisfactory reason was advanced for excluding the coast of America and no answer was given to the President's statement that "the restriction of search for pirates, to the African coast, is incompatible with the idea of such a crime." Nor could a possible fear of abolition be the real motive of the opposition as only five of the thirteen senators who voted against the treaty were from the Southern States.[24]

Adams was not the only one who had no hesitation in stating that the real motives of the opponents of the treaty were purely

[22] *Sen. Ex. Jour.*, III, 385.

[23] An editorial in the *National Intelligencer* of May 29, 1824, gives the arguments said to have been used in the Senate. This article was written by Senator Holmes of Maine, a Crawford supporter and one of the leading opponents of the treaty. Adams, *Memoirs*, VI, 368.

[24] This fact is commented upon in *Niles' Weekly Register* of June 5, 1824.

political. His interpretation, which is, of course, subject to the charge of prejudice, was that "the only object" of those who had defeated the treaty "was to use it as a weapon to raise a popular clamor against me."[25] Others less prejudiced and in a better position to know the facts agreed with him. Senator King told him, "that in the management of the opposition there had been great disingenuousness and rancor, and it had been clearly and plainly disclosed to the observation of every one that the main object of it was an electioneering engine against me."[26] On the evening after the Senate had finally acted upon the treaty Senator Taylor gave Adams an account of what had happened in the Senate, in which he said that "all the other partisans of Mr. Crawford had made of it a bitter and rancorous party matter."[27] Senator Johnson of Kentucky also thought the presidential election furnished the real but unavowed motive of the opposition.[28] Mercer, the member of the House of Representatives who had taken the lead there in the agitation against the slave trade, wrote Stratford Canning that the opposition to the treaty was a personal issue "connected with the Presidential question" and told Adams that "it was apparent and known to every one that the opposition now started against the Convention was merely personal, pointed against me with reference to the Presidential election, and but for that would not have existed."[29] Even Van Buren, one of the opposition, agreed with this interpretation of the Senate's action. In his Autobiography Van Buren wrote that "we opposed the treaty and defeated it by a decided vote," a statement which, with the accompanying text, shows that by "we" he

[25] *Memoirs*, VI, 366.

[26] *Ibid.*, p. 350. That Senator King was expressing his true opinion and not merely polite sympathy is shown by the facts that he wrote to his son, "Entre nous this rejection of the Convention in my belief is produced by the presidential Election" and to his friend Gore, "The friends of Crawford expect by these objections to discredit Adams." King, VI, 571, 573.

[27] Adams, *Memoirs*, VI, 348.

[28] *Ibid.*, p. 337.

[29] *Ibid.*, pp. 357, 361-362.

meant his party and that he, too, considered the vote a party matter.[30]

Another person who anxiously watched the fate of the treaty in the Senate and who cannot be accused of letting political motives influence his judgment was the British Chargé Addington. In a long dispatch to Canning, marked secret and confidential, he explained the nature and causes of the opposition to the treaty that had accumulated in the Senate.

Three causes combined to excite this opposition. Disinclination to concede the right of search; apprehension of ulterior measures being in contemplation by Great Britain for effecting the total suppression of slavery in all Countries, and thirdly and principally, Party Spirit.

The first objection, I have sufficient reason for supposing, was, in its broad and honest shape, confined to a few individuals. The majority appeared satisfied with the guards and limitations with which the right of search had been surrounded in the convention. This concession was, however, made by many a pretext for opposing the acceptance of that instrument by the Senate.

The second objection was felt and urged with somewhat greater sincerity by many of the Senators, especially those from the Southern or Slave holding states. . . .

The real cause of the obstruction, Sir, is Party Spirit. To this may be attributed the whole opposition which has been made to the measure. [He then explained the political situation.]

The arrival of the Convention had scarcely been announced before the opponents of Mr. Adams began to sound the alarm on his concession to Great Britain of the right of search, and this point they are evidently resolved to make a lever for discrediting him with the nation, and thereby crushing his hopes of attaining the Presidential Chair.

* * * * * * * * *

I have entered thus at length into explanations on this subject, because I conceive it to be of the most serious importance to the relations existing between Great Britain and the United States that His Majesty's Ministers should be made fully acquainted with the real causes of the opposition made by a portion of this Government to a measure which originated in another branch of it. . . .

The preceding hypothesis as to the real causes of the opposition to the Convention is not lightly entertained. It is founded on constant communication with many of the best informed Gentlemen in Congress, as well as on personal observation.

---

[30] P. 203.

I am assured that almost the whole opposition made to the measure in the Senate, is conducted by the adherents of the Secretary of the Treasury. Mr. Adams is also evidently under the same impression.[31]

An analysis of the decisive votes in the Senate on the treaty confirms these contemporary opinions. Certainly all of the thirteen who voted against the treaty were supporters of Crawford, as Addington reported to Canning.[32] And among the seven others who joined the thirteen in making the fatal amendment were several who were listed by Adams in his numerous canvasses of the political situation as being opposed to him even though they were not active Crawford men.[33]

Further confirmation of the political motives of the senators who mutilated the treaty can be found in the fact that attempts were made to use the treaty against Adams in the campaign during the following months. These apparently met with little success, at least in the opinion of Addington expressed in a report to his government on the course of the election. He wrote, "The attacks made upon the Secretary of State on the ground of his surrender of the right of search, do not appear to have made as yet any deep impression on the public mind, but they are reiterated again and again and may in the end excite in some portions of the people sentiments in his disfavour." [34]

However unsuccessful the maneuver may have been politically, it did succeed in killing the treaty. The general expectation that the alterations proposed by the Senate could not be accepted by Great Britain was realized. Canning offered to accept all the changes except the one omitting the coasts of America from the provisions of the treaty, since this would imply that the British were violating the law while the people in the United States were not. "To such an equality, leading

[31] Addington to Canning, May 21, 1824, *Public Record Office, Foreign Office* 5, vol. 185. Library of Congress Photostats.

[32] May 31, 1824. *Ibid.*, vol. 186.

[33] *Memoirs*, VI, 327, 328, 366.

[34] Addington to Canning, Aug. 2, 1824, *Public Record Office, Foreign Office* 5, vol. 186. Library of Congress Photostats.

to such an inference, his Majesty's Government can never advise his Majesty to consent. It would have been rejected if proposed in the course of negotiation. It can still less be admitted as a new demand after the conclusion of the treaty." [35] The question was discussed at a cabinet meeting on November 10, when it was decided not to accept this offer.[36] The only result from the correspondence on the subject was that Adams was given an opportunity to exercise his argumentative powers defending a position he did not approve, and to explain again to the British Foreign Office the peculiar nature of the treaty-making power of the United States.[37]

While it seems certain that the treaty was lost through the attempt of political opponents to discredit Adams, there is little or no trace of the effect of politics or of the constitutional struggle with the President to be seen in the fate of a similar treaty signed on December 10, 1824, with the recently recognized Republic of Colombia. This treaty enjoys the distinction of being the first to be absolutely rejected by the Senate.

The most remarkable feature of the rejection of this treaty was that the terms of the treaty were identical with those the Senate had approved in the treaty with Great Britain. As a result of the resolution adopted by the House of Representatives, Colombia was one of the governments invited by the United States to cooperate in the suppression of the slave trade. But before definite terms had been discussed the action of the Senate on the treaty with Great Britain was known. Guided by this information, Richard C. Anderson, the Minister of the

[35] *Am. State Papers, For. Rels.*, V, 365.

[36] Adams, *Memoirs*, VI, 426.

[37] A committee of the House of Representatives at the next session reported on the slave trade and, in reaffirming the position of the House, even hinted at the possibility of considering the treaty binding despite the action of the Senate. The report ended by saying that the committee "will not regard a negotiation to be dissolved, which has approached so near consummation, nor a convention, as absolutely void, which has been executed by one party, and which the United States, having first tendered, should be the last to reject." *Register of Debates in Congress*, Feb. 16, 1825, *Appendix*, pp. 73-75.

United States to Colombia, offered Colombia as a project for a treaty, the identical provisions of the British treaty as amended and approved by the Senate. In reporting his action to the Secretary of State he wrote, "I thought I could not err in offering articles which had passed the various tests to which these had been subject." [38] Since Colombia had no possessions in either Africa or the West Indies the objections which Great Britain had to the amendment of the Senate, omitting the coasts of America from the first article of the treaty, did not apply. The treaty was readily signed in a form that contained only four trifling variations in phraseology from the treaty to which the Senate had given its advice and consent six months previously.

The history of the treaty in the Senate is brief. It was sent to the Senate on February 22, 1825, but it was not considered until the new administration had been installed.[39] Then, on the last day of the session, March 9, the treaty was taken up and quickly killed. The question, whether the Senate would give its advice and consent to the first article, was put and only twelve senators voted in the affirmative while twenty-eight were opposed. No other changes were proposed, and on the question of consenting to the treaty with the exception of the first article all forty votes were in the negative, as without that article the treaty was meaningless.[40]

An examination of the vote shows that the twenty-eight decisive votes were cast by eleven of the thirteen senators who had voted against the treaty with Great Britain—the other two being no longer members—together with eight who had voted for the British treaty, and nine new members. While most of the political opponents of Adams were among the twenty-eight, so also were a large proportion of his friends; and among the twelve voting for the first article were such leading opponents

[38] His report and the treaty are given in *Am. State Papers, For. Rels.*, V, 729-735. See also Raimundo Rivas, *Relaciones Internacionales entre Colombia y los Estados Unidos*, pp. 26-27.

[39] *Sen. Ex. Jour.*, III, 416.

[40] *Ibid.*, pp. 445-446.

as Van Buren, Jackson, and Benton. Of the twelve only Jackson of Tennessee and the two senators from Missouri came from slave states. So it may be, as is usually stated, that the implied threat to the institution of slavery contributed to the defeat of the treaty. Certainly its loss cannot properly be charged to politics, or to a contest with the President, for scarcely any attention at all was given to the treaty by anyone.[41]

The loss of the next treaty also occurred under circumstances which free the members of the Senate from any suspicion of acting through political motives. On July 10, 1826, after a long and discouraging period of negotiation, frequently interrupted by the rapid changes in Mexican politics and the susceptibilities of Mexican politicians, a treaty of amity, commerce, and navigation with Mexico was signed.[42] The last article of the treaty provided that ratifications should be exchanged at Washington within eight months. When all but a month of that period had expired the President submitted the treaty to the Senate with a message calling their attention to the need for haste.[43] The advice and consent of the Senate was given on February 26, 1827, on condition that four changes be made in the treaty.[44] The vote of the Senate was unanimous on two of the

[41] As the result of the negotiations with the United States, Colombia, like Great Britain, passed a law for inflicting the punishment of death on persons engaged in the slave trade. The *American Annual Register* for the years, 1825-26, p. 180. The newspapers merely reported the rejection of the treaty, after the injunction of secrecy was removed, without commenting on the cause of it. *Niles' Register,* Mar. 12, 1825 and Mar. 26, 1825; *National Intelligencer,* Mar. 10, 1825. There is almost no mention of the treaty in the journals of the members of the Senate or of the administration. Adams records its rejection in his diary without expressing any opinion. This uncharacteristic omission is explainable by the great demands on him in his new office. It is also evident that a treaty with Colombia was regarded as of little consequence compared to the same treaty with Great Britain.

[42] The treaty with the correspondence relating to it are in *Am. State Papers, For. Rels.*, VI, 578-613. An excellent account of it and the subsequent negotiations on the subject during the following five years is in William R. Manning, *Early Diplomatic Relations between the United States and Mexico,* pp. 205-251.

[43] *Sen. Ex. Jour.*, III, 568.

[44] *Ibid.,* pp. 570-572.

proposed amendments and almost so on the others, as only one senator voted against each. On the question of consenting to the treaty as amended the vote was thirty-nine to three in the affirmative. The practical unanimity of the Senate definitely proves the absence of political motives.

None of the alterations made by the Senate was of great significance and all were accepted by Mexico a few years later in another treaty.[45] Moreover, the conditional ratification of the United States was not known to Mexico when that country allowed the time for the exchange of ratifications to expire without ratifying the treaty. So the action of the United States Senate was not the primary cause of the loss of the treaty, but it did provide an excuse with which Mexico could meet any complaints of the United States for her failure to ratify. There was, however, an even better reason that should have estopped the United States from complaining of Mexico's failure to ratify the treaty. The constitution of Mexico required that treaties should receive the consent of its Congress. Accordingly Mexico should have been granted, especially by the United States, the same right to amend, reject, or to take no action at all which the United States had successfully claimed for itself because of a similar constitutional arrangement.

Nevertheless, Mexico was upbraided for her action, or lack of it, in much harsher terms than Lord Harrowby had dared to use with the United States under similar conditions some years before. In 1829 the Secretary of State instructed the Chargé of the United States in Mexico to bring to the serious attention of that government " the various acts and omissions by which the United States have been aggrieved, and against which they have just cause for remonstrance and complaint." [46] Among these was the Mexican action on the treaty of 1826, a subject which was discussed at some length. After describing the negotiations and the prompt approval of the treaty with " beneficent " changes by the United States Senate, the Secretary of

[45] *Am. State Papers, For. Rels.,* VI, 948.
[46] *25th Cong., 2d sess., H. Doc.,* No. 351, p. 41.

State said, "But this promptness and the rectitude of their intentions were rendered unavailing by a spirit of procrastination, which, with the best inclination to view it in a favorable light, cannot be ascribed to any motives consistent with a friendly disposition towards the United States." He then complained that when after great delay the treaty was submitted to the Mexican Congress, "the committee of foreign affairs made an elaborate report upon it, objecting to some of its most liberal and just stipulations, and recommending its ratification, clogged with conditions apparently inserted for no other purpose than that of retarding or rather entirely defeating, the final conclusion of the negotiation." [47]

The fourth treaty during this period, for whose loss the Senate can be held responsible, was a treaty with Switzerland, signed at Paris on March 6, 1835. Its object was to secure to citizens of each country a reciprocal right of succession to personal and real property within the jurisdiction of the other. When Livingston, then United States Minister to France, through whom the negotiations were conducted, as the United States had no diplomatic representative in Switzerland at that time, received authority to negotiate the treaty the Secretary of State informed him that:

> Similar stipulations in regard to the disposal of the property of aliens, are, as you are doubtless aware, familiar to our diplomacy, and will be found on turning to a collection of American treaties, to have been, heretofore, embodied in several of them. The tenth article of our recent treaty with Russia is an example to which I beg leave to refer you, and may serve as a guide in the negotiation now proposed.[48]

The treaty was accordingly signed and dispatched to Washington.[49] It was given to the Senate on December 24, 1835, but was not considered by that body until the following May 30.[50] After being debated on two more days the treaty was

[47] *Ibid.*, p. 45.

[48] McLane to Livingston, April 30, 1834, No. 20, MS. State Department.

[49] Livingston to Forsyth, Feb. 3, 1835, No. 78; March 12, 1835, No. 83; March 26, 1835, No. 85. MSS. State Department.

[50] *Sen. Ex. Jour.*, IV, 496, 553.

rejected on June 11, as only fourteen senators were willing to give their advice and consent and twenty-three refused to do so.[51] In the meantime, diplomatic relations had been broken off with France because of the dispute over the payment of American claims, and the Swiss government was not even informed of the fate of the treaty. Nor was the new Minister who went to Paris informed, for, when he was approached on the subject by the Swiss Chargé d'Affaires, he had to confess his complete ignorance of the treaty and of the reasons for its rejection. He requested the Secretary of State to supply the information because, he said, "I understand that neither he [the Chargé] nor the Swiss government has received any information upon the subject, and a proper comity would seem to require some communication should be made to them." [52] Some eight months later he was answered by the Secretary of State who said, "The grounds of this decision are not officially known to me, and it would be useless now to enter into speculations regarding them." [53]

Speculation concerning the reasons of the Senate is hardly more profitable now. An examination of the vote on the treaty shows that twelve Democrats and two Whigs favored the treaty, while eight Democrats and fifteen Whigs opposed it. The almost solid alignment of the Whig senators against the treaty raises the suspicion of political reasons aimed at the Democratic administration. The fact that eight of the twenty Democrats, or more than one-third, also voted against the treaty would ordinarily clear the opposition of an accusation of political motives, but in this case it tends to substantiate the charge. Six of the eight Democrats were of the states' rights wing of the party, led by Calhoun, and were as bitterly opposed to Jackson and the majority of the party which he controlled

[51] *Ibid.,* pp. 553, 556, 559. The entire executive session on each of these days was not devoted to the treaty, as the consideration of it is only one of many items recorded.

[52] Cass to Forsyth, Jan. 27, 1838, No. 45, MS. State Department.

[53] Forsyth to Cass, Sept. 3, 1838, No. 25. MS. State Department.

as the Whigs.[54] Moreover, it was the year for a presidential election and at a time when political motives are most likely to prevail. Against this view the strongest argument is the utter insignificance of the treaty. It is difficult to believe that anyone thought it could have any political influence, and almost certainly no one did.[55]

A different and very interesting suggestion concerning the reasons of the Senate has been made in a recent article by a student of the subject.[56] He shows that in seven instances between 1830 and 1860 the Senate rejected, dropped, or amended treaties regulating the inheritance and disposal of real property and, from the nature of the amendments and attending circumstances, concludes that the action of the Senate was caused by a desire to avoid any infringement on the right of the states to pass laws limiting the ownership of land by aliens. While much evidence is submitted in support of this view it is by no means conclusive. Within a very few years of the rejection of the Swiss treaty other treaties with similar provisions secured the approval of the Senate.[57] The ratification of these can, perhaps, be explained on the grounds that only a portion of each treaty related to the inheritance and disposition of property, and that the Senate did not wish to endanger the rest by striking that part out, or on the grounds that the Senate was inconsistent due to inattention, as it has often been.[58] A

[54] They were Calhoun and Preston of South Carolina, King of Georgia, King and Moore of Alabama, and Nicholas of Louisiana. *Sen. Ex. Jour.*, IV, 559.

[55] A search has not revealed a single reference to the treaty except in the official documents cited. There is not even a mention of its rejection in the papers because the injunction of secrecy was not removed, probably no one thought it important enough. The negotiations and rejection of the treaty have attracted almost as little attention since then, as the only account of it disclosed by a careful search is that cited below.

[56] Ralston Hayden, "The States' Rights Doctrine and the Treaty-Making Power," *American Historical Review,* XXII, 566-585.

[57] Russia, 1832; Venezuela, 1836; Peru-Bolivia, 1836; Sardinia, 1838.

[58] Hayden, p. 573. On the other hand, some ten years later when the states' rights view had greater strength in the Senate, some treaties similar to the Swiss

greater obstacle to this attempt to explain the action of the Senate by the states' rights doctrine is the vote in the Senate. The six Democrats may have been influenced by their states' rights views, but the same cannot be said of the fifteen Whigs, who were enough to defeat the treaty even if all the Democrats voting had favored it. It is much more probable that the majority of the Whigs were expressing political animus rather than their principles.

treaty and containing no other provisions were approved. Hesse, 1844; Württemberg, 1844; Saxony, 1845; Nassau, 1846.

CHAPTER IV

AN IMPORTANT VICTIM OF POLITICS

I cannot but hope that the treaty would be sanctioned by the Senate, should the time be prolonged to the next session, when the Presidential election will be over, and the party motives that have led to laying the treaty on the table, shall have passed away. JOHN C. CALHOUN.[1]

It cannot be disguised that party considerations influenced many of those, who voted against the ratification, to oppose it. The question of the annexation of Texas to this Government has (as you doubtless have seen from the newspapers of this country) become strictly a party question between the democrats and whigs in the pending contest for the next Presidency. ISAAC VAN ZANDT.[2]
J. P. HENDERSON.

A question of foreign policy, presented in the form of a treaty submitted to the Senate, dominated the election of 1844. The renewed supremacy of foreign policy as a political issue was not due to a revival of interest in relations with European powers, but was the result of the westward expansion of the land-hungry people of the United States. One section of this significant migration spread into Mexico, then created the Republic of Texas and incidentally produced the issue on which the election of 1844 turned. The period, " the roaring forties," was characterized by vigorous assertions of the supreme confidence the young country felt in its " manifest destiny " to expand its political control over the whole continent. A thoughtfully inclined person then considering the aggressive and exuberant temper of the people, so unfavorable to the reciprocal concessions to other nations which are the basis of

[1] From a letter written when Secretary of State. Henry Wheaton, *Elements of International Law* (sixth edition), cvii.

[2] Letter of the Texan representatives in Washington to Anson Jones, the Secretary of State of Texas. George P. Garrison, ed., *Diplomatic Correspondence of the Republic of Texas,* Part II, 285.

peaceful relations, would have found it difficult to believe that foreign relations would quickly cease to be a dominant factor in American life. Yet the attention of the several succeeding generations became so engrossed in the deadly domestic struggle that the election of 1844 was the last in the century to be dominated by an issue of foreign policy and only on rare occasions did such issues play even a minor part.

The political stage on which the treaty carrying the dominant issue of the election of 1844 was to meet its fate, was peculiarly arranged. In 1840 the Whigs had been successful, electing Harrison the first President of their political faith, Tyler Vice-President, and securing a majority in both Houses of Congress. Just one month after his inauguration Harrison died, to the consternation of the Whig leaders, for they had not considered the possibility of having Tyler as President. Tyler had been a prominent Democrat as a member of the House of Representatives for five years, as a governor of Virginia, and as a member of the Senate for nine years. But he was of the aristocratic Virginia wing of the party and a firm supporter of states' rights, so that when Jackson and the boisterous western Democrats got control of the party and showed a conspicuous lack of consideration for the rights of states in the nullification controversy, Tyler joined the opposition. He had been nominated by the Whigs in 1840, for what they thought was a harmless place, to attract other Democrats who had been similarly disgusted with Jacksonian democracy.

Opposition to Jacksonism was the one bond of union between the Whigs and Tyler, since the latter did not change his political principles when he changed parties. The result was that the Whigs had to pay a disastrous price for whatever support they received by nominating Tyler, because he broke with them very soon after succeeding to the presidency. Although a break was inevitable, the circumstances under which it came increased the bitterness on both sides. The immediate cause was a bill creating a national bank to which the Whigs were pledged. This measure was a political necessity as their victory had been chiefly due to the panic of 1837, popularly believed to have been the result of the financial policy of the Democrats. After Tyler's veto of one bill, another was passed by Congress with changes that were supposed to have been approved by the President, but it too was vetoed. Charging bad faith the highly indignant Whig leaders in Congress issued a manifesto reading Tyler out of the party. All the members of the Cabinet expressed their loyalty to the Whig party by resigning. Webster alone remained for a short time to complete the negotiations he was conducting with Great Britain.

The Democrats naturally rejoiced at this turn of events and made the most of it. They gladly accepted office under Tyler and supported his vetoes of Whig policies. Under Tyler the gradual shifting of the control of the Democratic party which had been proceeding quietly in the various local units was accelerated. It was becoming more and more evident that the wing of the party committed to states' rights and to the defense of slavery would dominate. But Tyler was not even the leader of this element in the Democratic party whose principles he steadfastly championed. He was a President without a party, yet the political powers of the President are so great that it was not impossible that he might build up a party and popular following of his own or might become the acknowledged leader of the party to whose principles he subscribed. At least two Vice-Presidents, almost as badly handicapped as Tyler by the lack of political support when succeeding to the presidency, have since demonstrated how easily it can be done, and the possibility was not unappreciated then. If he could achieve some brilliant success that would be very popular with the voters his chances would improve. Not unnaturally the Whigs and those leaders of the Democratic party who hoped to be that party's candidate in 1844, or to share in the victory of the prospective candidate, were anxious to prevent such a personal success. The treaty for the annexation of Texas seemed to many to offer him an opportunity to win a popular following.

The Senate, in which the Whigs had a majority during Tyler's administration, was requested to give its advice and consent to fifteen treaties. Five of these were lost because of the Senate's action upon them. Seven of the fifteen were of such slight importance that no possible political advantage could be squeezed out of them, and they were readily approved without changes by unanimous votes in the Senate. The other three, which received the sanction of the Senate and were put into effect, consisted of an extradition treaty with France, an article added to this treaty, and the Webster-Ashburton Treaty. The extradition treaty with France, signed on November 9, 1843, was approved without amendments by the exact constitutional majority, twenty-four Whigs and six Democrats voting for it while fifteen Democrats opposed it.[3] The additional article to it, signed on April 15, 1844, received the advice and consent of the Senate, after it was amended by the insertion of definitions of "robbery" and "burglary," by a vote of twenty-nine to eleven, the minority being composed of ten Democrats and one Whig.[4] Thus in both the case of the treaty and the additional article the tendency to a party vote was present, although not strong enough to have fatal effect.

The highly important Webster-Ashburton treaty was helped through the Senate by unusual circumstances, some fortuitous and some carefully planned by Webster. Among the former the most important was that the political parentage of the treaty was doubtful. Webster, the Secretary of State who negotiated it, was a Whig; the President was, as has been explained, of no party but had Democratic principles; the rest of the cabinet were Democrats. This mixture made it doubtful if partisan advantage could be gained by claiming credit for either the negotiation or the defeat of the treaty. Fate was also kind to

[3] *Sen. Ex. Jour.*, VI, 230.

[4] *Ibid.*, p. 346. This additional article was really not put into effect as, rather than incorporate the amendments of the Senate in the notes for exchanging ratifications, France signed a new article on Feb. 24, 1845, embodying the changes required by the Senate. This new article was in turn submitted to the Senate and received its approval. *Ibid.*, p. 435.

the treaty in having the Senate act upon it in August 1842, when it was less likely to get tangled up in presidential ambitions that it would have if the time had been nearer to an election for that office. The discovery by Jared Sparks of a map in the French archives which seemed to substantiate the British claims on the northeastern boundary was pure luck; but Webster's use of it in persuading the Senate to accept the settlement reached was practical statesmanship, and was singularly justified by the fact that the British had discovered in their archives another map which seemed to prove the American claims and which was used in defending the treaty in Parliament. Webster also included in the treaty a provision by which the United States was to pay the States of Maine and Massachusetts one hundred and fifty thousand dollars each for their assent to the boundary line fixed by the treaty. Such a provision properly had no place in an agreement with Great Britain, but it was considered likely to mollify the opposition of those states and of their representatives in the Senate. The negotiations resulted in two treaties, one dealing with the boundary and the other with the slave trade and extradition; but at the last moment, even after copies had been dispatched to England, the two were joined in one instrument in the hope of securing the consent of the Senate more easily. Another precautionary measure that Webster took was to consult frequently and privately with members of the Senate during the negotiation, a practice which Senator Benton denounced as highly irregular and as forestalling the judgment of the Senate so that the treaty was "ratified out of doors." [5]

[5] Thomas H. Benton, *Thirty Years' View,* II, 424. The vote in favor of the treaty was thirty-nine to nine, with eight Democrats and one Whig in the minority. Accounts of the treaty are given in Jesse S. Reeves, *American Diplomacy under Tyler and Polk,* pp. 1-57; William A. Dunning, *The British Empire and the United States,* pp. 88-120; George T. Curtis, *Life of Daniel Webster,* II, 94-139; Ephraim D. Adams, "Lord Ashburton and the Treaty of Washington," in *American Historical Review,* XVII, 764-782. These accounts are concerned mainly with the negotiations and only mention incidentally the remarkable campaign Webster conducted to secure the consent of the Senate to the treaty.

Of the five treaties that were lost, the first to meet with disaster was a treaty of commerce with Texas which was signed on July 30, 1842.[6] The treaty was put in the hands of the Senate several weeks later, but no action was taken on it until March 3, 1843, the day before the session ended. Then, as on so many other occasions, the Senate struck out of the treaty the provisions containing the principal concessions on the part of the United States and gave its consent unanimously to what was left. By a vote of thirty-two to nine, the Senate rejected the fifth article, which would have permitted Texan cotton to be sold in the United States free of duty for five years, and the fourth article, which provided for the free navigation of the Red River, Sabine River, boundary rivers, and the lower Mississippi.[7] Although both these articles were reciprocal and, under the fifth, manufactures or produce from the United States could enter Texas free of duty, they included the chief benefits Texas would have received from the treaty. Without them, Van Zandt had warned Senator Archer, "the fragments would not be worth preserving," and such was the view taken by the government of Texas. So the treaty was lost.[8]

The thirty-two senators who voted for the alteration of the treaty included twenty-five Whigs and seven Democrats, while the nine votes opposing the change were cast by eight Democrats and one Whig. The fact that practically half of the Democrats joined the Whigs seems to warrant the conclusion that politics had little to do with the vote. Further justification for

[6] The treaty and some correspondence relating to it are given in Garrison, *Diplomatic Correspondence,* Part I, 576-580, 619-628, 642-644. Van Zandt, the Texan representative in Washington, disregarded the usual rules and addressed a long letter to Senator Archer, the chairman of the Committee on Foreign Relations in which he explained the merits of the treaty. *Ibid.,* Part II, 139-148.

[7] *Sen. Ex. Jour.,* VI, 188.

[8] Garrison, *Diplomatic Correspondence,* Part II, 148. In a private letter written to the Secretary of State of Texas, Van Zandt considered the treaty rejected and said, "Some of the people of this country are disposed to think that they can claim what they please at our hands and we will yield it, of course." Anson Jones, *Memoranda and Official Correspondence Relating to the Republic of Texas,* p. 213.

this view is found in the reasons assigned for the action of the Senate by persons reporting the transaction. A large variety of reasons were given, ranging from the opposition of holders of repudiated Texan bonds,[9] to a distrust of Texas because "of our own demagogical madness and diabolical insubordination at home." [10] But no one suggested that the reason might be politics, although the same persons were quick to see political motives a year later.[11] The loss of this treaty was of no consequence as events turned out, yet its fate might well have convinced some of the hesitating leaders of Texas that close relations and annexation to the United States would prove impossible to accomplish.

The next treaty to be lost was another victim of the propensity of the Senate for making changes in treaties. One of the most fruitful sources of irritation between the United States and Mexico during the decade before 1846 was the large number of claims which citizens of the United States had against Mexico. In 1839 a treaty was negotiated for their settlement, but before all had been adjudicated the commission provided by the treaty was obliged to dissolve in accordance with the time limit fixed by the treaty.[12] On the 30th of January, 1843, another treaty was signed, which provided a new method for paying the claims which had been settled, and which contained a promise on the part of Mexico to make another convention

[9] Garrison, *Diplomatic Correspondence,* Part I, 614.

[10] *Ibid.,* Part II, 130.

[11] For other reasons given, see *ibid.,* Part II, 132-134, 149. The British representative in Texas reported several interesting explanations. Ephraim D. Adams, ed., *British Diplomatic Correspondence Concerning the Republic of Texas,* pp. 166-167. Fear of the competition of Texan cotton cannot have been the reason as four of the nine votes in favor of leaving that provision in were cast by senators from Mississippi, South Carolina, Alabama, and Georgia. The real reason seems to have been the desire not to jeopardize the settlement of the claims against Mexico which were apparently about to be paid. Lyon G. Tyler, *The Letters and Times of the Tylers,* II, 256.

[12] Malloy, II, 1101. John Bassett Moore, *History and Digest of the International Arbitrations to Which the United States Has Been a Party,* II, 1231 ff.

for the settlement of the claims not decided under the treaty of 1839.[13] After much urging from the United States the promised treaty was signed on November 20, 1843.[14]

In his letter to the Secretary of State reporting the successful negotiation of the treaty, Waddy Thompson, Minister of the United States to Mexico, justly claimed that he had secured all the points that had been designated as the " most material " in his instructions. One deviation of some importance was made from the draft of a treaty which had been given to him; instead of meeting in Washington, as the State Department desired, the commission which would pass upon the claims was to meet in Mexico City. Thompson had argued that the claims presented to the previous board were all against Mexico and that as the claimants resided in the United States it would be a hardship to make them all travel to Mexico. To this the Mexican plenipotentiaries replied that the former commission had met in Washington and they were justified in insisting that this one should meet in Mexico, as it could also settle claims of the citizens and government of Mexico against the United States. " I thought," wrote Thompson, " that there was much reason in their demand; and as it was a matter of punctilio, and as, with a Spaniard, punctilio is everything, I was well satisfied that it would be a *sine qua non,* and therefore yielded it in consideration of their allowing me to name the arbiter—a much more important concession." [15] Apparently the President had no objections to this provision, for in his message transmitting the treaty to the Senate he commended the promptness and good faith of Mexico in fulfilling its pledge in the treaty of January,

[13] Malloy, II, 1105. The payments were not made as they fell due, a circumstance which added to the general irritation.

[14] The treaty, the instructions, and the diplomatic correspondence leading up to it are given in *28th Cong., 2d sess., H. Doc.,* No. 158.

[15] *Ibid.,* p. 20. " I could not see any great importance as to the place where the commission met, the more especially as nearly all of the seven claims which alone were to be submitted to this commission depended upon documentary evidence entirely, and all these documents were in the public archives of Mexico." Waddy Thompson, *Recollections of Mexico,* p. 226.

1843, and said, "I am happy to believe that this Convention provides, as fully as is practicable, for the adjustment of all claims of our citizens on the Government of Mexico." [16]

The Senate, however, cared little for matters of "punctilio" or for Mexican sensitiveness, and by unanimous votes amended the treaty so that the commission would meet in Washington.[17] One other alteration was made by the Senate. Only twenty-five senators were willing to give their advice and consent to the sixteenth article and seventeen refused.[18] This article, which provided for the settlement of all claims of either government against the other, was eliminated by a party vote as fifteen of the seventeen were Democrats and nineteen of the twenty-five were Whigs. But the loss of the treaty cannot be charged to politics, as there is no evidence to show which of the amendments was responsible for the subsequent failure of the Mexican government to accept the treaty. From the circumstances and from the comments of Thompson it is a reasonably safe deduction that the amendment made unanimously by the Senate would alone have been used by the Mexican government as an excuse for refusing to exchange ratifications. As it was, the changes in the treaty required by the Senate were called to the attention of the Mexican Government and repeated requests were made for action, but not even a note was written in reply, although verbal assurances were given that the matter would be considered.[19] Whether in calmer times these changes would have been accepted by Mexico is doubtful. As matters actually stood, the knowledge of the impending treaty for the annexation of Texas, which was signed a few weeks after the Senate acted, made it certain Mexico would not accept the altered

[16] *Sen. Ex. Jour.*, VI, 205. Tyler says that the President would not have approved the treaty with this provision in it but offers no contemporary evidence to substantiate this statement. Tyler, II, Appendix B, 691.

[17] *Sen. Ex. Jour.*, VI, 228.

[18] The treaty was then approved by a vote of thirty-six to three. *Ibid.*, p. 229.

[19] *28th Cong., 2d sess., H. Doc.*, No. 19, pp. 7, 28; and *H. Doc.*, No. 144, p. 19.

claims convention. Paying, or agreeing to pay the claims of citizens of the United States, was now sure to be particularly distasteful to the Mexican Government and the alterations of the Senate offered justification for evading the settlement. The only result of the negotiations was to increase the bitterness between the two countries and, thus, to contribute to the causes of the war.[20]

The next treaty to fall a victim to the Senate was the treaty of April 12, 1844, for the annexation of Texas, one of the most important treaties ever submitted. It decided the election of the President in that year. It proposed a policy which, when carried out by other means, was the chief cause of the war with Mexico and which was therefore indirectly responsible for the subsequent acquisition of territory that contributed so materially to the forces culminating in the Civil War. Naturally, in this case as in almost no other, the political struggles over the treaty have received marked attention.[21]

It is unnecessary to discuss the previous attempts to acquire Texas; the tangled political situation in that country; the flirtations of that government with Great Britain; the difficult posi-

[20] Justin H. Smith, *The War with Mexico,* I, 74-81, 189-190. In his annual message of December 8, 1846, Polk reviewed the history of this treaty and after referring to Mexico's refusal to accept the "reasonable" amendments of the Senate, said, "Mexico has thus violated a second time the faith of treaties by failing or refusing to carry into effect the sixth article of the convention of January 1843." Richardson, *Messages and Papers of the Presidents,* V, 2328.

[21] The most comprehensive and best study is Justin H. Smith, *The Annexation of Texas.* His account of both the diplomatic negotiations and the political struggles in the United States is based on the best sources and is written with a sober judgment that compels acceptance of his general conclusions. See also, Jesse S. Reeves, *American Diplomacy under Tyler and Polk,* pp. 58-189. The published diplomatic papers of Texas and of Great Britain have already been noted in other connections in this chapter. The most important papers submitted to Congress can be found in *28th Cong., 1st sess., S. Doc.,* No. 341 and *H. Doc.,* No. 271; *28th Cong., 2d sess., S. Doc.,* No. 79. Some of these were published in the newspapers as the injunction for secrecy was removed from them. See *Niles' Register* of June 8, 1844. The papers and letters of the time, some of which will be quoted below, are naturally full of references to the treaty.

tion of Houston and Anson Jones which compelled them to conduct Texan affairs so as to be prepared for any of several contingencies, with the result that it cannot be absolutely stated whether either really favored annexation or would have preferred independence; or the course of the immediate negotiations leading to the treaty.[22] The important considerations for present purposes are that the policy of independence was open to Texas, that there was present in Texas a party which desired independence rather than annexation, and that the rejection of the treaty offered an opportunity to this party for obtaining its desire. The only thing prior to the submission of the treaty to the Senate, that must be considered is the political situation into which the treaty was introduced. It reached the Senate on the eve of the most decisive part of the presidential campaign, during the period when candidates and issues were to be chosen.

The position of Tyler has been stated. Belonging to neither party, it was still possible for him to create one of his own should he be able to present the country with an issue popular enough to secure a following; or he might be able to capture the nomination of the Democratic party if it would adopt his issue and take him with it. The candidate of the Whigs was sure to be Clay. It was difficult to prevent Clay from being nominated at any time; in 1844 it was well nigh impossible and he was accepted without question by everyone as the future nominee of the party he led. Superficially it seemed equally certain that Van Buren would be the Democratic candidate, for immediately after his defeat in 1840 he had been proposed again and by 1844 Democratic conventions in twenty-four of the twenty-six states had declared for him.[23] Actually, however, there was much dissatisfaction at the prospect of having Van Buren again as nominee and many rivals were pushing or being

[22] Houston and Jones both claimed exclusive credit for annexation and accused each other of opposing it. The conclusion of the historian who has most thoroughly studied the entire episode is that both were right in their accusations and that both really preferred independence for Texas. Smith, *The Annexation of Texas*, pp. 372-381.

[23] Edward Stanwood, *A History of the Presidency from 1788 to 1897*, p. 206.

pushed for the coveted position. Calhoun, Cass, and Buchanan each had supporters and even R. M. Johnson of Kentucky made a tour through the North and stood in places where the lightning might strike him. The friends of each united in opposing Van Buren as the man who blocked the way. But as they could agree on no one else it seemed probable that Van Buren would be the nominee of an unenthusiastic and disunited party, until the treaty for the annexation of Texas suddenly changed the vista.[24]

To a small but vociferous minority of his contemporaries it appeared that Tyler had negotiated this treaty to extend and strengthen the institution of slavery. Some twenty years later this became the generally accepted view in one section of the country where the idea of a long and deliberate conspiracy by "the slave power" was firmly held.[25] To his political opponents it appeared that Tyler had an even more reprehensible purpose, namely, his reelection and their defeat. In the eyes of the Whig politicians it was clear, as A. H. Stephens wrote, that "the whole annexation project is a miserable political humbug, got up as a ruse to divide and distract the Whig party at the South." [26] In the eyes of many of both parties Tyler was making a desperate bid for the Democratic nomination. Adams noted in his diary that "It is John Tyler's last card for a popular whirlwind to carry him through; and he has played it with

[24] *Ibid.*, pp. 208-209. Smith, pp. 234-239. Tyler, II, 303-304. Benton describes a conspiracy with secret committees working feverishly, even in collusion with the Whigs, to accomplish the defeat of Van Buren. *Thirty Years' View,* p. 585. The Calhoun adherents were particularly bitter against Van Buren. J. Franklin Jameson, ed., *Correspondence of John C. Calhoun,* pp. 834-838, 850, 852-857, 862-864, 875-878, 892, 897, 906-908, 917. Charles H. Ambler, ed., *Correspondence of Robert M. T. Hunter, 1826-1876,* pp. 41-48, 51-65.

[25] This belief is typically reflected in Henry Wilson, *History of the Rise and Fall of the Slave Power in America,* I, 586-620, and in Herman E. Von Holst, *The Constitutional and Political History of the United States,* II, 610-657.

[26] Ulrich B. Phillips, ed., *The Correspondence of Robert Toombs, Alexander H. Stephens, and Howell Cobb,* pp. 57-58. The opinions expressed in the leading newspapers of the country are traced in Smith, pp. 180-193.

equal intrepidity and address." [27] Clay took the same view in a letter to Charles Elliot, who had temporary left his duties as British representative in Texas and was recuperating in Virginia.[28] The Texans in Washington reported that Tyler was endangering the treaty by using it as a means of getting elected.[29]

The judgment of history is more favorable to Tyler than was that of any considerable portion of his contemporaries, for according to it, Tyler's primary motive was not the hope of political reward but the laudable "ambition to do something brilliant for the country and gain fame in its history." [30] Still, he was not unaware of its political possibilities and when his supporters attempted to make capital out of it they acted with his approval.[31] The treaty was signed April 12, 1844, and was sent to the Senate ten days later accompanied by a message of unusual length from the President and by the diplomatic correspondence relating to it.[32] Not only was this the year for a presidential election but it was almost the crucial moment of the campaign, for the Whig convention was to meet in Baltimore on May 1, and the Democratic convention in the same city twenty-six days later.

The first few days after the treaty reached the Senate were days of relative calm while anxious politicians awaited their cues. On the 27th of April all doubt was ended. The *National Intelligencer* of that date published a letter in which Clay set

[27] *Memoirs,* XII, 22. See also the bitter attack of Senator Jarnagin, in which he said, "The truth is, this whole business is a fraud, a plan, with which John Tyler intends, if he can, to bamboozle the American people in the approaching Presidential election." *Congressional Globe,* 28th Cong., 1st sess., *Appendix,* p. 685.

[28] *British Diplomatic Correspondence Concerning the Republic of Texas,* p. 349.

[29] Jones, pp. 344, 357.

[30] Smith, p. 103.

[31] Tyler, II, 317.

[32] The treaty, the various messages of the President, and the diplomatic papers are in *28th Cong., 1st sess., S. Doc.,* No. 341.

forth his views. Clay had been aware of the negotiations and had carefully considered what position he should take on the new issue. The tour he was making through the South gave him an opportunity to estimate public opinion and to consult with his political friends in that section. The result was that he decided the South was not nearly so anxious to acquire Texas as had been thought. He knew that some of the Whigs in the North were very bitterly opposed to any suggestion of annexation and Webster was then engaged in spreading this sentiment with the hope, some said, of securing the Whig nomination himself. Moreover, Van Buren, who he confidently expected would be his opponent in the election, was known to be opposed to annexation, and so Clay could neutralize this issue between them by opposing annexation too. The combination of these reasons was enough for Clay, and in his letter written from Raleigh, North Carolina, he opposed annexation at that time chiefly because it would mean war with Mexico. This apparently gave him an opportunity to change his position later, if necessary.[33] As the Whigs had a majority in the Senate, Clay's letter meant the defeat of the treaty unless they would reject their leader and declare for Texas. This they had no intention of doing, especially as there was not time to learn public opinion on the question in the three days between his letter and the convention. Clay was nominated unanimously amid great enthusiasm and the platform adopted did not mention Texas.[34]

On the same day that Clay's letter appeared, a letter stating Van Buren's views was published, a coincidence that appeared to Tyler to be the result of a plot to eliminate him and the issue from the election.[35] Like Clay, Van Buren had studied the situation carefully and had consulted his friends with the result that he, too, did not take a stand against annexation but only against it at that time and under those circumstances. If Mexico should be reconciled, or if a foreign power should attempt to gain Texas, or if the people of the United States

[33] Smith, pp. 239-240. [34] *Ibid.*, pp. 246-247. [35] Tyler, II, 308.

should clearly express their desire for annexation, Van Buren would favor the measure. Unfortunately for him, Van Buren did not, like Clay, have an enthusiastic and united party behind him and his convention did not meet until a month later, so that public opinion in those sections favoring immediate annexation had time to make itself heard, and the opponents of Van Buren within the party had a peg on which to hang their opposition.[36]

The favorable vote of which Texas had been assured before the treaty was signed was now clearly impossible.[37] The treaty remained in the hands of the Committee on Foreign Relations until May 10, when it was reported without amendment.[38] On the same day Crittenden, Clay's closest friend in the Senate, introduced a resolution calling upon the President for information about military measures taken in anticipation of war since the commencement of the annexation negotiations.[39] When this information was supplied by Tyler—and he had to admit some military preparations—the Whigs and Van Buren men decided to give this valuable campaign material to the public. A resolution removing the injunction of secrecy from the treaty and documents—a secrecy already violated—had been previously introduced; it was now amended to include the latest documents and pressed to a vote. The wording of the resolution saying that annexation " is a subject of great importance, on which the will of the people of this Union ought to be consulted ", and saying that because of the peculiar circumstances in this instance publication " cannot be drawn into precedent for different cases in time to come," shows its extraordinary character. The friends of the treaty rallied to its defense with amendments excepting the military information from publication and postponing the final decision of the Senate on the

[36] Smith, pp. 242-246. Jameson, pp. 585, 953.

[37] Garrison, Part II, 239-243. In January 1844, Upshur instructed Murphy to tell Houston that the senators had been canvassed and " a clear constitutional majority of two-thirds are in favor of the measure," *28th Cong., 1st sess., S. Doc.*, No. 341, p. 47.

[38] *Sen. Ex. Jour.*, VI, 271.

[39] *Ibid.*, p. 274.

treaty until a reasonable time should be allowed to hear from the people. But these suggestions were rejected and the treaty, messages, and documents were made public by the votes of the Whig majority aided by Van Buren's friends.[40] More skirmishing followed. McDuffie tried to get "the correspondence of Mr. Clay and Mr. Van Buren with our ministers at Mexico relative to the annexation of Texas to the United States proposed by Presidents Adams and Jackson," but the majority would not let this evidence be published.[41]

The formal decision of the Senate had not been given when the Democratic convention met on May 27, but the end was clearly foreseen.[42] On the same day a second convention also assembled in Baltimore. It had been called with Tyler's approval by a committee of his personal friends and supporters, and with no dissension or delay Tyler was nominated under the banner of "Tyler and Texas."[43] In this way the Democrats in the other convention were notified that unless they nominated a man favoring annexation they would have to meet the competition of that issue at the polls.

No such harmony prevailed in the Democratic convention. Although at one time some thought with Adams, that Tyler had "forced himself upon the whole Democracy as their exclusive candidate," it was apparent by the time the convention met that he had little or no hope of securing that nomination.[44] It had also become evident that Van Buren was probably doomed, and when the convention retained the two-thirds rule, all hope of his nomination was ended. Who would secure the

[40] Tyler's message and the proceedings in the Senate are in *ibid.*, pp. 279-283. The views of some of the press on learning of the military steps are given in Smith, pp. 229-230.

[41] *Sen. Ex. Jour.*, VI, 284.

[42] Jones, pp. 343-346.

[43] Tyler, II, 314-321. Smith, pp. 247-248.

[44] *Memoirs,* XII, 22. Gadsden wrote to Calhoun on May 3, 1844, "No inconsiderable portion of the Democracy are ripe for hoisting the Tyler flag and of rallying under an Administration party to carry out the President's policy as explained in his message." Jameson, p. 953. Smith, p. 247.

6

prize was a doubtful question not settled until after some of the most interesting contests and adroit manipulation that have ever taken place in a national convention. Other factors, in addition to Polk's stand on annexation, were responsible for his nomination. Among them were the skill of his managers and the fact that he was not identified with any of the factions, so that all could unite on him and have a fair chance at the fruits of victory. But it was the treaty for the annexation of Texas that supplied the issue which enabled his enemies to eliminate Van Buren.[45]

The Senate could now complete its consideration of the treaty with the added knowledge that the Democratic platform and nominee were committed to immediate annexation, or " re-annexation," as they called it. Something of what was said in the executive sessions of the Senate is preserved, as the injunction of secrecy was taken from many of the long, formal speeches, and they were printed in the *Congressional Globe*.[46] The reasons advanced in the speeches on both sides need not be examined here because, in this case, the natural suspicion that they contained arguments to defend a position taken for other motives is almost a certainty. The fact of publication shows they were addressed to the voters for political effect. Moreover, as in many other instances, deductions as to reasons and motives should not be based on the speeches of a few, but rather on the votes of the often silent majority.[47] There seemed to be little real opposition to annexation itself. The Texan representatives reported to their government that " the majority of those who voted against ratifying the treaty, are in favour of annexing Texas at some future period," and similar

[45] *Ibid.*, pp. 248-257. A great deal of light is cast on the convention by the letters from Pillow to Polk, *American Historical Review,* XI, 832-843.

[46] In the Appendix of the *Globe* of the 28th Cong., 1st sess. Smith summarizes the most important, pp. 246-271.

[47] In a stimulating article, entitled "A Plea for the Study of Votes in Congress," in the *Annual Report of the American Historical Association* for 1896, pp. 323-334, Orin G. Libby points out the ease with which speeches have led to false conclusions that an examination of the vote would have prevented.

reports were made to both the Mexican and British governments.[48]

A final attempt to postpone the decision of the Senate, until the opinion of the people could be expressed, was abandoned, probably because the senator making it was informed by the Texan representative that Houston would regard such a step as equivalent to rejection. The vote was taken on June 8, 1844.[49] Only sixteen favored the resolution giving the advice and consent of the Senate to the treaty, while thirty-five opposed it.[50] The sixteen favorable votes were cast by fifteen Democrats and one Whig, Henderson of Mississippi. The thirty-five negative votes were cast by twenty-eight Whigs and seven Democrats. The Democrats who broke from their party on this issue were Van Buren men, like Benton and Wright, who either resented his defeat in the convention or felt themselves too deeply committed against annexation to reverse themselves. The latter feeling, if sincere, soon disappeared, for eight months later every Democratic vote was given to the joint resolution annexing Texas. One Democrat, Hannegan of Indiana, who was reported to be in favor of the treaty, did not vote. The factional fights in the Democratic ranks merely added to the majority; it was the partisan vote of the Whigs that was responsible for the rejection of the treaty.[51]

Later, when the political and military contests over slavery dominated the attention of the country, it was frequently stated

[48] Garrison, Part II, 285. The British and Mexican despatches are cited by Smith, p. 279.

[49] Jones, p. 364.

[50] *Sen. Ex. Jour.*, VI, 312.

[51] The vote on the treaty is analyzed by parties and by states in *Niles' Register* of June 15, 1844; in Smith, p. 273. The position of Benton was interesting. As a Southwesterner, as a close associate of Jackson who was ardently and openly supporting the treaty, as an expansionist and an old friend to Texas it would be natural to expect him to fight vigorously for the treaty. On the other hand, he was intimately connected with Van Buren, whom, it was said, he hoped to succeed as President, and he cordially disliked both Tyler and Calhoun. Smith, p. 258.

that the rejection of the annexation treaty was due to that issue.[52] It is true that much was said about slavery and that, in his diplomatic correspondence with the British government, Calhoun maintained that the treaty had been negotiated solely to defend the institution of slavery in the neighboring states of the United States which he said, was threatened by the intention of Great Britain to force abolition on Texas. These letters were submitted to the Senate with the treaty and other documents and, when published, aroused a storm of angry comment from the abolitionists.[53] But despite Calhoun's attempt to put the treaty on the issue of slavery and despite the counter-demonstration from the anti-slavery people in the North, the vote in the Senate shows that that issue was not stronger than party lines in 1844. Fifteen of the twenty-six senators from states south of the Mason and Dixon line voted against the treaty, and five of the sixteen votes for the treaty were from northern states. In only one case—that of Henderson of Mississippi, who was the one Whig to vote for the treaty—did slavery offer an explanation for the position taken.

The subsequent presidential election was determined by the issue which the treaty had furnished at the cost of its life. Clay tried in vain to keep the question out of the campaign, and in his Alabama letters equivocated still more in an effort to please all the voters. As in all elections there were numerous issues involved and it is impossible to determine the exact weight each had in the result, but the annexation of Texas was the decisive issue. Polk's stand on it induced Tyler, who would have split the Democratic vote in the South, to withdraw in his favor, and gave Polk the victory by a narrow margin.[54] The result of the election was generally interpreted as evidence that the country desired the annexation of Texas and at the next session of Congress a joint resolution was passed to accomplish

[52] Some recent writers still say so. Channing, V, 543. John M. Mathews, *The Conduct of American Foreign Relations,* p. 166.

[53] *28th Cong., 1st sess., S. Doc.,* No. 341, pp. 48-53.

[54] The course and significance of the election is fully treated by Smith, Chap. xv.

it. Annexation by treaty would still have been impossible, for, although the wayward Democrats headed by Benton had retraced their steps, perhaps to ensure their position for patronage and other favors, and voted with their party, twenty-five Whigs voted against the joint resolution.[55]

To those interested only in results it is enough that Texas accepted the offer of annexation extended to her and that the great benefits resulting from that union have been secured for the United States. Others may well tremble at the narrow escape from disaster, for an independent Texas guaranteed by Great Britain and France would have been disastrous. The rejection of the treaty could easily have persuaded the Texans that annexation was not feasible and that safety lay in following those leaders who wanted independence with the guarantee of Great Britain and France. That both these powers seriously considered such a guarantee and were once very close to signing one is now well established.[56] The fortunate combination of circumstances which prevented the project from being completed was the political situation and the opposition of public opinion in France to such an advanture, the obstinate refusal of Mexico to acknowledge the independence of Texas, the belief in Texas that annexation could still be accomplished, and to some extent public opinion in Great Britain. None of these could be counted on with certainty. Yet the risk was run by the United States, and not because of any sincere difference of opinion among those in control of foreign policy but because of the hope of partisan advantage.

Overshadowed greatly in importance by the Texan question, another treaty was lost at the same time and for the same reason. On March 25, 1844, a commercial treaty had been signed with Prussia, acting for itself and on behalf of the other German states of the Zollverein. The treaty was not the result

[55] *Congressional Globe,* Feb. 27, 1845, p. 362.

[56] By Smith, pp. 382-413, and Ephraim D. Adams, *British Interests and Activities in Texas,* although they differ in the reasons to which the failure of the proposal is ascribed.

of impulsive action, nor should it have been identified exclusively with the Tyler administration, for the negotiation really started in 1837 after the House of Representatives had passed a resolution requesting the President to negotiate with foreign countries for a modification of the duties on tobacco imported from the United States.[57] Other commodities, including rice and lard, were added to the list from time to time, but the promotion of the tobacco trade remained the primary object of the negotiations. Instructions to secure reductions in the duties on these commodities were sent to Henry Wheaton, an authority on international law, who was then Minister at Berlin. With great persistence, Wheaton endeavored to persuade the members of the Zollverein of the advantages to be gained from complying with the wishes of the United States. His sole achievement after great efforts, especially at the congresses of the Zollverein at Dresden in 1838, at Stuttgart in 1842, and at Berlin in 1843, was a reduction in the duty on rice.[58]

However, Wheaton was told that a treaty for the reduction of the duties on tobacco could be made, if equivalent reductions were made in the tariff of the United States on some German products selected from a list of articles which would not compete with the manufactures of the United States. This suggestion was heartily approved by the authorities in Washington and Wheaton was instructed to sign such a treaty. By the terms actually agreed upon the principal imports from the Zollverein were divided into three classes on which the United States agreed not to levy duties greater than twenty, fifteen, and ten per cent *ad valorem.* The United States also agreed

[57] *Congressional Globe,* February 28, 1837, p. 213.

[58] The best account of this negotiation is in the Introductory Remarks by William B. Lawrence to the sixth edition of Wheaton's *Elements of International Law,* pp. lxxxvii-cx. A briefer account is in George M. Fisk, *Die handelspolitischen und sonstigen volkerrechtlishen Beziehungen zwischen Deutschland und den Vereinigten Statten von Amerika,* pp. 81-91. Much of the correspondence between Wheaton and the State Department is in *25th Cong., 2d sess., H. Doc.,* No. 258; *26th Cong., 1st sess., H. Doc.,* No. 229; *27th Cong., 1st sess., S. Doc.,* No. 55; *28th Cong., 1st sess., S. Doc.,* No. 1, pp. 17-24.

not to raise the existing duties on the wines of Prussia or to impose higher duties on the wines of the other states of the Zollverein than on those of Prussia. The states of the Zollverein agreed to reduce the duties on tobacco and lard to a stipulated rate, not to raise the existing duties on rice, and not to impose any duty on raw cotton.[59] The diplomatic efforts culminating successfully in this agreement had continued through seven years and had been approved by the men of both parties who had served as Secretary of State during that period.[60]

The treaty was sent to the Senate on April 29, 1844, with a message from the President in which its advantages were stressed. After calling attention to the fact that this was the first reduction that had ever been obtained in the heavy duties on American tobacco in foreign markets, and after mentioning the concession on rice, lard, and cotton, Tyler said,

> I cannot but anticipate from its ratification important benefits to the great agricultural, commercial, and navigating interests of the U. States. The concessions on our part relate to articles which are believed not to enter injuriously into competition with the manufacturing interest of the U. States, while a country of great extent and embracing a population of 28,000,000 of human beings will more thoroughly than heretofore be thrown open to the commercial enterprise of our fellow-citizens.[61]

The treaty, thus hopefully launched on its hazardous journey through the Senate, soon met with disaster. On May 30, it was reported without amendment from the Committee on Foreign Relations, but was recommitted two days later.[62] The treaty was again reported back to the Senate on June 14, this time with a recommendation that it be rejected and with a long statement

[59] Both the English and German texts are given in Alfred Zimmermann, *Geschichte der preuszisch-deutschen Handelspolitik,* pp. 599-606.

[60] The one Whig Secretary of State during this period was Webster. His approval of the project is shown by his report to the President of May 24, 1841. *27th Cong., 1st sess., S. Doc.,* No. 1, pp. 28-32.

[61] *Sen. Ex. Jour.,* VI, 262-263. A long letter from Wheaton to Tyler dated March 27, 1844, gives his views on the treaty. Tyler II, 326-328.

[62] *Sen. Ex. Jour.,* VI, 295, 302.

explaining this recommendation.[63] With an unusual solicitude for the prerogatives of the House of Representatives, the sole reason given by the Committee on Foreign Relations was that the treaty would necessitate a change in the laws regulating commerce and raising revenue, which under the Constitution were powers of Congress. "If Congress think the proposed arrangement a beneficial one, it is quite easy to pass a law which shall impose the rates of duty contemplated by it, to take effect when satisfactory information is conveyed to the President that the stipulated equivalents are properly secured." [64] On the following day a motion to lay the treaty on the table carried by a vote of twenty-six to eighteen. This was equivalent to rejecting the treaty, as the session of Congress was to last only two days longer and the treaty required an exchange of ratifications within four months of the date of signature.[65]

The reason assigned by the committee for defeating the treaty does not seem sincere and there were a number of precedents, notably Jay's Treaty, for treaties involving a modification of the revenue laws.[66] It would seem plausible to expect that economic motives might have been responsible, and some evidence to substantiate such an explanation is furnished by the Secretary of the Treasury who, in his Annual Report for 1845, states that the treaty was opposed by the manufacturing interests of the United States.[67] Calhoun placed the Senate's action on different grounds. In a letter to Wheaton, dated June 28,

[63] *Ibid.*, pp. 333-336.

[64] Just how the stipulated equivalents could be secured from foreign governments without a treaty the committee did not say. It did, however, add that it did not think the benefits of the treaty were great.

[65] *Ibid.*, p. 347. Tyler resubmitted the treaty the following December in an effort to save it by having the time for the exchange of ratifications extended. The Committee on Foreign Relations reaffirmed the position it had taken. *Ibid.*, pp. 357, 406. In any case the effort was futile as Wheaton reported to Calhoun that the Zollverein refused to extend the time. Jameson, pp. 1063-1065.

[66] They are cited in Crandall, pp. 183-199.

[67] *29th Cong., 1st sess., H. Doc.*, No. 6, p. 12.

1844, he said, "The true cause . . . I believe to be, the bearing which it was feared it would have on the Presidential election. Mr. Clay's friends, who are a decided majority in the Senate, felt confident of his election, under the old issue, as it stood when Congress met; and were averse to admit any new question to enter the issue." He went on to say that if the time for ratification could be extended until after the election he hoped to secure the consent of the Senate because of "the very inconclusive reasons assigned by the committee on foreign relations for its rejection." [68]

An examination of the vote which laid the treaty on the table shows that Calhoun was right and that responsibility lay with party politics alone and not with the conflicting economic interests of farmers and manufacturers. The twenty-six votes in favor of tabling were cast by twenty-five Whigs and one Democrat, while the eighteen votes that tried to save the treaty came from seventeen Democrats and one Whig.[69] Economic pressure may have accounted for the two votes that broke away from party lines. The Democrat who voted against the treaty represented Pennsylvania, where tariff concessions were apt to be unpopular, and the one Whig vote for the treaty came from the tobacco-growing state of Connecticut. With these possible exceptions economic motives were not dominant, for Whig senators from the great tobacco-raising states of Maryland, Virginia, North Carolina, and Kentucky, in whose behalf the negotiations were begun, voted against the treaty. So did the other Whig senators from the agricultural South and West, which might expect to benefit from the lower duties on German goods, while the Democrats even from the manufacturing states favored the treaty.

The political aspect of the Senate's action on the treaty is further shown by a letter from Jackson to Polk, in which the old leader gave campaign advice to the new one, saying "Let . . . the vote of our senators against the treaty with the Ger-

[68] Wheaton, p. cvii.

[69] Fisk, p. 90, says it was a strictly party vote.

man league be fully exposed to the people. The treaty secured such important benefits. . . . There never was such treachery to the laborer of the South and West, as the rejection of this treaty. I have been greatly astonished that the Democratic papers have said so little about it. It must, when explained to our farmers, arouse them against Whigery." [70] But Jackson's unfavorable criticism of his party's editors was not entirely justified, since the treaty had been frequently used by them as an issue in the campaign.[71]

The last of the treaties which were submitted by Tyler and killed by the Senate did not suffer from either political motives or the constitutional struggle between President and Senate. Its insignificance saved it from those forces, but increased the danger of death through neglect, a danger already considerable because the treaty was made and submitted to the Senate in the twilight zone pending a change in administrations. It was a commercial treaty with New Granada, signed on December 20, 1844, and submitted to the Senate the following February.[72] Some light on the unimportance of the treaty, and incidentally on the manner in which the State Department conducted its affairs, is thrown by a letter written in 1846 by Secretary of State Buchanan to the Chairman of the Senate Committee on Foreign Relations. In this, after referring to the fact that the treaty was still before the Senate, he said, "No copy of this Treaty remains in the Department, nor do I recollect its special provisions. Will you be good enough to request Mr. Dickens to return this Treaty, also, with the action of the Senate upon it." [73]

The Senate, however, never acted on the treaty. The reasons for its hostile neglect are obscure. The Secretary of State evidently believed that senatorial objections to some of the pro-

[70] Tyler, III, 149.

[71] There is an article reviewing the comments of the press on the political use of the treaty in *Niles' Register* of Aug. 24, 1844.

[72] *Sen. Ex. Jour.*, VI, 399.

[73] John Bassett Moore, ed., *The Works of James Buchanan,* VII, 172-173.

visions of the treaty were responsible. When instructing the representative of the United States in New Granada to negotiate a new commercial treaty, he called attention to the existing commercial treaties with Venezuela and Ecuador and said that "Mr. Blackford, shortly before his departure from Bogotá, deemed himself warranted by the circumstances in concluding and signing a Treaty upon a different basis; but this did not receive the approbation of the Senate. Without directly rejecting it, they suffered it to fall, by declining to act upon it." [74] Whether that is the true explanation or whether sheer indifference was responsible might be questioned. The absence of any struggle in the Senate for or against the treaty, the lack of any public or private comment about it and the insignificant nature of its provisions make it clear that neither politics nor insistence on its constitutional prerogatives caused the Senate to kill this treaty by refusing to act on it.

[74] *Ibid.*, p. 184.

CHAPTER V

SOME MINOR EXAMPLES, 1845-1865

I repeat the remark I have heretofore made, that the Presidential election has too much to do with the question of the ratification of the Treaty. More Senators than one will probably give their votes in reference to the probable effect upon the election. It is deeply to be regretted that the best interests of the country should be affected by such considerations. JAMES K. POLK.[1]

And now we are favored by the Republican Senators with a burst on their own side of equally paltry passions and unstatesmanlike intrigue. New York *Times*.[2]

In the twenty years between the administrations of Tyler and Johnson there were two distinct periods when questions arising from the relations of the United States with foreign powers played a leading part in the history of the country. The first was marked by the war with Mexico. The second included the Civil War, when relations with Great Britain were such a decisive factor. Neither crisis produced any defeated treaties. The single treaty resulting from the war with Mexico was ratified. Fortunately, no treaty involving critical issues had to be negotiated with Great Britain during the Civil War. It is, therefore, permissible in a study of the defeated treaties to consider the twenty years as one period.

It was a period of increasing activity for the treaty-making power, since the Senate was requested to give its advice and consent to one hundred and eighteen international agreements.[3]

[1] Milo M. Quaife, ed., *The Diary of James K. Polk,* III, 371.

[2] June 1, 1860, referring to the action of the Senate on the treaty of Dec. 14, 1859, with Mexico.

[3] As in the other periods this statement is based on an examination of the *Executive Journal of the Senate.* In a number of cases where the Senate required amendments the other power objected to having the amendments appear only in the act of ratification and so new treaties embodying the changes were

The vast majority of these were incidental to the routine business of foreign relations, which, when undisturbed by unusual developments, receives little attention from the public and only spasmodic supervision from the Senate. While some treaties of this character are carefully scrutinized and amended, others, even with similar provisions, are readily approved after a perfunctory examination.

Six of the perfected treaties contained important provisions that merited and received special attention from the Senate. These were the Oregon treaty of June 15, 1846, the treaty of December 12, 1846, with New Grenada, which guaranteed the neutrality of the Isthmus of Panama, the treaty of Guadalupe Hidalgo, the Clayton-Bulwer treaty, the Gadsden treaty, and the Canadian reciprocity treaty of 1854.[4] It is interesting to note that most of these were helped through the Senate by unusual conditions. The obvious wisdom of removing the danger of war with Great Britain while engaged in hostilities with Mexico was an important factor in securing the consent of the Senate to the Oregon treaty. The treaty of peace with Mexico, signed at Guadalupe Hidalgo in 1848, at one time seemed likely to be made a party issue, but after some hesitation the Whig senators refused to take the responsibility of rejecting it, although they attempted, according to Polk, " to effect its rejection indirectly, by putting it in such a form that Mexico will not ratify it." [5] The treaty of December 30, 1853,

signed. Thus the treaty of Jan. 30, 1857, with Baden was the same as that of March 10, 1856 with the amendments of the Senate; the treaty of Aug. 21, 1857 with the Netherlands replaced that of May 29, 1856; the treaty of June 21, 1867, with Nicaragua replaced that of March 16, 1859; the treaty of Dec. 13, 1856, with Persia replaced that of Oct. 9, 1851. *Sen. Ex. Jour.*, X, 145, 239; 109, 276; XI, 218; XVI, 152; VIII, 373; X, 233. Although the second treaty was submitted to the Senate each time, the two have been counted as one even in the case of Nicaragua where eight years intervened.

[4] The treaty of March 31, 1854, which Perry made with Japan was not regarded as important by contemporaneous opinion in the United States.

[5] Quaife, III, 376. Polk's diary, in which he recorded numerous conversations with members of the Senate about the treaty, shows how narrowly it escaped from being a political issue. It was not the ability of the senators to resist the tempta-

which Gadsden negotiated with Mexico, came out of the Senate with all its essential features altered so radically that it was expected that Santa Ana would refuse to accept it, as he undoubtedly would have liked to do, but his extreme need for money saved the treaty. Although present political motives were not paramount in the Senate's action on this treaty.[6] The treaty for commercial reciprocity with Canada, which Lord Elgin signed for Great Britain on June 5, 1854, is said to have received much help in the Senate from Lord Elgin's social entertainments. It has been referred to as the treaty "floated through on champagne."[7]

Of the one hundred and eighteen agreements with foreign powers the Senate can be held responsible for the failure of eighteen to be perfected. Most of the eighteen were of very minor importance and were lost under circumstances which preclude the possibility of political motives or constitutional struggle on the part of the Senate.

Seven of these were extradition treaties. The treaties of Sep-

tion of political motives but the doubts of the political wisdom of rejecting the treaty, that saved it. *Ibid.*, pp. 363-377.

[6] Paul N. Garber, *The Gadsden Treaty,* pp. 118-139.

[7] James Ford Rhodes, *History of the United States,* II, 8-9. This reference is based on the lively account of Laurence Oliphant, then secretary to Lord Elgin, in which he tells how the Democratic senators, who Marcy said would oppose the treaty, were lavishly entertained and persuaded to approve the treaty, much to the surprise of the Secretary of State. *Episodes in a Life of Adventure,* pp. 37-44. How much weight should be assigned to this influence is open to question; but, if there is any truth at all in his account, the negotiations illustrate the use of doubtful means of persuasion by both parties. The procedure of the United States was, perhaps, less creditable, for earlier in the negotiations a special agent, Israel D. Andrews, was sent to Canada where he distributed some thousands of dollars to editors and politicians to promote a favorable attitude toward the proposed treaty. Charles C. Tansill, "The Canadian Reciprocity Treaty of 1854," *Johns Hopkins University Studies,* XL, No. 2, pp. 66-74. In a long letter to the British Foreign Secretary, Lord Elgin expressed his vigorous disapproval of this special agent and especially of the claim which he had made to the effect that Lord Elgin had authorized him to pay money to members of the Senate. John L. Morison, *The Eighth Earl of Elgin,* pp. 177-186.

tember 15, 1846 with Switzerland,[8] of February 11, 1853 with Belgium,[9] of June 20, 1855 with Nicaragua,[10] of May 27, 1856 with Chile,[11] of July 10, 1856 with Venezuela,[12] and of May 29, 1862 with Salvador,[13] were all amended by the Senate and failed because the other parties would not accept the amendments. In every case the amendments of the Senate were adopted by unanimous votes and the treaties were then approved unanimously or by overwhelming majorities, so that the action of the Senate was clearly non-partisan. The content of the amendments shows that the action of the Senate was not due to a contest with the President for power. The other defeated extradition treaty was that of July 20, 1850 with Mexico, upon which the Senate never took any definitive action. Although the President requested the opinion of the Senate on the treaty after it had been in their hands two years and, although it was reported some eighteen months later by the Committee on Foreign Relations, no attempt was made in the Senate to vote on the treaty.[14] It was the victim of indifference rather than politics. The reasons for the changes made by the Senate in these treaties need not be examined, but it might be well to mention that the Senate was not consistent in its action on extradition treaties, because others, with some of the same provisions which it removed from these treaties, were approved without opposition during the same period.[15]

[8] *Sen. Ex. Jour.*, VII, 237.

[9] *Ibid.*, X, 462.

[10] *Ibid.*, p. 147. The vote on the treaty was 34 to 4.

[11] *Ibid.*, p. 233. The vote on the treaty was 36 to 3.

[12] *Ibid.*, p. 231. The final vote was 37 to 2.

[13] *Ibid.*, XII, 369-370.

[14] *Ibid.*, VIII, 207, 408; IX, 216.

[15] John Bassett Moore, *A Treatise on Extradition and Interstate Rendition,* I, 108-112. The reasons of the Senate for amending the treaties as understood by the State Department can be found in a letter from Buchanan to Rush. Sept. 25, 1847. John Bassett Moore, ed., *The Works of James Buchanan,* VII, 419-421. Curiously enough another extradition treaty was lost because the Senate failed

Two other unimportant treaties, that failed of consummation because of the Senate, regulated the right of inheriting and acquiring property by the citizens of each country in the jurisdiction of the other. Such a treaty with Hesse-Cassel was signed on May 2, 1846. This and five more treaties on the same subject were negotiated by Henry Wheaton with various German states. Four were approved by the Senate without any changes and by unanimous votes, while a fifth, after being amended to conform to the others, was also ratified. But the treaty with Hesse-Cassel, which contained essentially the same provisions, was never considered by the Senate. The reason for the neglect of this treaty, if there were one, does not appear and was not known by the Secretary of State.[16] The second defeated treaty regulating the right to inherit property also failed because the Senate did not act upon it. It had been signed with Belgium on August 25, 1852, and during the next seven years references to it appear in the records of the Senate. Once it was reported with an amendment from the Committee on Foreign Relations and twice the same committee reported it to the Senate without amendments, but each time it was tabled by unanimous consent.[17] From some of the circumstances it has been suggested that this may have been one of the treaties that was lost because of the reluctance of the Senate to interfere with the powers of the states to legislate on the

to amend it. In submitting the treaty with Prussia that had been signed on Jan. 29, 1845, President Polk recommended that it be amended so that each country would have to surrender its own citizens. *Sen. Ex. Jour.,* VII, 7. That was the general policy of the United States and one on which the Senate had insisted in the case of several other extradition treaties. But in this instance after a lapse of several years the treaty, as the Secretary of State said in the official explanation he sent abroad, "was most unexpectedly taken up, and, in the hurry of business suddenly acted upon by the Senate," which unanimously agreed to it without changes. Buchanan, *Works,* VIII, 150. The President, however, on this occasion stood for consistency, refused to ratify the treaty, and unsuccessfully attempted to negotiate another. *Sen. Ex. Jour.*, VII, 462-464.

[16] Buchanan to Donelson, Oct. 12, 1847, *Works,* VII, 431-432.

[17] *Sen. Ex. Jour.*, VIII, 447; IX, 57, 69; XI, 45, 75, 77, 92.

right of owning property.[18] Whether this is the real explanation or not, it is clear that politics was not responsible for the loss of either of these treaties, for if political motives had been involved there would certainly have been an effort made to save them. It is equally clear that there was no senatorial jealousy of the powers of the Executive to explain the failure of the Senate to approve these two treaties.

On March 4, 1853, a treaty of friendship, commerce and navigation had been signed with Paraguay. The treaty had been carelessly phrased. The United States was referred to as the "North American Union" and the "United States of North America." This unusual phraseology was amended by the Senate so as to conform to the customary and legal title of the United States, and one other trifling amendment was made.[19] The amendments were adopted and the treaty was approved by unanimous votes. The President of Paraguay had previously ratified the treaty in its original form but he now refused to ratify it again. Although the changes made by the Senate served as the excuse, the real reason for Paraguay's action is to be found in the strained relations between the two countries caused by other matters, especially by the attack upon the United States vessel "Water Witch" by a Paraguayan fort.[20]

Amendments by the Senate again provided an excuse in the case of the treaty defining the rights, privileges, and duties of consuls, which had been signed with Chile on December 1, 1856. The changes made by the Senate were of slight importance and, as the votes on them and on the question of consenting to the treaty were unanimous, political motives were certainly not involved in the loss of the treaty.[21]

A treaty between Great Britain and the United States pro-

[18] Ralston Hayden, "The States' Rights Doctrine and the Treaty-Making Power," *American Historical Review,* XXII, 581-582.

[19] *Sen. Ex. Jour.,* IX, 316-319.

[20] The diplomatic correspondence relating to the ratification of the treaty is in *35th Cong., 1st sess., H. Doc.,* No. 2, especially pp. 48-50.

[21] *Sen. Ex. Jour.,* X, 204, 233-234.

viding for an exchange of copyright privileges was signed on February 17, 1853. It was twice reported to the Senate without amendments from the Committee on Foreign Relations, but the Senate neither rejected nor approved it.[22] As in so many other cases, information about the treaty became public despite the rules of the Senate for secrecy, and a number of petitions against the treaty were presented to the Senate.[23] Again, the insignificance of the treaty and the absence of any contest makes it reasonably certain that the action, or rather the inaction, of the Senate was not due to party politics or to a struggle with the President over the treaty-making power.

Another treaty that was defeated through the failure of the Senate to take any action upon it was the treaty of July 20, 1855, for commercial reciprocity with Hawaii. According to its terms ratifications were to be exchanged within eighteen months.[24] Although the treaty was considered in the Senate on five different occasions no serious attempt was made to push the question to a vote.[25] In a report upon the relations of the United States with Hawaii prepared for the President by the State Department many years later it is said that the treaty failed "by reason of the pressure of more important and absorbing questions."[26] A more satisfactory but still incomplete explanation was given by Seward in 1867 when he was considering negotiating another reciprocity treaty with Hawaii. He wrote that the action of the Senate was due mostly to "an apprehension on the part of the Senators from Louisiana that the

[22] *Ibid.*, IX, 69, 146, 216. George H. Putnam, *The Question of Copyright*, p. 378.

[23] *Sen. Ex. Jour.*, IX, 237, 238, 240, 249, 259.

[24] The treaty can be found in the *Compilation of Reports of the Committee on Foreign Relations* (*56th Cong., 2d sess., S. Doc.*, No. 231), VIII, 148-149.

[25] *Sen. Ex. Jour.*, X, 147, 155, 197, 200, 257. Each time the treaty was laid on the table without any opposition, except on the last day the treaty was considered, March 13, 1857. Then a motion to table it was voted down by thirty to fourteen, but after further debate the Senate adjourned without acting on the treaty. The next day the session ended.

[26] *52d Cong., 2d sess., S. Doc.*, No. 77, p. 10.

sugar from those islands would interfere with the demand for sugar, the production of that State." [27] What the true reason or combination of reasons was, is immaterial for present purposes since it is clear from the history of the treaty in the Senate that neither political opposition nor struggle with the President was responsible for its defeat.

In the twelve years prior to the outbreak of the Civil War no part of the foreign relations of the United States presented more complex problems or received more attention than the relations with Central America, and with Great Britain in respect to Central America. The primary interest of the United States was, of course, in the possibility of a canal and for that reason as well as the Monroe doctrine the threatened extension of English control caused great concern. The very active negotiations both before and after the Clayton-Bulwer treaty, which had been expected to end all the irritating problems, resulted in the signing of a number of treaties by the United States. Several of these failed to be perfected, either because they were objectionable to the President, or because he merged them in other negotiations, or because the other parties failed to ratify them. In one case only was the Senate responsible for the failure of the treaty to be completed. On October 17, 1856, Dallas, the Minister of the United States in London, and Lord Clarendon signed a treaty to settle all the questions between the two countries relative to Central America. When the treaty reached the Senate a number of amendments were made, all by large majorities.[28] One of them proved to be unacceptable

[27] Seward to McCulloch, Jan. 17, 1867, *Compilation of Reports of the Committee on Foreign Relations,* VIII, 148.

[28] *Sen. Ex. Jour.,* X, 242-248. The American negotiator of the treaty on learning how the Senate had mangled the result of his labors gave vent to his wrath and, like so many of his predecessors and successors, denounced the constitutional treaty-making arrangement. He wrote that "The amendments made to the treaty by the Senate are a series of miserable little criticisms, doctrinal and verbal, unworthy the dignity of the body and the gravity of the occasion," and that "Our system constitutes, as the final negotiator of treaties, a popular body of sixty-two members! They amend such instruments with all the freedom they

to Great Britain and, since the United States would not change its views as expressed by the Senate, the treaty was lost. The nature of this amendment, the reasons for it and for the refusal of Great Britain to accept it need not be considered,[29] as the votes of the Senate on it and on the treaty show that neither political considerations nor constitutional struggles determined the action of the Senate. The decisive amendment had been inserted by a non-partisan vote of thirty-eight to one[30] and, while the vote on the resolution giving the advice and consent of the Senate to the treaty was close, being thirty-two to fifteen, it was not on party lines.[31]

On December 14, 1859, two remarkable treaties were signed with Mexico which, if perfected, might easily have led to the absorption of Mexico into the United States, for they would have permitted direct intervention under conditions that were almost certain to appear or that could be easily alleged by an aggressive administration in the United States. One, called a treaty of "transits and commerce," provided that Mexico should grant to the United States in perpetuity the right of transit by three great highways across Mexico. The

amend ordinary bills, engrafting each his peculiar notion, and indulging claptrap and bunkum without stint. This is diplomacy run riot: and one must not be astonished at finding foreign Powers occasionally restive under its operation." Beckles Wilson, *America's Ambassadors To England,* p. 303.

[29] These can be found in the diplomatic correspondence which is given in the most complete form in *Parliamentary Papers, 1860, Commons,* LXVIII. Accounts of the treaty are given in Mary W. Williams, *Anglo-American Isthmian Diplomacy, 1815-1915,* especially pp. 226-230; Ira D. Travis, *The History of the Clayton-Bulwer Treaty,* pp. 177-184.

[30] *Sen. Ex. Jour.,* X, 243.

[31] *Ibid.,* p. 248. Thirteen of the negative votes were Democratic, but at least fifteen Democratic senators voted for the treaty. H. Barrett Learned, "William Learned Marcy," *The American Secretaries of State and Their Diplomacy,* VI, 223. The treaty did, however, suffer from one of the minor ills to which treaties in the Senate are subject. It was considered in the interim between a presidential election and the advent of the new administration. Accordingly its chances of dying were, as Dallas wrote to Lord Clarendon, "aggravated by the debility incident to a retiring Administration." Wilson, p. 303.

United States was to enjoy special privileges, such as freedom from duty on goods and free transport of mail, and on two of the highways it could transport troops and military supplies on the same terms as the Mexican government. Mexico agreed to employ her military forces to protect goods and persons in transit, and upon failure to do so the United States could supply the needed protection upon the request of Mexico or of the legally appointed local authorities. Even this consent was not essential; in exceptional cases of imminent danger to life or property the United States could intervene without it. The treaty also provided for special commercial privileges for the United States. In return for these concessions Mexico was to receive $4,000,000, one half to be paid her immediately and the balance to be used to meet claims of citizens of the United States.[32]

The other treaty was even more extraordinary, for it not only provided for intervention anywhere in Mexico on what might be slight grounds but also stipulated that Mexico should pay the cost. It said in part:

> If any of the stipulations of existing treaties between Mexico and the United States are violated, or the safety and security of the citizens of either Republic are endangered within the territory of the other, and the legitimate and acknowledged government thereof may be unable, from any cause, to enforce such stipulations, or to provide for such safety and security, it shall be obligatory on that Government to seek the aid of the other in maintaining their due execution, as well as order and security in the territory of that Republic where such violation and

[32] Soon after the treaties were submitted to the Senate, they appeared in full in the newspapers despite the rule for secrecy. New York *Times* of Feb. 15, 1860, *National Intelligencer* of Feb. 18, 1860. They are also published in full in Edward E. Dunbar, *The Mexican Papers,* No. 3, pp. 90-95. Summaries are given in Hubert H. Bancroft, *History of Mexico,* V, 774; Howard L. Wilson, "President Buchanan's Proposed Intervention in Mexico," *American Historical Review,* V, 693-695. An account of the negotiations, based upon the records of the State Department, is given by James M. Callahan, "The Mexican Policy of Southern Leaders under Buchanan's Administration," *American Historical Association, Annual Report,* 1910, pp. 135-151. J. Fred Rippy, *The United States and Mexico,* pp. 223-227.

discord occur; and in every such special case the expenses shall be paid by the treasury of the nation within whose territory such intervention may become necessary.

There was not a little truth in the statement of the New York *Times,* when making the treaty public, that "It stands almost alone among the documents of our diplomatic history for the simplicity and scope of its provisions, as well as for the magnitude of the consequences which it involves."[33] Only the magnitude and intensity of the domestic struggle into which the country was rushing prevented these treaties from receiving the attention which would certainly have been devoted to them in ordinary times. The explanation for the signature of Mexico to such terms is that an unusually severe civil war was in progress there and the "liberal" party headed by President Juarez was in desperate need of money to maintain itself in power.[34] Buchanan, in addition to following the expansionist tendencies of his party, saw in the treaties a means of preventing the European powers from intervening in Mexico, as appeared likely.[35]

Whatever may have been the merits of the foreign policy reflected in the treaties, it had little chance of being adopted. Political passions were aroused in 1860 as perhaps never before and the vote was taken when the nominating conventions had raised them to even greater intensity. Because the Republican members numbered more than one-third of the Senate, any treaty that was made a party issue was sure to fail. In a letter to Stephens, Toombs said, "We are getting on badly. The Black Reps. are now strong enough to do mischief in the Senate and are using their power. . . . They will also defeat the

[33] Feb. 15, 1860. The editors could not resist the temptation to brag a little of their ability to circumvent the rules of the Senate, and said, "We are once more enabled to lay before our readers the draft in full of an important National Treaty, in advance of its official publication." In Europe the treaties were regarded as preliminary steps to annexation. Wilson, pp. 699-701.

[34] The Buchanan administration aided them by permitting the exportation of war material from the United States and in other ways. Bancroft, V, 773.

[35] *Works,* XII, 260.

Mexican treaty when action is had on it."[36] His prophecy was fulfilled, and the treaty of "transits and commerce" was rejected on May 31, by a vote of eighteen to twenty-seven in favor of the resolution of ratification.[37] The treaty "to enforce treaty stipulations and maintain order" was killed by the same blow. Being even more objectionable to the Republicans, it was never pushed to a vote.

In this instance some of the arguments used in the Senate are known, not through official records, but from the current newspapers from which the executive sessions of the Senate kept few secrets.[38] Some of the objections to the treaties were that they were made with a faction and not the regular government; that they represented a departure from the established policy of refusing to meddle in the affairs of other nations; that United States troops would have to be in Mexico continually "as the armed Janissaries of some Mexican satrap"; that the commercial advantages in the treaties were in favor of Mexico.[39] Undoubtedly of more influence, although it was not reported as having been used as an argument in the Senate, was the belief expressed by Greeley in his bitter denunciation of the treaties in the New York *Tribune* that the whole scheme was designed to secure more territory from which to erect slave states as Calhoun had done in 1844.[40] To this the

[36] Ulrich B. Phillips, ed., *The Correspondence of Robert Toombs, Alexander H. Stephens, and Howell Cobb,* p. 464.

[37] *Sen. Ex. Jour.,* XI, 199. Almost a month later this action was reconsidered by a majority vote, but the consideration of the treaty was immediately postponed by unanimous consent until the following December. *Ibid.,* pp. 228-229. This did not reverse the rejection because the terms of the treaties required an exchange of ratifications within six months.

[38] Every time any action was taken on the treaty the papers of the next day had accounts of it, with votes and other details. They were not always accurate but a comparison with the *Executive Journal of the Senate* shows them substantially so.

[39] New York *Tribune,* Feb. 28, Feb. 29, Mar. 5, June 1, 1860. *National Intelligencer,* June 4, June 11, 1860. Dunbar, pp. 96-103.

[40] Feb. 27, 1860.

Times replied that slavery was impossible in Mexico and that the treaties would help the North rather than the South, a view several Southern senators were reported to have taken.[41]

The records of the Senate corroborate the statements then made in the papers that the votes of the Republican senators were responsible for the defeat of the treaties. Twenty-one of the twenty-seven votes against the resolution giving the consent of the Senate were cast by Republicans.[42] All of the eighteen votes in favor of the treaty were cast by Democrats, of whom four were from Northern states. The two treaties must clearly be listed among the victims of party votes in the Senate.

At about the same time another treaty, but one of far less importance, was lost in the Senate. For many years a number of claims, based upon injury to the persons or property of citizens of the United States in Cuba and upon the illegal exaction of duties in Cuba, had been presented to Spain without success. At one time the validity of the "Cuban claims" was admitted by Spain and payment was expected, but the hopes thus raised were not fulfilled. After more negotiations a convention was signed on March 5, 1860, which provided for the speedy settlement of them and for the establishment of a joint commission to adjudicate all the outstanding claims of the two countries against each other. The treaty, Buchanan informed the Senate, was entirely satisfactory to the citizens of the United States holding the claims.[43]

Unfortunately for them, however, the terms of the treaty permitted Spain to present the *Amistad* claims to the proposed commission. These claims, which Spain had against the United States, went back to 1839, when a boat owned by Spanish subjects—the *Amistad*—sailing from one Cuban port to another, was seized by the negroes who formed its cargo and was later captured by a warship of the United States. The latter took the *Amistad* to the United States and libelled the boat, cargo,

[41] New York *Times* of June 1, 1860.

[42] *Sen. Ex. Jour.*, XI, 199. Wilson, p. 696.

[43] *Works*, XI, 28-29; XII, 236-237.

and negroes for salvage. The Spanish Minister demanded the restoration of the boat and cargo under the treaty of 1795. After much litigation the negroes were set free and the boat was sold to satisfy the claims of the salvors.[44] Spain continued to press her claims but, despite the recommendations of four Presidents to Congress to pay them, no action was taken.[45]

Although the treaty did not recognize the validity of the *Amistad* claims but merely permitted Spain to present them to the commission for adjudication, this was too great a concession for the Republican members of the Senate. The *Amistad* claims involved the question of slavery and they would not permit the settlement of claims which partly depended upon a recognition of the institution.[46] The result was that when the vote was taken on June 27, 1860, seventeen Republican Senators opposed the treaty and none voted for it. No Democrats voted against the treaty and twenty-five of them joined with Crittenden in favor of the treaty.[47] Again a party vote in the Senate was responsible for the defeat of a treaty.

One more treaty failed of ratification because of the Senate during this period.[48] The intervention of European powers

[44] John Bassett Moore, *A Digest of International Law,* V, 852-854.

[45] Messages to Congress by Polk, Dec. 7, 1847; Fillmore, Jan. 17, 1853; Pierce, Dec. 5, 1853; and Buchanan, Dec. 8, 1857, Dec. 6, 1858, Dec. 19, 1859.

[46] At least that is the explanation given for the rejection of the treaty by Buchanan, *Works,* XII, 237; and by the papers, for news of the action of the Senate on this treaty, too, leaked out, and while not meriting much attention in those exciting times, its fate was noticed. New York *Times* of June 28, 1860; New York *Tribune* of June 30, 1860.

[47] *Sen. Ex. Jour.,* XI, 227.

[48] In the interim between the election of 1860 and the assumption of office by the new administration the advice of the Senate was requested by the President upon a proposed treaty. Although no treaty was actually submitted to the Senate and although the Senate cannot be held responsible for the failure of the proposals, the transaction is worth noting. The British government proposed that a treaty be made submitting to arbitration the boundary dispute over the island of San Juan in the channel separating Vancouver Island from the continent. This proposal was passed on to the Senate on Feb. 21, 1861, with a request for its approval before concluding such a treaty.

in Mexico, which Buchanan had attempted to forestall, became more probable after the outbreak of the Civil War in the United States. Unwilling to permit a dangerous situation, involving possible violation of the Monroe doctrine to develop, and unable to resort to force, the administration in Washington attempted to protect its policy by diplomacy. It proposed to guarantee the payment of the Mexican debts for a period of years or to lend Mexico the money to pay them and thus remove the excuse for intervention. In this instance Lincoln departed from the general rule and, before signing the treaty, submitted on December 19, 1861, a draft of it to the Senate for its approval, requesting an early consideration of it "as the subject is of momentous interest to the two Governments at this juncture."[49]

Over a month later the President sent another message to the Senate with the latest dispatches from Mexico and again urged the Senate to act quickly.[50] Within several weeks the Committee on Foreign Relations submitted an inconclusive report in which it was stated that in view of the changing conditions "it is impossible for the Senate to advise the President with regard to all the terms of a treaty with Mexico so as to supersede the exercise of a considerable discretion on the part of our minister there, under instructions from the President."[51] But the Senate disagreed with its committee as to the possibility of directing the negotiations and resolved that "it is not advisable to negotiate a treaty that will require the United States to

Sen. Ex. Jour., XI, 278-279. Six days later the Committee on Foreign Relations reported a resolution advising the President to make such a treaty, but in the few remaining days of that Congress no action was taken, and on March 13, 1861, the new Senate ordered its secretary to lay before the new President a copy of the message of February 21, with the accompanying original documents, evidently to learn his wishes before taking action. *Ibid.*, pp. 282, 303. The records contain no further references to the proposal.

[49] *Ibid.*, XII, 24.

[50] *Ibid.*, p. 102.

[51] *Ibid.*, pp. 121-126. The report is also published in *Compilation of Reports of the Committee on Foreign Relations*, VIII, 132-136.

assume any portion of the principal or interest of the debt of Mexico, or that will require the concurrence of European powers." [52] The resolution was adopted by a vote of twenty-eight to eight.

Before news of this advice reached Mexico the important events that were occurring there caused Corwin, the Minister of the United States, to decide he must act immediately or it would be too late. Accordingly he signed the provisions that had been tentatively proposed and sent them with the ratification of the Government of Mexico to Washington. Lincoln sent the treaty to the Senate with a message explaining that while the previous action of the Senate prevented him from accepting it, yet he "thought it just to our excellent minister in Mexico, and respectful to the Government of that Republic," to submit the treaty to the Senate.[53] He seemed to indicate a wish for a reversal of the decision of the Senate, for he added, "the importance of the subject thus submitted to the Senate cannot be over-estimated, and I shall cheerfully receive and consider with the highest respect any further advice the Senate may think proper to give upon the subject." But the Senate had nothing further to say and with no one opposing, the treaty was laid on the table where it remained.[54] Political opposition to the administration was not involved in the decision of the Senate, for over two-thirds of the members of the Senate belonging to the President's party voted for the resolution saying the negotiations were inadvisable. Nor is there anything in the records or events to indicate that the Senate's motive was a desire to assert its powers against the President's in the conduct of foreign relations.

[52] *Sen. Ex. Jour.*, XII, 134.

[53] *Ibid.*, p. 370. Strictly speaking there were two treaties, one providing for a loan to Mexico, the other fixing the compensation of the commissioners to be appointed under the terms of the treaty making the loan. As the second is solely auxiliary to the first, it has here been considered as an additional article and the two counted as one.

[54] *Ibid.*, p. 401.

CHAPTER VI

THE DEFEATS OF A DISCREDITED ADMINISTRATION

Political adversaries, finding your negotiations crowned with complete success, contrary to their own predictions, will begin to cavil at the several treaties which you will have made, on the ground that they fall short of what might and ought to have been secured. This is the habitual experience of diplomacy. WILLIAM H. SEWARD.[1]

The treaty fell a victim to the storm of political hatred then raging in this country, and in the session of 1868, after an adverse report, the United States Senate dropped it. HENRY CABOT LODGE.[2]

The election of 1864 gave the Republican party control of the government with large majorities in Congress so that an expectation of a period of harmony, when few or no treaties would be defeated by the Senate for political reasons, would have seemed to be justified.[3] But the control of the Republicans was not secure. After the tragic death of Lincoln, the presidency was lost to the party, for Johnson offered what resistence he could to what proved to be the dominant wing of the party. In doing this Johnson was not an apostate, as he was so frequently called by his bitter opponents, for he had never been, or claimed to be, a Republican. The convention which had nominated him and Lincoln in 1864 was that of the

[1] Seward to Reverdy Johnson, Oct. 26, 1868, in John Bassett Moore, *History and Digest of the International Arbitrations to Which the United States Has Been a Party,* I, 506.

[2] Referring to the treaty for the purchase of the Danish West Indies in a report submitted by him from the Committee on Foreign Relations on March 31, 1898. *57th Cong., 1st sess., S. Doc.,* No. 284, p. 18.

[3] James H. Hopkins, *A History of Political Parties in the United States,* p. 113, gives the membership of the Senate for the thirty-ninth Congress, which met in 1865, as 40 Republicans and 11 Democrats, and for the fortieth Congress as 40 Republicans and 14 Democrats. Changes took place during each Congress as members died or resigned and new members were admitted.

"National Union Party," and both during the convention and in the subsequent campaign the name and traditions of the Republican party were carefully avoided or minimized in an effort to obtain the support of all "union men," like Johnson, irrespective of political parties. The Republican party as such did not participate in the election but was "if not dead, at least in a state of suspended animation, and . . . so far as it was capable of expressing an opinion of its own condition, it admitted that it was dead." [4]

Even in Congress its control was threatened at one time. This was due to the fact that after the war the party found itself in the embarrassing position of having achieved its purpose. The extension of slavery, which had been the chief issue that created the party, was settled by the abolition of slavery. It was not to be expected that the men who had pledged their political faith on that issue would continue their allegiance after the question had been definitely settled and new issues had arisen. When reconstruction became the outstanding issue, it was at first doubtful whether the bulk of the party would follow Johnson and the Conservatives or the Radicals. The mistakes of Johnson, the shrewd management of his opponents, and events in the South, however, soon drove practically all who had hesitated into the arms of the Radicals so that these could claim to be, and were, the Republican party.

The fight between Johnson and Congress was the bitterest and most spectacular which has yet occurred in the many contests between the executive and the legislature. It originated and was fought principally on the question of reconstruction, but quickly spread to all the other fields where either the President or Congress could frustrate the policies of the other. The result was that any proposal identified with the Johnson administration was sure to meet in Congress with opposition that had no connection with its merits. Evidence of this is seen in the exercise of the treaty-making power for only one treaty

[4] William A. Dunning, "The Second Birth of the Republican Party," *American Historical Review,* XVI, 56.

of the twenty-eight treaties perfected during Johnson's administration involved more than routine matters. The one treaty which could be claimed as an achievement by the administration was for the purchase of Alaska from Russia. The willingness of the Senate to approve this act of the Johnson administration was due to two special factors.[5] There was an exceedingly naïve but widespread belief that Russia had sent her fleet to American waters and had run the risk of war with Great Britain and France solely out of friendship for the United States. The purchase of Alaska was regarded as a means of repaying Russia for that service.[6] This laudable sentiment was stimulated and the purchase was further aided by a quiet and judicious distribution to newspaper writers and members of Congress of money provided by the Russian Minister.[7]

Four other treaties, negotiated by Johnson's administration and concerned with issues transcending the routine of foreign relations, failed to receive the advice and consent of the Senate. The first to be signed was that of May 21, 1867, providing for commercial reciprocity with Hawaii.[8] More than commercial arrangements were involved in the treaty; the privileged position it would give the United States implied an obligation of protection and was regarded as a step toward annexation. The Senate was informed on this point, for Johnson in his annual

[5] At first, according to the reports of the Russian Minister, senators came to him and said they would not vote for the treaty, not because they had any objections to it but simply because it bore Seward's name. Frank A. Golder, "The Purchase of Alaska," *American Historical Review,* XXV, 421.

[6] Russia acted, of course, in self-interest. The European situation made it appear that war with Great Britain and France was imminent and the fleet was sent to American waters to avoid being shut up in the Baltic. Frank A. Golder, "The Russian Fleet and Civil War," *American Historical Review,* XX, 801.

[7] William A. Dunning, "Paying for Alaska," *Political Science Quarterly,* XXVII, 385-398. The evidence of bribery among members of Congress concerns the appropriation to pay for Alaska after the treaty had been ratified. Corroborative evidence from the Russian archives can be found in Golder, "The Purchase of Alaska," pp. 411-425.

[8] Some of the diplomatic correspondence can be found in *52d Cong., 2d sess., S. Doc.,* No. 77, pp. 130-147; *56th Cong., 2d sess., S. Doc.,* No. 231, pp. 145-160.

message to Congress, while the treaty was in the hands of the Senate, referred to the unwillingness of the United States to see Hawaii pass under foreign control and said, " A reciprocity treaty . . . would be a guaranty of the good will and forebearance of all nations until the people of the islands shall of themselves, at no distant day, voluntarily apply for admission into the Union." [9]

For over a year the Senate took no action on the treaty, being occupied with the impeachment trial and other pressing problems. When the treaty was finally reached it was immediately laid on the table by a vote of thirty to twenty-one.[10] At the time this was equivalent to rejection, but a few months later the Senate received a second treaty, signed July 28, 1868, which extended the time for the exchange of the ratifications of the reciprocity treaty.[11] The attempt to save the treaty proved futile, for when, on June 1, 1870, the Senate voted on the resolution of ratification only twenty favored it and nineteen members opposed it.[12]

The small number of votes cast on the treaty—only a few more than half of the membership of the Senate—is indicative of the slight attention the treaty received both from the senators and the public. Although the public knew from Johnson's message that a reciprocity treaty was pending, there was no mention of it in the newspapers. Evidently it was not deemed of sufficient importance to warrant a violation of the rules of the Senate, for no news of its provisions leaked out. The absence of comment makes the search for the reasons of the Senate's decision more than usually difficult. Some writers have said the opposition to the treaty came from the sugar growers of the Southern states and from the friends of annexation, who felt that reciprocity would postpone that project.[13] This inter-

[9] Richardson, *Messages and Papers of the Presidents,* VIII, 3887.

[10] *Sen. Ex. Jour.,* XVI, 354.

[11] *Ibid.,* p. 424.

[12] *Ibid.,* XVII, 466.

[13] John W. Foster, *American Diplomacy in the Orient,* p. 367. J. Laurance Laughlin and H. Parker Willis, *Reciprocity,* p. 74.

pretation is evidently based on several statements made by Seward. It has already been pointed out that he said the similar treaty with Hawaii in 1855 was opposed by the senators from Louisiana because of their interest in sugar.[14] The other source of opposition was suggested by him in a letter to the Minister of the United States at Honolulu. He wrote that certain unnamed circumstances made him believe "that a strong interest, based upon a desire for annexation of the Sandwich Islands, will be active in opposing a ratification of the reciprocity treaty."[15]

Neither of these suggestions affords a satisfactory explanation of the opposition of the Senate to the treaty. It is true that both senators from Louisiana voted in favor of tabling the treaty. But they did not vote on the resolution of ratification, nor were they recorded as being paired either for or against the treaty, thus indicating indifference rather than active hostility. There is no evidence, except Seward's statement made prior to the action of the Senate on the treaty, that the desire for annexation influenced any votes. Seward favored annexation, but almost no one else did, as he was forced to admit.[16] Writing to Hawaii, some nine months after the letter quoted above, he said that

> public attention sensibly continues to be fastened upon the domestic questions which have grown out of the late civil war. The public mind refuses to dismiss these questions even so far as to entertain the higher but more remote questions of national extension and aggrandizement. The periodical Presidential and Congressional elections are approaching. Each of the political parties seems to suppose that economy and retrenchment will be prevailing considerations in that election and the leaders of each party therefore seem to shrink from every suggestion which may involve any new national enterprise, and especially any foreign one.[17]

The reluctance of the public to assume any new obligations,

[14] See page 90.

[15] *52d Cong., 2d sess., S. Doc.,* No. 77, p. 139.

[16] Frederic Bancroft, *The Life of William H. Seward,* II, 489.

[17] Seward to Z. S. Spalding, July 5, 1868, *52d Cong., 2d sess., S. Doc.,* No. 77, p. 140.

an obvious though intensely disappointing fact to Seward, probably accounted for much of the opposition to the treaty. Certainly politics was not involved, for only a few of the small minority of Democrats voted each time and these were divided.[18] The votes also show that hostility to Johnson and the acts of his administration will not alone explain the defeat of the treaty, because among those voting in favor of the treaty both times were several of his bitterest enemies, including Sumner himself.

When Seward wrote regretfully of the lack of public interest in "the higher but more remote questions of national extension and aggrandizement," he undoubtedly had in mind the reception given the treaty of October 24, 1867, which he had negotiated with Denmark for the purchase of St. Thomas and St. John, two of the Danish West Indian islands. During the Civil War the lack of a naval base in the West Indies was keenly felt, and the Danish islands were expected to supply the deficiency, the expectation being based on favorable reports by naval authorities.[19] But the Secretary of the Navy, who had wanted to purchase such a naval base during the war at almost any price, now opposed the purchase at cabinet meetings, offering in his customary blunt and vigorous manner what seemed to him and to some of his colleagues to be good and sufficient reasons.[20] To Welles it was clear that the talk of a naval base was merely a cloak to Seward's real motives,

[18] Buckalew, Davis, and Hendricks voted for tabling the treaty; Doolittle, now a Democrat, McCreery, and Patterson against. Only three Democrats voted on the resolution of ratification, Casserly and Stockton favoring it while Vickers voted in the negative.

[19] James Parton, *The Danish Islands,* pp. 63, 71. Parton's account of the negotiations is probably the fullest and best. He was employed to write this pamphlet by the Danish negotiator who supplied him with confidential documents. Edward L. Pierce, *Memoir and Letters of Charles Sumner,* IV, 619. Pierce has a good account. *Ibid.,* pp. 613-624. See also Bancroft, II, 479-486. Extracts from the more important diplomatic despatches are given in Moore, *Digest of International Law,* I, 601-610.

[20] John T. Morse, ed., *Diary of Gideon Welles,* III, 95-96, 98, 124.

for Seward, he said, "Has become almost a monomaniac on the subject of territorial acquisition, that being the hobby on which he expects to be a candidate for President."[21] While the latter part of his comment was based chiefly on his antipathy to Seward, who no longer had any serious hopes of becoming President, Welles was right in attributing to Seward the desire for expansion as an end in itself. As his biographer says, "Seward was a very conspicuous prophet of territorial expansion."[22]

It was another instance of a prophet without honor in his own country. Denmark had entered upon the negotiations with some hesitation, but quickly completed her part of the transaction by ratifying the treaty after holding a plebiscite on the islands to secure the assent of the inhabitants to the cession. News of these steps with much other information was transmitted to the Senate from time to time.[23] But the Senate did not act on the treaty. The time for the exchange of ratifications was extended by an additional article. Still the Senate made no move.[24] Evidence of the attitude of the Senate, and incidentally of several violations of the Senate rules of secrecy, exists in a letter from General Raasloff, the Danish negotiator, to Senator Doolittle. He wrote, under date of February 5, 1869:

> A few days ago somebody who insisted upon being well-informed assured me that the Comm. for f. Relations—before the Christmas holidays & recess—agreed to reject the St. Thomas Treaty immediately after the recess. He says that the members of the Com. had talked the matter over with Mr. Sumner, and that they were all agreed. My arrival—he further stated—had prevented the execution of the preliminary decision the Com. had come to, and that now the Com. would prefer to let the matter lay over to the next administration after 4th of March.
>
> This latter assertion, being essentially in accordance with what you wrote to me last week in answer to my inquiry I believe to be well-founded. . . .

---

[21] *Ibid.*, p. 125. The Russian Minister believed that Seward was interested in the purchase of Alaska because he hoped it would restore him into public favor. Golder, "The Purchase of Alaska," p. 425.

[22] Bancroft, II, 470.

[23] *Sen. Ex. Jour.*, XVI, 151, 166, 178, 443, 452, 483.

[24] *Ibid.*, p. 425.

I prefer now myself to let the matter pass over till after the 4th of March and I should be happy to know that the Com. will not again change & suddenly act adversely, without waiting for the Memorandum which I have promised them and which I am now preparing.[25]

The new administration came into office but Grant did not favor the treaty, saying it was "a scheme of Seward's and he would have nothing to do with it." [26] This, one senator reported, was the general attitude of the Senate.[27] General Raasloff, by this time Secretary of War in the Danish cabinet, found his political future was at stake and returning to the United States made strenuous efforts in behalf of the treaty, employing special counsel, having pamphlets written, giving dinners, and twice securing the unusual privilege of appearing before the Committee on Foreign Relations.[28] In 1870 that committee reported the treaty with a recommendation that it be rejected, but it was allowed to expire without action, that being considered a gentler method and one less likely to embarrass Raasloff at home.[29]

"We cannot conceive what strong or solid reasons the Senate can give for refusing to ratify this treaty," wrote Henry Adams in a contemporaneous account.[30] He continued,

Say it is our humor,—is Denmark answered, or is our national credit redeemed in the world's eyes? Seven years ago our whole nation wanted

---

[25] MS. Doolittle Papers.

[26] Pierce, IV, 622. *The Nation,* May 30, 1872.

[27] Pierce, IV, 623.

[28] *Ibid.,* pp. 328-329, 619-620.

[29] *Sen. Ex. Jour.,* XVII, 405; Bancroft, II, 486; Pierce, IV, 329, 622-624. The kindness was ineffectual as the failure of the treaty ended Raasloff's political career. *Ibid.,* p. 622.

[30] "The Session," *North American Review,* CVIII, 628. Woodrow Wilson, writing in 1884, cited this treaty as an example of what he called the "treaty-*marring* power" of the Senate. His words contained a prophecy the fulfillment of which he was to experience personally many years later. "During the single congressional session of 1868-9, for example, the treaty-*marring* power of the Senate was exerted in a way that made the comparative weakness of the executive very conspicuous and was ominous of very serious results." *Congressional Government,* p. 50.

St. Thomas; now we need it no longer; a few years hence we may again require it; and the world must learn submission to these passing whims!

The reason that has been generally accepted is that the Senate was merely expressing its animosity to Johnson. Even the Committee on Foreign Relations, many years later, gave political hatred as the cause of the defeat of the treaty in the report quoted at the head of this chapter. It was, as Grant said, "a scheme of Seward's" and that was reason enough for rejecting it.[31]

Although the bitterness of the Republican party toward Johnson and his administration was great enough to account for the loss of the treaty and did, in fact, play some part in deciding its fate, other factors more creditable to the Senate were also involved. Seward was doubly unfortunate as a prophet of expansion. He was not only faced by a hostile Senate but also had the added handicap of having public opinion generally against expansion.[32] The exuberance of the forties had been worked off in the war and the demand for economy and retrenchment was a powerful force against purchases of territory. Seward could see the trend of public opinion even against his wishes, as has been noted in connection with Hawaii. He noted the same influence working against this treaty, saying, "The desire for the acquisition of foreign territory has sensibly abated. . . . In short, we have already come to value dollars more, and dominion less." [33] The purchase of Alaska had been accomplished in spite of this factor because of special circumstances, but at the time Sumner announced that the pur-

[31] "The President and the Department of State had negotiated this treaty; therefore, if for no other reason, the Senate would not consent to it." Anna L. Dawes, *Charles Sumner,* p. 282. *The Nation* of May 30, 1872, XIV, 348. Willis F. Johnson, *America's Foreign Relations,* II, 63. Soren J. M. P. Fogdall, *Danish-American Diplomacy, 1776-1920,* p. 107.

[32] Theodore C. Smith, "Expansion After the Civil War, 1865-1871," *Political Science Quarterly,* XVI, 412-436.

[33] Frederick W. Seward, *Autobiography of William H. Seward,* III, 369.

chase " must not be a precedent for a system of indiscriminate and costly annexation." [34]

On November 25, 1867, a resolution was introduced into the House of Representatives which declared that " in the present financial condition of the country any further purchases of territory are inexpedient, and this House will hold itself under no obligations to vote money to pay for any such purchase unless there is greater present necessity for the same than now exists." [35] The resolution was adopted after Washburne, who introduced it, stated that it was intended to serve notice upon Denmark, and after the rules had been suspended by a two-thirds vote.[36] Soon after the treaty had been signed the islands were visited by an earthquake and a hurricane, accompanied by tidal waves, to the joy of the opponents of the treaty who promptly added ridicule to their economic arguments.[37] Not a single member of the Committee on Foreign Relations favored the treaty, a fact which raises the presumption that other factors besides hostility to Johnson were present.[38]

However honest some of the opposition to the treaty may have been, the United States subsequently decided a mistake had been made and that sound policy demanded the acquisition of the islands. In 1892, negotiations were begun, but proved futile. In 1902, a treaty for their purchase was signed and, although the Senate acknowledged its former error by promptly

[34] *The Works of Charles Sumner,* XI, 232. The argument of economy was used vigorously in the House when the appropriation for the Alaska purchase money was introduced. *Congressional Globe,* June 30, 1868, pp. 3620 ff.

[35] *Ibid.,* p. 792.

[36] *Ibid.,* Nov. 25, 1867, pp. 792-793.

[37] Rhodes, VI, 213-214; Bancroft, II, 485-486. Parton, pp. 33-34, had a hard time minimizing these catastrophes. The New York *Tribune* of Dec. 17, 1867, said, " St. Thomas is to be purchased to give us ' a foothold in the Gulf.' Recent events indicate our foothold is likely to be shaky."

[38] Pierce, IV, 623-624, includes quotations from three former members of the committee to him. Since the above was written an intensive study has been made of the struggle for ratification. Based on rich and varied materials it confirms the account given here. Charles C. Tansill, *The Purchase of the Danish West Indies,* pp. 78-153.

approving this treaty, it again failed because the Danish upper House rejected it. In 1917, the purchase was finally accomplished at a much higher price than had been acceptable in 1867.[39] The defeat of the treaty by the Senate left the United States in an exceedingly awkward position. If Denmark, having been committed to the policy of selling the islands, had offered them to one of the great powers of Europe, the United States would have had to permit a violation of the Monroe doctrine as ordinarily defined, or would have had to defend the unjustifiable policy of denying Denmark the right to sell to anyone else and still refusing to buy them ourselves. The prospect of the cession of the islands to a European power caused several administrations uneasiness, but fortunately Denmark never put the queston to the test.

The fate of the treaty affords a good illustration of the embarrassment that the power of the Senate to reject treaties can give to the other party to the negotiations. The possibilities of causing Denmark great injury by thus committing her publicly to a foreign policy which might easily have aroused the antagonism of other European powers, and then failing to complete the transaction, are obvious and have often been pointed out.[40] The humiliation of Denmark was greater because the inhabitants of the islands by an overwhelming vote signified their preference for annexation to the United States. Indeed a resolution was introduced into the House authorizing the President to extend the protection of the United States over any of the islands in the Antilles whenever the government or people should desire such protection. In speaking for the resolution Benjamin F. Butler very pointedly suggested that the people of St. Thomas "voted that they preferred to belong to this country" and thereby "shut themselves off from Den-

[39] *Ibid.*

[40] Parton's account of the injury done Denmark may perhaps be dismissed on the grounds of prejudice, pp. 43-50. But see Henry Adams, "The Session," pp. 627-629; *The Nation,* XIV, 349; and the frantic letters from Raasloff to Sumner in Pierce, IV, 619-622.

mark."[41] No attention was paid to this dishonorable suggestion, but the whole affair was one which might well have caused other powers to hesitate a long time before entering into similar negotiations with the United States.

The two remaining treaties which Johnson submitted to the Senate and which that body refused to approve were both with Great Britain and were both signed in London by Reverdy Johnson on January 14, 1869.[42] One, known as the Johnson-Clarendon treaty, dealt with the highly important subject of claims, while the other—of much less consequence—provided for the settlement of the northwestern boundary at San Juan island. The dispute over the title to this small island had its source in the Oregon treaty of 1846, which fixed the boundary as the forty-ninth parallel "to the middle of the channel which separates the continent from Vancouver's Island; and thence southerly through the middle of the said channel, and of Fuca's Straits, to the Pacific Ocean."[43] Unfortunately there was more than one channel. It was not easy to determine which was meant, and the title to San Juan depended on what

[41] *Congressional Globe,* Jan. 13, 1869, pp. 333-334.

[42] On the same day a treaty relating to the construction of a canal across the isthmus of Darien was signed with Colombia, and it also failed to be perfected; but the United States Senate cannot be held responsible for its failure. The treaty was sent to the Senate and was discussed there on several occasions without being acted upon. Meanwhile it was rejected by the Federal Senate of Colombia and no further attention was given to it by the United States Senate. Whether it would have been accepted by the United States Senate is open to question, but as the time for the exchange of ratifications had not expired before news of Colombia's rejection arrived, the Senate must be given the benefit of the doubt. *Sen. Ex. Jour.,* XVII, 136, 163, 174-175. *Appleton's Annual Cyclopaedia, 1869,* pp. 108-111, 704. George E. Baker, ed., *The Works of William H. Seward,* V, 34, 605. The treaty and diplomatic papers are given in *46th Cong., 2d sess., S. Doc.,* No. 112, pp. 8, 25-38. On Jan. 26, 1870, another treaty on the same subject was signed with Colombia. It was submitted to the Senate but before action was taken it was amended by the Congress of Colombia in such a way that the treaty was not acceptable to the United States. It was not, however, withdrawn by the President from the Senate but was apparently just dropped. *Ibid.,* pp. 9, 38-84. *Sen. Ex. Jour.,* XVII, 415, 535.

[43] Malloy, I, 657.

channel was used. The conflicting claims of the two countries led to a dispute which was too remote to endanger friendly relations by itself, but which might have supplied the spark to explosive materials supplied by more important disputes. It did, however, cause much local friction and in 1859, when the island was occupied by military forces from both countries, bloodshed was narrowly averted.[44] The negotiations for the settlement of the question were interrupted by the Civil War, but with the return of peace they were resumed and led to the treaty of January 14, 1869. This referred the question to the arbitration of the President of the Swiss Confederation.[45] It was the solution which the Senate Committee on Foreign Relations approved in the closing days of Buchanan's administration.

Although the cable enabled Seward to submit a copy of the treaty to the Senate several days after it was signed, his hopes of seeing the treaty ratified before the few remaining weeks of his official life expired were disappointed.[46] The treaty was still waiting for a decision from the Senate when the new administration assumed office, and, though President Grant was willing to accept it, the Senate did not.[47] The treaty was considered on two occasions, but when, on the next to the last day of the session, Sumner moved that it be considered again, the motion was defeated by a vote of twenty-two to twenty-four.[48] An examination of the votes gives no positive clue as to motives, for Democrats, Radical Republicans, and Conservative Republicans were on both sides. Moreover, in this instance

[44] The shooting of a pig belonging to the Hudson's Bay Company precipitated the crisis in 1859. Andrew Fish, "The Last Phase of the Oregon Boundary Question," *Quarterly of the Oregon Historical Society,* XXII, 161-224.

[45] Moore, *International Arbitrations,* I, 196-236. The treaty and the immediate negotiations preceding it can be found in *Diplomatic Correspondence,* 1868, Part I, 328-332, 354-356, 361, 366-369, 377, 400-406.

[46] *Sen. Ex. Jour.,* XVI, 441.

[47] Sumner wrote John Bright on Jan. 19, 1869, that he discussed the treaty with the President-elect and found he had no objections to it. Pierce, IV, 368.

[48] *Sen. Ex. Jour.,* XVII, 175, 187, 240.

postponement was not equivalent to rejection since the treaty permitted ratifications to be exchanged within a year and the Senate would have ample time after it met early in the following December to give its consent to the treaty. As a matter of fact, it did not desire to save the treaty and took no action until the time limit expired.

In his instructions to the British commissioners in 1871, Earl Granville stated that the United States government had explained to him the failure of the Senate to act by saying it was caused by the delay in carrying through Parliament the measures necessary for the conclusion of the pending naturalization treaty.[49] This was a reasonable explanation because the naturalization treaty was of great interest due to the Fenian troubles and at one time Seward had instructed Reverdy Johnson not to sign the boundary treaty until Great Britain had agreed to the naturalization treaty.[50] On the other hand opposition was expressed to the San Juan treaty on its merits.[51] The American commissioners in 1871 informed the British commissioners that the treaty "had not been favorably regarded by the Senate."[52]

Other factors which certainly had some influence in deciding the Senate were the hostility to the Johnson administration and the desire to leave the settlement of this and the more important claims problem to the incoming administration. Sumner, who tried to get the Senate to approve this treaty, recognized that "the feeling towards Mr. Seward will not help the treaties"—a moderate statement in the light of the extreme bitterness that had been displayed toward him and Johnson.[53] The few months that a defeated administration remains in office have often proved to be a period of governmental paralysis in

[49] *Foreign Relations,* 1873, Part III, 376.

[50] *Ibid.,* 1868, Part I, 354-355.

[51] *Parliamentary Papers, House of Commons, Sessional Papers,* 1868-9, Vol. 63, *North America,* No. 1 (1869), pp. 41, 57.

[52] *Foreign Relations,* 1873, Part III, 405.

[53] Pierce, IV, 368.

making or carrying out policies. Seward referred to this in a letter to Reverdy Johnson, saying

The confused light of an incoming administration is already spreading itself over the country, as usual rendering the consideration of political subjects irksome if not inconvenient. With your experience in legislative life you will be able to judge for yourself of the prospects of definite action upon the treaties during the remainder of the present session.[54]

The defeat of the treaty was probably due to the fact that it coincided in time with the claims treaty as much as to anything. The Johnson-Clarendon claims treaty served as a rallying point for those who resented the conduct of Great Britain during the war, those who were indignant at the British suppression of the Fenian uprising, and those who hated Great Britain anyway. The resulting outburst of passion created an atmosphere that contributed to the defeat of the San Juan treaty together with the more important claims treaty. There was nothing in the latter treaty itself to justify such a clamor. On the contrary the treaty seemed to Henry Adams, with his bitter experiences in England fresh in his mind, to be a great victory. "Our national history," he wrote, "furnishes no other example of such diplomatic triumph. . . . Our Government has conceded nothing, however, except the principle of arbitration." [55] The treaty was modeled on the claims convention of 1853 and it provided for the arbitration of all the claims of citizens of either country against the other.[56]

The treaty went to the Senate on January 19, 1869.[57] An

[54] Moore, *International Arbitrations,* I, 506.

[55] Henry Adams, "The Session," *North American Review,* CVIII, 637. It is interesting to compare this with the account of his brother, Charles Francis. Writing in 1901, the latter said, "The Johnson-Clarendon Convention was open to criticism at many points, and its rejection by the Senate was altogether defensible." *Lee at Appomattox and Other Papers,* p. 101.

[56] The treaty and the immediate negotiations preceding it are in *Foreign Relations,* 1868, Part I, 328-404. See also *Sessional Papers,* 1868-9, vol. 63, *North America,* No. 1 (1869). Moore, *International Arbitrations,* I, 495-516. Bancroft, II, 492-500. Bernard C. Steiner, *The Life of Reverdy Johnson,* pp. 233-248.

[57] *Sen. Ex. Jour.,* XVI, 441.

adverse report was made by the Committee on Foreign Relations on February 18.[58] It was not acted upon until the next session when, on April 13, 1869, it was rejected almost unanimously.[59] One senator, a Democrat, voted for it and fifty-four, of both parties, refused to give their advice and consent. There was practically no debate on it in the Senate, for it was considered only on the day it was rejected and most of that executive session was probably consumed by the startling speech Sumner made on the treaty.[60] This was the speech in which with characteristic rhetoric and vituperation he demanded the payment of several billion dollars to compensate the United States for indirect damages and for the prolongation of the war due to the unfriendly conduct of Great Britain.[61] The Senate removed the injunction of secrecy from Sumner's speech, which was immediately published in practically every paper in the country, and thus seemed to announce that Sumner's views were the views of the Senate and that it had rejected the treaty because the indirect claims of the United States had not been included.

There is, however, abundant evidence that this interpretation would be wrong and that many of the members of the Senate did not vote against the treaty for the reasons alleged by Sum-

[58] *Ibid.*, p. 483.

[59] *Ibid.*, XVII, 163.

[60] The British Minister informed his government that Chandler and a few others followed Sumner and spoke to the same effect. *Sessional Papers*, 1868-9, vol. 63, *North America*, No. 1 (1869), p. 52.

[61] *Works*, XIII, 53-93. It is now agreed by all American scholars that these indirect claims were preposterous. Rhodes says, " Of all the outrageous claims of which our diplomatic annals are full, I can call to mind none more so than this. VI, 339. The publicity attaching to Sumner's speech has caused censure to be directed almost solely at him, yet both Seward and Charles Francis Adams had urged claims based upon Great Britain's recognition of a state of belligerency. The lack of substance in them has, perhaps, been best exposed by the son of the latter, in *Lee at Appomattox and Other Papers*, pp. 96-101. So many American politicians had used hostility to England as a means of political preferment that it was, perhaps, natural that John Bright should regard Sumner's speech as a bid for the presidency. Rhodes, VI, 341.

ner. One senator, visiting England the following month, wrote a letter to the London *Times* stating that the Senate "simply agreed to the conclusion at which Mr. Sumner arrived. . . . and not to the processes by which he reached that conclusion, or the arguments by which he supported it." [62] This unofficial disclaimer received official corroboration in the instructions that the new Secretary of State sent to the new Minister at London and which were read to the British Foreign Secretary. In them Fish said:

> This adverse judgment, while unanimous, or nearly so, in its conclusion, was not reached by any single train of argument, nor from any one standpoint of policy, nor with any single standard of estimate of the claims either of the nation or of its citizens.
>
> * * * * * * *
>
> Both with the people and in the Senate, different minds, viewing it from different standpoints, each measuring by its own standard and judging in its own way, arrived at the one conclusion.[63]

To a friend Fish put the matter more concisely, "*But the fact is,* many Senators dissented from the argument while agreeing to the conclusion." [64] Even Sumner himself wrote to John Bright only a few months before he delivered his speech, that the treaty "would have been ratified at any time last year almost unanimously." [65]

The opposition to the treaty of the senators who did not agree with Sumner's reasoning has been ascribed to various

[62] William Salter, *The Life of James W. Grimes,* pp. 368-370. Grimes was then a member of the Senate but resigned on account of ill health before the next session. His letters to Fessenden show the effects of Sumner's speech in Europe. *Ibid.,* pp. 370, 372, 376.

[63] *41st Cong., 3d sess., S. Doc.,* No. 11, p. 3.

[64] Fish to S. B. Ruggles, May 18, 1869, cited in Charles Francis Adams, p. 208. The best proof of this is that the Senate accepted the Treaty of Washington about two years later under which the indirect claims were not included. John Bigelow wrote to a friend in England, "Sumner's basis has few adherents, if any, besides himself and Motley." But this was in October 1869 when public passions had cooled. *Retrospections of an Active Life,* IV, 322.

[65] Pierce, IV, 368.

causes. The gravity of the questions involved induced the Secretary of State to offer explanations to the British government and in them he admitted that other factors than the merits of the treaty were involved. "The time and the circumstances under which the convention was negotiated," he wrote, "were very unfavorable to its acceptance either by the people or by the Senate. The nation had just emerged from its periodical choice of a chief magistrate, and having changed the depository of its confidence and its power, looked with no favor on an attempt at the settlement of the great and grave questions depending, by those on the eve of retiring from power, without consulting or considering the views of the ruler recently intrusted with their confidence, and without communication with the Senate, to whose approval the treaty would be constitutionally submitted, or with any of its members." [66]

This interpretation of the Senate's motives was the one that seemed the best explanation to Seward, Johnson, and to many writers, only they worded it in harsher terms. To Seward it was clear that "the fact that they were made by President Johnson's Secretary of State and Minister was reason enough for refusing to accept them." [67] A few years later *The Nation,* after commenting on the small difference between the Johnson treaty and the settlement Grant obtained, said, "The real objection to his treaty was that it was negotiated by a Johnsonian Democrat, who was too polite to the British aristocracy at a time when we hated the British aristocracy." [68] "The question of the ratification of this convention by the United States was almost wholly political or personal. . . . The feeling against the President had reached the point of spite against the administration, and Seward was the object of bitter antagonism, because it was believed that but for his influence, and that of his political friends, the impeachment trial might have

[66] Fish to Motley, May 15, 1869, *41st Cong., 3d sess., S. Doc.,* No. 11, p. 3. Motley's report of his interview with Lord Clarendon is given in pp. 5-10.

[67] Frederick W. Seward, *Autobiography of William H. Seward,* III, 395.

[68] *The Nation* of Feb. 17, 1876, XXXII, 106.

succeeded . . . the Republicans were not disposed to put the seal of success upon negotiations that had been carried on by Johnson's well-hated administration. Perhaps the most effective complaint was the one that said the convention overlooked the moral wrong. . . . But any objection was good enough if it helped to defeat the convention." [69]

While political and personal spite might account for the defeat of the treaty, they cannot satisfactorily explain the practical unanimity of opinion in the Senate. Indeed that consideration led Motley to state to Lord Clarendon that "The rejection of the claims treaty, however, was not in the slightest degree an affair of party, as was sufficiently proved by the vote in which Senators of every shade of political opinion had emphatically united." [70] Some of the senators must be credited with opposing the treaty on its merits. Sincere objections to it were made because, as Clarendon was told, "it embraced only the claims of individuals, and had no reference to those of the two Governments on each other; and lastly, that it settled no question and laid down no principle." [71] Much was made at the time of the unfortunate conduct of Reverdy Johnson in England, where he made effusive speeches and mingled on friendly terms with several who had been prominent enemies of the North during the war.[72] Under different political circumstances at home these indiscretions might well have been overlooked. As it was, they were seized upon as a means of

[69] Bancroft, II, 499-500. "There was extreme antipathy, personal and partisan, between the outgoing and the incoming administrations, and nothing so dear to Seward's heart as ratification of his final treaty could be anticipated." William A. Dunning, *The Bitish Empire and the United States,* p. 244.

[70] *41st Cong., 3d sess., S. Doc.,* No. 11, p. 7.

[71] *Sessional Papers,* 1870, vol. 69, *North America,* No. 1 (1870), p. 1.

[72] Rhodes, VI, 337. Steiner, pp. 243-246. Bigelow wrote, "Johnson seems to be possessed with a devil—one or more." *Retrospections,* IV, 245. Welles noted in his diary that Johnson "is doing neither himself nor the country credit in England. By last accounts he was corresponding and dining with Laird. There is, in much of his conduct, and especially in this, a degree of servility that is disgusting." III, 488.

attacking the treaty and may have decided some votes in the Senate.

How much weight should be assigned to each of the several reasons actuating the Senate is impossible to determine. Hostility to Great Britain [73] and hostility, both partisan and personal, to the Johnson administration were sure to defeat the treaty. The objections to it on its merits merely made the decision almost unanimous.[74]

Once again a foreign government had been given a painful lesson on the necessity of remembering which branch of the government controlled the treaty-making power of the United States. As Lord Clarendon observed to Motley, when the latter was attempting to explain the action of the Senate, "it could

[73] In reporting Sumner's speech to his government the British minister said, "Your Lordship will observe that Mr. Sumner claims to be animated with an anxious desire that peace should be maintained with Great Britain; yet I know of no arguments more calculated than those contained in his speech to excite the passions of his countrymen, and to inflame that animosity which, unhappily, it is but too apparent they still feel against England." *Sessional Papers,* 1868-9, vol. 63, *North America,* No. 1 (1869), p. 53.

[74] Writing the same month the treaty was rejected, Henry Adams put the rejection on still different grounds. He supposed a foreign diplomat meditating on the motives of the Senate in rejecting the treaty. "He would dismiss at once the idea that this action was due to a mere passing ebullition of spite against the late Cabinet. The determination to reject is not restricted to the opponents of Mr. Seward. . . . The mere gratification of a long-nursed wrath against England might explain the action of some Senators, but not of all. We regret to add, that the diplomatist would not entertain the idea that the Senate was influenced by any virtuous devotion to the improvement of international law; for he would feel confident, and with reason, that if England offered to cede Canada to the United States, on condition of being relieved of these claims, the Senate would immediately assent, without giving a second thought to international law or establishing any new principle whatever. In fact, the more he considered and reconsidered all other motives for an absolute rejection of the treaty, the more confident would his conclusion be, that the idea of territorial aggrandizement lay at the bottom of Senators' minds—or, in other words, that these claims were to be reserved and used to lead or force England into a cession of territory." *North American Review,* CVIII, 638. Subsequent events proved this was true of Sumner, but apparently not of the other members of the Senate.

not be denied that this result might induce more caution in future, as when dealing with plenipotentiaries from the United States it would be necessary for a government to remember that there was a greater power behind them—namely, the Senate." [75] Unfortunately for them, they did not always remember.

In 1868 there was a revision of all the standing rules of the Senate. The new rule, then the thirty-eighth, prescribing the proceedings on treaties was phrased in new language. This varied from the old rule only in one respect, but the change was of great importance. It provided that except on the final question to advise and consent to the ratification all motions and questions should be decided by a simple majority vote. The reasons for making this departure from the old procedure do not appear. No explanation is given in the report of the select committee appointed to revise the rules, nor was any comment made in the Senate when the new rules were debated and adopted.[76] The effect of this change was to increase still further the power of those opposing a treaty, for under it amendments could be inserted or reservations added by an ordinary majority vote. A small group of senators wishing to defeat a treaty, but not numerous enough to do so, could henceforth achieve their purpose by an indirect method. By joining with others, who favored the treaty only with changes, they could force amendments which would make the treaty unacceptable to some who had favored it in its original form. These new opponents, added to the few who had opposed the treaty in any form but who helped to make the changes in it, might constitute more than one-third of the Senate. Thus the treaty would be defeated. This was exactly the method used in defeating the Versailles treaty in 1919.

[75] *41st Cong., 3d sess., S. Doc.,* No. 11, p. 7.

[76] *40th Cong., 2d sess., S. Rept.,* No. 56. The revised rules were reported to the Senate on Feb. 21, 1868, but were debated only on Mar. 25, 1868, when they were adopted. No reference at all was made to the rule on treaties. *Congressional Globe,* pp. 2087-2094. The rule has remained without significant changes down to the present day.

CHAPTER VII

A PERIOD OF SENATORIAL DOMINATION, 1869-1898

The United States Senate having a Republican majority, which was unwilling to give the Democratic party any advantage in the impending presidential election, rejected the treaty. "We cannot allow the Democrats to take credit for settling so important a dispute," a leading Republican senator told me at the time in justifying the attitude taken by his party.

SIR CHARLES TUPPER.[1]

The Treaty, in getting itself made by the sole act of the executive, without leave of the Senate first had and obtained, had committed the unpardonable sin. It must be altogether defeated, or so altered as to bear an unmistakable Senate stamp—and thus be the means both of humiliating the executive and of showing to the world the greatness of the Senate.

RICHARD OLNEY.[2]

From the time that Grant entered the White House until the Spanish-American war domestic issues continued to dominate politics and public attention in the United States. They did not, however, enjoy the almost undisturbed domination which had prevailed during the quarter of a century after 1815, for now questions arising from the foreign relations of the country repeatedly challenged their supremacy. The greatly improved means of communication which brought all parts of the world into closer contact with the rest, the further development of the economic organization of the world on international lines which made each country more concerned with events elsewhere, and the rapid expansion in wealth and population, particularly in the United States, were all factors that tended to make foreign relations more important. The process was largely unnoticed, as fundamental changes usually are,

[1] Sir Charles Tupper, *Recollections of Sixty Years,* p. 192. The treaty referred to was the Fisheries Treaty of 1888 in the negotiation of which Sir Charles Tupper had participated.

[2] Olney to Henry White, May 14, 1897. MS. Olney Papers.

and the people of the United States were not conscious of their gradual growth to the status of a world power with its interests and responsibilities. They only noticed that more and more frequently their attention was diverted from domestic affairs to questions at issue with some foreign power. None of those questions preceding the war with Spain was of sufficient importance to play a dominant or even large part in any election, but an appreciable number claimed some public attention and offered what John Hay later called, "a contingent chance of petty political advantage."

It was undoubtedly fortunate that the treaties submitted to the Senate did not assume a greater importance because, after the meeting of the forty-fourth Congress in 1875, neither party has ever had a two-thirds majority in the Senate.[3] Moreover, during these years the Senate, acting as a body and irrespective of party, was engaged in a constant campaign, sometimes marked by spectacular events and sometimes passing unnoticed, to establish itself as the dominant part of the government. With conspicuous success the Senate asserted and extended its powers against both the House of Representatives and the President, its victories over the latter being due, in part at least, to the mediocre abilities and lack of force that characterized most of the men who occupied the presidency between Lincoln and Roosevelt.[4] These constitutional struggles had disastrous effects on several treaties that had the misfortune to serve as battlegrounds.

[3] In ten of the twenty-two years after Grant a majority of the Senate did not belong to the same party as the President. Such a condition materially aids the opposition to the President and increases the opportunities for political motives, as the opposition then controls the Committee on Foreign Relations with its powers of obstruction and negation without publicity.

[4] The process received serious attention, especially in its later stages, from contemporary observers. The following titles are typical of the best among the many articles on the subject: Henry Loomis Nelson, "The Overshadowing Senate," *Century Magazine,* Feb., 1903. Samuel W. McCall, "The Power of the Senate," *Atlantic Monthly,* Oct., 1903. A. Maurice Low, "The Usurped Powers of the Senate," *American Political Science Review,* Nov., 1906.

The more numerous contacts of the United States with the rest of the world were reflected in the number of treaties negotiated, and in the twenty-nine years preceding the treaty that ended the Spanish-American war the Senate decided the fate of one hundred and thirty-four treaties.[5] The Senate can be held responsible for the loss of twenty of these.[6] Among the perfected treaties only one, the treaty of 1871 with Great Britain, was of major importance, while among the defeated treaties were all the others that were concerned with other than the routine and trivial problems of international relations. Looking back on this record in 1898, when it was apparent that another important treaty would have to be negotiated the Ambassador of the United States to Great Britain expressed his despair to a friend by saying, "I have told you many times that I did not believe another important treaty would ever pass the Senate."[7]

The first treaties to be defeated during this period were among the important ones and deservedly received considerable attention. These were the two treaties with the Dominican Republic, signed on November 29, 1869, on the personal insistence of President Grant. In so doing Grant proved that when he refused to aid the treaty for the purchase of the Danish West Indies it was not because he objected to expansion but because it was "a scheme of Seward's." One of the treaties was for the annexation of the Dominican Republic to the

[5] This does not include the numerous treaties and additional articles which merely extended the time for the exchange of the ratifications of another treaty.

[6] Several others failed because the other parties refused to ratify although the Senate had approved them without amendments. In 1874 Grant asked the advice of the Senate on a draft of a treaty for reciprocity with Canada, and after some delay was answered that it was inexpedient to negotiate such a treaty. *Sen. Ex. Jour.*, XIX, 355, 502. As no treaty was submitted to the Senate and as Grant merely said that a proper reciprocity treaty would be beneficial and was not prepared to say that the terms outlined were proper, this project has not been counted with the defeated treaties.

[7] John Hay to Henry Adams, May 27, 1898. William Roscoe Thayer, *The Life and Letters of John Hay,* II, 170.

United States, while the other provided for the lease to the United States of Samana Bay and peninsula.[8] The negotiations had been conducted by Colonel Babcock, formerly on Grant's staff and now nominally a private secretary, and a treaty had been signed before the members of the Cabinet even knew that one was contemplated.[9] To make the transaction appear more regular Babcock was sent back to Santo Domingo and new treaties were signed, this time by the representative of the State Department.[10]

The two treaties were sent to the Senate on January 10, 1870, where it might have been expected they would be favorably received, for more than two-thirds of the Senate were nominally of the President's party. Nevertheless, the fate of the Danish treaty spurred Grant to take many precautions to ensure a favorable decision on his favorite measure—the annexation treaty—and he " went so far as to make the issue one of personal weight, and condescended to do the work of a lobbyist almost on the very floor of the Senate Chamber using his personal influence to an extent scarcely ever known in American experience." [11] The members of the Cabinet who did not exert themselves in behalf of the treaty were asked to resign and the new appointments were apparently made to gain the support of certain senators to the treaty.[12] Grant called at Sum-

[8] The treaties and some of the diplomatic correspondence concerning them are in *41st Cong., 3d sess., S. Doc.*, No. 17, especially pp. 78-102.

[9] Jacob D. Cox, " How Judge Hoar Ceased To Be Attorney-General," *Atlantic Monthly*, LXXVI, 162-173. James G. Blaine, *Twenty Years of Congress*, p. 458. Hugh McCulloch, *Men and Measures of Half a Century*, p. 353. Rhodes, VI, 347-349.

[10] *41st Cong., 3d sess., S. Doc.*, No. 17, pp. 80-82, 94-96.

[11] Henry Adams, " The Session," *North American Review*, CXI, 58. Babcock's agreement was not submitted to the Senate with the other papers but became known later. In it was the pledge that " his Excellency, General Grant, President of the United States, promises *privately* to use all his influence in order that the idea of annexing the Dominican republic to the United States may acquire such a degree of popularity among members of Congress as will be necessary for its accomplishment." *Congressional Globe*, Dec. 21, 1870, p. 228.

[12] Cox, pp. 168-171. Fish offered his resignation but withdrew it on Grant's

ner's house and directly solicited his assistance for the treaty. This interview partly caused and greatly embittered the subsequent quarrel between the two, as Grant interpreted as a promise of support Sumner's reply,—"Mr. President, I am an Administration man, and whatever you do will always find in me the most careful and candid consideration." [13] The President also spoke to other senators in favor of the treaty.[14]

More formal methods of obtaining a favorable decision from the Senate were also used. Both treaties contained a provision requiring an exchange of ratifications within four months, and when that period had nearly expired Grant sent a message to the Senate urging favorable action.[15] The following day the Committee on Foreign Relations reported the treaty with a recommendation that the Senate should not give its advice and consent.[16] Although the treaty was frequently considered by the Senate, no action had been taken before the time limit expired. The annexation treaty, however, was not to be given up so easily and an additional article extending the time for exchanging ratifications was negotiated and submitted to the Senate. Accompanying it was a long message from the President in which the benefits to be derived from the treaty were stated in vigorous, if exaggerated, terms.[17] In addition to numerous economic and general advantages the President stated that the acquisition of the Dominican Republic would give the United States command of the Caribbean Sea and of the Isthmus, and that he already had reliable information that a European power

request. Extracts from his diary are given in Charles Francis Adams, *Lee at Appomattox and Other Papers,* pp. 218-223. New York *World,* March 25 and 26, 1871.

[13] Sumner's account of the interview may be found in one of his speeches in the Senate on Dec. 21, 1870, *Congressional Globe,* p. 243; and in his *Works,* XIV, 125-126. Pierce, IV, 433-436.

[14] Schurz gives an interesting account of the blunt way Grant approached him and of the frank conversation they had. *Reminiscences,* III, 307-309. See also William D. Foulke, *Life of Oliver P. Morton,* II, 148.

[15] *Sen. Ex. Jour.,* XVII, 389-390.

[16] *Ibid.,* p. 392.

[17] *Ibid.,* pp. 460-462.

was ready to offer two million dollars for Samana Bay alone so that the treaty was essential to uphold the Monroe doctrine. This last argument received added force from the fact that during the Civil War the Dominican Republic had annexed itself to Spain. But appeals to the Monroe doctrine had as little effect on the Senate as his glowing picture of the riches of Santo Domingo, so that when a vote was taken on June 30, 1870, twenty-eight senators voted against the treaty and the same number voted for it.[18]

Still Grant would not admit he was beaten and in his next annual message to Congress he repeated his arguments with a suggestion that a commission be created to negotiate a new treaty of annexation.[19] The most the President's friends could do was to authorize the appointment of a commission to visit the island and report on its political and economic conditions.[20] This was done and the report of the commission, which naturally contained information that made annexation seem highly desirable, was ultimately submitted to the Senate but no further action was ever taken.[21] The chief result of the creation of the commission was that, when the resolution was pending, it gave the opposition a chance to air their views on annexation before the public and to attack the administration.[22] Sumner made the most of the opportunity and in his most extravagant and vitriolic style denounced Grant and his policy.[23]

[18] *Ibid.*, p. 502. Some pairs were announced, seven members for the treaty and four against it.

[19] Richardson, *Messages and Papers of the Presidents,* IX, 4053-4055.

[20] Blaine, p. 460.

[21] The report is in *42d Cong., 1st sess., S. Doc.,* No. 9. In his last annual message to Congress some six years later Grant returned to the subject not to reopen the question but merely to "vindicate my previous action in respect to it." Richardson, *Messages and Papers of the Presidents,* X, 4366.

[22] The debates which can be found in the *Congressional Globe* from Dec. 20, 1870 to Jan. 11, 1871 were marked by great bitterness and savage personal attacks.

[23] The speech began, "The resolution before the Senate commits Congress to a dance of blood." *Ibid.* Dec. 21, 1870, pp. 226 ff. Pierce gives a favorable account of the speech. IV, 457-462.

The prominent part Sumner played and his subsequent removal from the chairmanship of the Committee on Foreign Relations, due largely but not solely to his opposition to the annexation of the Dominican Republic, have led many people to hold him responsible for the defeat of the treaty. Grant did so at the time, and others agreed with his view that it was a personal contest between the two.[24] So keen an observer as Henry Adams took the same view. Writing on the session in the *North American Review,* he said, " Senator Sumner again stood forward to assume the control and direction of foreign affairs. He again wielded the power of the Senate and declared the policy of the government. The President and Mr. Fish struggled in vain against this omnipotent senatorial authority. . . . Mr. Sumner flung them both aside and issued his orders with almost the authority of a Roman triumvir." [25]

But Sumner did not control the Senate in the way indicated, as events were soon to prove. Indeed, the negative votes were not due to Sumner's insistence, but the affirmative votes were due to Grant's. If the treaty had been considered solely on its merits, as they were then viewed, it would have received very little support in the Senate.[26] The public, which had objected to Seward's plan of annexation, because they valued " dollars more and dominion less," could see no compelling reason for this new attempt at expansion.[27] The same attitude was revealed

[24] Horace White, *The Life of Lyman Trumbull,* p. 342. John Sherman, *Recollections of Forty Years in the House, Senate and Cabinet,* pp. 398-399. McCulloch, p. 354. Blaine, p. 461.

[25] " The Session," p. 58.

[26] "At first very few Senators manifested any positive desire for annexation, and the mass of the Republicans were indifferent with a leaning toward opposition. Yet upon this indifferentism a deep impression was made by the terrible earnestness with which the President continued to press his policy." Frederic Bancroft and William A. Dunning, "A Sketch of Carl Schurz's Political Career," in Schurz's *Reminiscences,* III, 325.

[27] Smith, after surveying the comments of the newspapers, concludes, " The general attitude of the country was indifferent, lukewarm, unresponsive." *Expansion After the War, 1865-1871,* pp. 428, 433-436. He points out that some, like the New York *Tribune,* which had opposed the Alaska and Danish treaties

in the Cabinet when Grant made the startling announcement that Babcock had negotiated a treaty of annexation, for Cox blurted out, "But, Mr. President, has it been settled then, that we want to annex San Domingo?"[28] There were others who could not understand why anyone should wish to annex "San Domingo," and many advanced reasons why it should not be annexed.[29] Schurz made the most elaborate argument in the Senate against colonial expansion, especially in the tropics.[30]

In addition to the evident reluctance on the part of the public to support annexation schemes, the treaty suffered from several other handicaps. Baez, who signed the treaty for the Dominican Republic, had a precarious hold on that government and was apparently surrounded by a group of friends who had a pecuniary interest in promoting annexation. An atmosphere of corruption, concessions and speculation attended the entire transaction, and the opposition in the Senate was not slow to take advantage of the opportunity presented to them.[31] The

now changed front in order to uphold the administration and attacked Sumner and others, not for opposing annexation but for opposing Grant.

[28] Cox, p. 167.

[29] Henry Adams wrote, "Whence it came, why it was made, what influences supported it, are matters which no one has hitherto explained. One point alone was clear, and this was that the San Domingo treaty stood in flat opposition to the entire policy pursued down to that moment by the administration towards the West Indies, and it is as certain as anything resting on mere a priori reasoning can be, that neither Mr. Fish nor his colleagues as a body could possibly have sympathized in the proposed annexation, which was contrary to all their modes of thought and to their political education." "The Session," p. 57.

[30] *Congressional Globe,* Jan. 11, 1871, *Appendix,* pp. 25-34. Also in Frederic Bancroft, ed., *Speeches, Correspondence and Political Papers of Carl Schurz,* II, 71-122. See also *ibid.,* pp. 177-252, for Schurz's argument that Grant usurped the war powers by sending a naval force to Santo Domingo.

[31] Several months before the treaty was negotiated J. C. B. Davis, the Assistant Secretary of State, wrote to John Bigelow, "We are beset by a parcel of speculators, among whom is Fabens,—to take steps for annexing St. Domingo." Bigelow, IV, 306. The concessions and financial transactions of the Dominican Republic are given in *41st Cong., 3d sess., S. Doc.,* No. 17. Some of the unsavory features of the transaction can be found in *41st Cong., 2d sess., S. Rept.,* No. 234.

opposition also made much of the fact that a naval force was sent to the Island with Babcock, a proceeding which they denounced as a flagrant violation of the Constitution and which was necessary, they claimed, to maintain Baez in power long enough to sell his country.[32] Running through the debates were repeated appeals to the Senate to protect its constitutional powers from the alleged attacks of the President.[33] Under the circumstances the tie vote was a compliment to Grant's efforts and to the powers of the executive.

An examination of the vote on the treaty corroborates this conclusion. The twenty-eight affirmative votes were cast by Republicans, among whom were all who were conspicuous as regular party men and supporters of the administration. The twenty-eight negative votes were cast by the nine Democrats who voted and nineteen Republicans. The latter included three senators who joined the Liberal Republican party two years later, the independents like Ross and Fowler who had proved their independence and courage by refusing to find Johnson guilty when the party leaders had demanded it, and the more progressive of the organization men like the two Morrills.[34] While political considerations may have played some part in the unanimous vote of the Democrats against the treaty, and personal animosities may have had some influence on several negative Republican votes, the affirmative votes seem to have been cast almost solely for party reasons.

[32] Sumner used this point with harsh comments in his "dance of blood" speech. Grant's chief defender, Morton, did not make a very effective answer. Foulke, II, 160. Roosevelt was less vigorously attacked and more ably defended for his use of the navy under similar circumstances in 1905.

[33] "It is an attempt to destroy the prerogative of the American Senate, . . . an attempt to deprive the Senate of the United States of its power under the treaty-making clause of the Constitution." Senator Stockton. *Congressional Globe,* Dec. 21, 1870, p. 251. ". . . this furtive, unconstitutional project of the President . . . assuming the prerogative of the treaty-making power . . . are Senators ready to subordinate the power of the Senate to such a purpose, to such a project?" Senator Davis. *Ibid.,* Dec. 20, 1870, p. 195.

[34] *Sen. Ex. Jour.,* XVII, 502.

Two more treaties submitted to the Senate by Grant failed to receive the approval of that body. The first, like the treaties with the Dominican Republic, would have given the United States a political interest in an island, this time one of the Samoan group in the Pacific. But Grant showed no interest in this treaty. The administration was not committed to it and it attracted very little attention. The treaty had been made with a native chief of the island of Tutuila by a naval officer, Commander R. W. Meade, acting on his own responsibility without authority or instructions. It granted to the United States the exclusive privilege of establishing a naval base in the harbor of Pago-Pago, and in return for this concession there was only an implied promise of protection and friendship by the United States.[35] When submitting the agreement to the Senate, Grant said

> The advantages of the concession which it proposes to make are so great, in view of the advantageous position of Tutuila, especially as a coaling station for steamers between San Francisco and Australia, that I should not hesitate to recommend its approval but for the protection on the part of the United States which it seems to imply. With some modification of the obligation of protection which the agreement imports, it is recommended to the favorable consideration of the Senate.[36]

Whether it was damned by this faint praise, whether the opposition to overseas expansion blocked it, or whether it was simply neglected in the excitement of the presidential election, does not appear, but the treaty was never reported from the Committee on Foreign Relations and no efforts were made in its behalf.[37]

The last of Grant's unratified treaties was unimportant and, as it suffered in no way from political or constitutional motives on the part of the Senate, can be briefly treated despite its curious history. It was a naturalization treaty with Turkey, signed

[35] The treaty is given in *44th Cong., 1st sess., H. Doc.,* No. 161, which also includes the long report of the special agent sent to the islands the following year.

[36] *Sen. Ex. Jour.,* XVIII, 254.

[37] Brief accounts of it are given in John B. Henderson, *American Diplomatic Questions,* p. 213. Charles O. Paullin, *Diplomatic Negotiations of American Naval Officers,* pp. 350-351.

on August 11, 1874. Submitted to the Senate the following December, it was promptly and unanimously approved after several amendments had been made without opposition.[38] Fourteen years elapsed before Turkey accepted the Senate's amendments and offered to exchange ratifications, but President Cleveland thought that after so long an interval the Senate should have another opportunity to act on the treaty. Again the Senate promptly gave its unanimous approval, but again only conditionally.[39] Not to be outdone by the Senate the Turkish Government repeated its former action, or inaction, and seven more years went by before it offered to exchange ratifications. But apparently the Senate's amendments were not fully accepted by Turkey and the treaty ended its unduly protracted career.[40] The unanimity of the votes in the Senate, the insignificance of the whole affair as well as the other attending circumstances all exonorate the Senate from any suspicion of objectionable motives in amending this treaty.

The next treaty to be lost was of even less consequence. In 1878 Commodore Shufeldt, who had an eventful career as a diplomat during his long service in the navy, started on a mission to Africa and the Orient with general instructions from the State Department to extend and encourage American commerce and influence. Acting under these instructions Shufeldt on October 4, 1879, signed a treaty of amity and commerce with Sultan Abdallah, King of Johanna, one of the Comorro islands in Mozambique channel. The treaty was transmitted to the Senate on March 15, 1880, but no action was ever taken on it by that body.[41] Again no suspicion of political or constitutional motives can be raised because of the insignificance of the treaty and of the complete absence of any reference to it, such as there

[38] *Sen. Ex. Jour.*, XIX, 406, 491.

[39] *Ibid.*, XXVI, 467, 469. The new condition, however, merely clarified the earlier amendments.

[40] Anyone interested in the later proceedings can find them in *Foreign Relations, 1896*, pp. 929-937. See also, Leland J. Gordon, *American Relations with Turkey, 1830-1930*, pp. 205-208.

[41] *Sen. Ex. Jour.*, XXII, 269.

would surely have been had anyone considered that politics or anything save indifference was involved.[42]

The next treaty to be defeated had an unusual experience in some respects, as it was twice rejected by the Senate—the first time under a Republican administration and again under a Democratic administration. On July 13, 1882, a treaty was signed with Mexico providing for the reopening and retrying of the claims of Benjamin Weil and the La Abra Silver Mining Company against Mexico.[43] These claims had been presented to the commission created by the treaty of July 4, 1868, and substantial awards had been made which Mexico was to settle by a series of annual payments. Soon after the claims had been adjudicated Mexico discovered new evidence which, if true, would prove that both claims were fraudulent. The affair was aired in Congress and the President was requested to investigate the charges of fraud and if convinced of the necessity he was authorized to withhold the payments of the award until the claims had been retired.[44] The Secretary of State investigated and reported that the justice of the claims was exceedingly doubtful and that Congress should authorize some agency to examine and determine the charges judicially.[45] But no further steps were taken by Congress, and the awards were distributed to the claimants until Arthur became President. Then the dis-

[42] A summary of the provisions and a brief account of the treaty is in Paullin, p. 354. There is also a mention of it in the account of Shufeldt's voyage in Paullin, "The Opening of Korea by Commodore Shufeldt," *Political Science Quarterly*, XXV, 477-478.

[43] The treaty and the diplomatic correspondence immediately preceding it are in *50th Cong., 1st sess., S. Rept.*, No. 1630. There is a brief account of the two claims in Moore, *International Arbitration*, II, 1324-1328. The claims were the subject of litigation and negotiation for over twenty years and a large number of Congressional documents and reports are devoted to them. The one cited above and *48th Cong., 1st sess., H. Doc.*, No. 103, are perhaps the most important. The second volume of the *Compilation of the Reports of the Committee on Foreign Relations*, a book of over one thousand pages, is devoted exclusively to a report on the claim of the La Abra Silver Mining Company.

[44] *Statutes at Large*, XX, 114.

[45] *48th Cong., 1st sess., H. Doc.*, No. 103, pp. 581-582.

tributions were suspended and a treaty to retry the claims was negotiated.

The treaty went to the Senate on July 26, 1882, but the session was nearly over and a vote was not taken on it until the following January.[46] The treaty was then rejected by a vote of thirty-three to twenty in favor of the resolution giving the advice and consent of the Senate to it.[47] Immediately after the vote a motion was made by one of the senators, who had opposed the resolution, to reconsider the vote. By this means the treaty was kept before the Senate and during the next three years it was considered from time to time and petitions were received from the claimants. Finally on April 20, 1886, the Senate again reached a vote and the treaty was again rejected, this time by a vote of thirty-two to twenty-six in favor of it.[48] This ended all attempts to settle the question through the treaty-making power, and after a further delay of six years Congress conferred jurisdiction on the Court of Claims to investigate and determine both claims. Both were declared to be wholly fraudulent, and when the Supreme Court had approved this verdict Mexico received back the money held by the Secretary of State, plus the amount distributed to the claimants which the United States now reimbursed, minus the expenses of litigation.

An examination of the votes on the treaty shows that while the result was not determined by party politics the vote was colored by partisanship. When the treaty was first rejected the thirty-three affirmative votes were cast by twenty-one Republicans and twelve Democrats, while the twenty negative votes were those of five Republicans and fifteen Democrats. On the second and final rejection the treaty was approved by nineteen Republicans and thirteen Democrats and opposed by thirteen Democrats, eleven Republicans and the two Readjuster senators from Virginia. The trace of politics can be found in the fact that under a Republican administration only five Republicans opposed the treaty while under a Democratic administration

[46] *Sen. Ex. Jour.*, XXIII, 502.

[47] *Ibid.*, p. 595.

[48] *Ibid.*, XXV, 429.

eleven, or more than one-third of the Republicans who voted refused to approve it.[49]

The real cause of the rejection of the treaty must be sought elsewhere, as the almost equal division of the Democratic vote on both occasions precludes the idea that political considerations dominated. John W. Foster, who participated in the case as one of the legal representatives of Mexico, explained the fate of the treaty, after listing some of the distinguished lawyers with political connections on the claimants' side, by saying, "the combined influence of lawyers and claimants was then brought to bear to prevent the approval of the treaty." [50] More respectable reasons were present and may have decided the Senate's action, for there seemed to be doubts in some minds as to whether the reopening of the claims was a question which properly concerned Mexico and the treaty-making power or whether it should be handled by some other branch of the government, as it ultimately was.[51]

Even though the action of the Senate on the next treaty to be lost took place in the interim pending a change of administrations, not a trace of partisanship can be detected. For that reason and because the treaty concerned only the routine of foreign relations, it can be quickly dismissed. On June 23, 1884, an additional article to the treaty of commerce and navigation of July 27, 1853, with the Argentine Confederation was signed, but it did not reach the Senate until the following

[49] Only one Republican, Conger, who had voted for the treaty under Arthur changed his vote and opposed it under Cleveland. The others who opposed it under Cleveland were either new members or had refrained from voting on the first test. One Democrat, Call, voted against the treaty under Arthur and for it under Cleveland.

[50] John W. Foster, *Diplomatic Memoirs,* II, 284. Among the large number of lawyers defending the fraudulent claims were ex-Secretary of State and ex-Attorney-General Jeremiah Black, ex-Senator and ex-Secretary of the Treasury Boutwell, ex-Attorney-General Williams, ex-Congressman Robert C. Schenck, ex-Senator Joseph E. McDonald, George Ticknor Curtis, and the prominent firm of Shellabarger and Wilson.

[51] *50th Cong., 1st sess., S. Rept.,* No. 1630, pp. 2, 3, 7, 32.

January.[52] Before it was acted on, the new administration came into office and Cleveland withdrew the treaty from the Senate for reexamination.[53] He returned it to the Senate with an additional clause, signed June 25, 1885.[54] It was not until January, 1887, that the treaty finally received the advice and consent of the Senate in an amended form.[55] The amendments, which were trivial in character, were made by unanimous votes, and the treaty with amendments was approved unanimously. Argentina failed to ratify the treaty for reasons which need not be examined here. While the amendments of the Senate did not cause the loss of the treaty, they offered a technical justification for Argentina's refusal to ratify had the treaty been important enough to require any.

Four other treaties went to the Senate to meet with defeat in that same period of waiting for the shift of power to the Democratic President who had been elected in November but would not enter office until March. Three clearly suffered from party votes. The most important of these was an incident in the diplomatic history of the interoceanic canal which was the subject of so much negotiation in the half-century following the expansion of the United States to the Pacific coast. The evident intention of the French company led by De Lesseps to di
a canal across Panama under the concession granted by Colo
bia aroused the United States to action. An attempt was
to get rid of the Clayton-Bulwer treaty, which the Unit
had come to regard as an oppressive restriction on i
policy toward the proposed canal. When Great Brit
ted this attempt by asserting her rights under t
Bulwer treaty, and no modification seemed att
agreement was completely disregarded and a trea
with Nicaragua on December 1, 1884. This
vened the Clayton-Bulwer treaty which had
canal to be jointly owned and protected by
The United States also guaranteed the inte

[52] *Sen. Ex. Jour.*, XXIV, 443.

[53] *Ibid.*, XXV, 47.

[54] *Ibid.*, p

[55] *Ibid.*,

[56] The treaty can be found in *55th Cong.*, 2

ng
om-
made
d States
ts proper
ain frustra-
he Clayton-
ainable, that
ty was signed
directly contra-
provided for a
two countries.
f Nicaragua.[56]
No. 1265, pp.

The treaty went to the Senate ten days after it was signed with a long message explaining its merits and the necessity for it.[57] After numerous debates a vote was reached on January 29, 1885, when a majority, but not the required two-thirds, was willing to give its advice and consent to the treaty.[58] Thirty-two senators favored the treaty and twenty-three opposed it. Despite this vote the Secretary of State said he expected the treaty would be approved ultimately and he instructed the representative of the United States in Nicaragua to use his best efforts in persuading Nicaragua to ratify the treaty.[59] What little hope there was for the treaty was based on the fact that a motion to reconsider the vote, introduced by one of the senators who had voted against the treaty, was unanimously agreed to several weeks later, when the further consideration of the treaty was postponed to March 3.[60] That date passed without action and the treaty was left to the new administration. Soon after his inauguration Cleveland withdrew the treaty from the Senate and did not resubmit it.

In his first annual message Cleveland explained why he had not resubmitted the treaty to the Senate by saying that he opposed "a policy of acquisition of new and distant territory or the incorporation of remote interests with our own." [61] He also reasserted the then traditional policy of the United States in respect to the canal and thus, by implication at least, reaffirmed the Clayton-Bulwer treaty. The fact that no attempt was made

20-27. Soon after it was submitted to the Senate the rules of secrecy were violated and the [illegible] treaty appeared in the New York *Tribune* of December 18, 1884. The diplomatic setting of the treaty is described in Travis, pp. 211-240; Williams, pp. 274-286.

[57] *Sen. Ex. Jour.*, XXIV, 377-380.

[58] *Ibid.*, p. 453.

[59] *49th Cong., 2d sess., S. Doc.*, No. 50, especially pp. 11, 13-14, 16. Nicaragua did ratify the tr[illegible]y. It complicated her relations with her neighbors, who first learned of the [illegible]y through the columns of the New York *Tribune*. *Ibid.*, pp. 6-7, 9, 12, 1[illegible]

[60] *Sen. E*[illegible]XXIV, 456, 481.

[61] Rich[illegible]ages and Papers of the Presidents*, XI, 4912.

in the Senate to remove the guarantee of the territorial integrity of Nicaragua has led most writers to conclude that a reluctance to violate the Clayton-Bulwer treaty was responsible for the senatorial opposition to the treaty. This view is further substantiated by the testimony of several of the senators who were members at the time. Speaking in the Senate some eight years later Senator Frye said,

It is in the memory of many Senators who are here now that for long months we discussed that treaty. It will be remembered, too, that in the midst of the contest the ghost of the Clayton-Bulwer treaty, a treaty that had been as dead as Julius Caesar for a quarter of a century, was summoned into this chamber and succeded in preventing the treaty from receiving the necessary two-thirds vote, though it did command a very large majority.[62]

Senator Morgan, one of the four Democrats who voted for the treaty gave the same explanation of its defeat.[63]

An examination of the vote makes this explanation seem highly improbable, if not certainly incorrect. The thirty-two votes in favor of the treaty were cast by twenty-seven Republicans, four Democrats, and one Readjuster. The twenty-three votes against the treaty were cast by twenty-one Democrats, one Readjuster, and one Republican. The one Republican opposing the treaty, Edmunds, did so merely to be permitted under the

[62] *Congressional Record,* Feb. 13, 1893, p. 1514.

[63] *Ibid.,* p. 1522. In his *Recollections of Forty Years,* pp. 852-853, John Sherman said, "I do not feel at liberty to state the causes of delay nor the ground taken, nor the votes given either for or against it, as the injunction of secrecy in respect to it has not been removed, but I have regarded as a misfortune its practical defeat by the want of a two-thirds vote. . . . This objection [guarantee of integrity] to the treaty could have been easily removed by negotiation as Mr. Bayard, a Member of the Senate when the treaty was pending and Secretary of State under President Cleveland, very well knew. Thus, by an unfortunate division in the Senate and the action of the President, the construction of the canal by the United States was prevented." This rare sense of delicacy about breaking the rules of the Senate was unnecessary for his book was not published until 1896 and the injunction of secrecy had been removed on January 6, 1891, and the votes on the treaty had been explained, as quoted above, with Sherman present.

rules of the Senate to move that the vote be reconsidered.[64] So the Republicans were solidly for the treaty and the Democrats were almost a unit against it[65] An alignment of this character is incompatible with the idea that such a consideration as the desire not to violate the Clayton-Bulwer treaty determined the vote of the Senate. There was, perhaps, a possibility for an honest difference of opinion as to whether or not the Clayton-Bulwer treaty was still in force, or was voidable, or even whether it applied, but honest differences of opinion on technical legal matters or on ethical questions do not follow party lines. When all the Republicans vote one way and all the Democrats another, partisanship is chiefly responsible for the division no matter what reasons may be advanced by both sides. Some of the Democrats undoubtedly opposed the treaty because it was a Republican measure and because they wanted the question left to the incoming Democratic administration, while some of the Republicans just as certainly supported the treaty because it was an administration measure. The views of these as to whether the Clayton-Bulwer treaty was a " ghost " or alive were determined by the accident of party allegiance.[66]

[64] Standing Rule XIII of the Senate provided " When a question has been decided by the Senate, any Senator voting with the prevailing side may, on the same day or on either of the next two days of actual session thereafter, move a reconsideration; and if the Senate shall refuse to reconsider, or upon reconsideration shall affirm its first decision, no further motion shall be in order unless by unanimous consent." These motions are decided by a majority vote. Edmunds really favored the treaty. Sherman, p. 852.

[65] Party votes are the exception rather than the rule in Congress and even when they occur a few members usually leave the majority of each party. As the result of a careful statistical study, almost the only one of its kind, A. Lawrence Lowell stated that only between seven and eight per cent of the public bills enacted by Congress are made the subject of a party vote at some stage of their passage. " The Influence of Party upon Legislation in England and America," *Annual Report of the American Historical Association, 1901*, I, 321-542.

[66] Despite injunctions for secrecy full details of the votes and party alignment appeared in the papers. New York *Times,* Jan. 30, 1885. New York *Herald,* Jan. 30, 1885. The latter paper had a long despatch from Washington explaining the reasons for the defeat of the treaty. After explaining that many Democrats had favored it until Senator Bayard, who, it was known, was going to be

On the same day that Cleveland withdrew the treaty with Nicaragua from the Senate he also withdrew two other treaties which had been sent there by the defeated Republican administration and which were still pending. Both provided for commercial reciprocity with islands in the West Indies and, because they involved the same principles and met the same fate, they can be considered together. One, with Spain, had been signed on November 18, 1884; the other, with the Dominican Republic, on December 4, 1884. Both treaties were published in full in the newspapers, the Spanish treaty being cabled from Spain where a copy had been obtained by bribing an official,[67] while in the case of the Dominican treaty, the leak was in this country.[68] The treaty with Spain provided for commercial reciprocity with Cuba and Porto Rico, so that as soon as it was made public the newspapers of the country received and published many protests from persons interested in the tobacco and sugar industries, and many petitions were sent to the Senate.[69] The

Cleveland's Secretary of State, caused them to change their minds, the paper said, "Mr. Bayard therefore secured the rejection of the treaty . . . by, in a manner, coercing his fellow democrats to vote against its ratification. He was able to do this only because his language and attitude put upon the minds of democratic Senators the moral conviction that it is Mr. Cleveland's desire that the treaty should be rejected."

[67] Foster, *Diplomatic Memoirs,* I, 259. The New York *Times* on the day it published the treaty said, "As it was not practicable to secure a copy of the treaty in this country in advance of its submission to the Senate, the *Times* has had the entire document cabled to it from Madrid." Dec. 8, 1884. This was regarded as quite a coup and for several days the *Times* printed extracts of the views of the other papers on its feat. It also started a discussion of secrecy in the Senate and the treaty-making power. There were many editorials on these subjects, see especially New York *Herald,* Dec. 7 and 12, 1884, and a resolution was introduced into the House on Dec. 8th, providing for a constitutional amendment which would have made the consent of the House of Representatives necessary for treaties. The Senate removed the injunction of secrecy from the treaty on Dec. 11, 1884. *Sen. Ex. Jour.*, XXIV, 385.

[68] The New York *Herald* of Dec. 18, 1884 made this treaty public. See also, *Sen. Ex. Jour.,* XXIV, 396.

[69] New York *Times,* Dec. 9, 10, 12, 1884. New York *Herald,* Dec. 9, 12, 13, 1884. *Sen. Ex. Jour.*, XXIV, 351, 376, 381, 383, 388.

merits of the economic policy involved cannot be examined here, nor can the peculiar political conditions which made reciprocity treaties important at intervals from 1883 to 1900. As a rule the Democrats opposed the treaties and the Republicans split into two groups, the one opposing the treaties being composed of the ultra-protectionists and those representing the economic interests adversely affected. The other group which favored reciprocity usually included the majority of the party.[70]

The two treaties were submitted to the Senate on December 9 and 10, 1884.[71] The administration made efforts to secure favorable action, sending a laudatory report to the Senate,[72] and negotiating four additional articles to the Spanish treaty "in deference to the representations made on behalf of important commercial interests." [73] But a defeated administration often finds it difficult to push measures in its last Congress and no vote was taken on the treaties. Cleveland's opposition was "a foregone conclusion." He withdrew them from the Senate and did not resubmit them.[74] The Senate can justly be held responsible for their defeat because they were in its hands almost three months and would have been approved but for the opposition in that body..

The sources of the opposition have already been revealed. The general hostility of the Democrats to reciprocity, the opposition of some of the Republicans based either on principle or on personal antagonisms, and the weakness of a defeated administration were all factors. Exactly how much weight should be assigned to each cannot be determined because no vote was taken, but the opposition of the Democrats was decisive.[75] An

[70] Both these questions are fully developed by J. Laurence Laughlin and H. Parker Willis, *Reciprocity*.

[71] *Sen. Ex. Jour.*, XXIV, 375, 380.

[72] *48th Cong., 2d sess., S. Doc.*, No. 10.

[73] *Sen. Ex. Jour.*, XXIV, 493.

[74] Laughlin and Willis, p. 125.

[75] The New York *Herald*, a Republican paper advocating the treaties, recognized they were lost as soon as it was evident they were being opposed by the incoming administration. Jan. 30, 1885.

interesting explanation of the causes for the defeat of the treaties, showing how little they were considered on their merits, has been given by John W. Foster who, as Minister, had negotiated the Spanish treaty and had been recalled to the United States to assist the State Department in securing the advice and consent of the Senate, so he was both interested and in a position to follow events. He said,

> The Republican Party had been beaten in the national election, and Mr. Cleveland was about to enter upon the Presidency with a policy opposed to commercial reciprocity. While there were Democratic Senators who were warm advocates of the Cuban treaty, the influence of the incoming Administration was thrown against it.
>
> Neither was there a unanimous support by Republican Senators. Mr. Blaine, the defeated candidate for the Presidency, felt resentment at not being continued in the Arthur Cabinet after the death of President Garfield and at the alleged want of hearty support from the Administration in the recent campaign. He spent the winter in Washington when the treaty was before the Senate, and, although he became a few years later the champion of reciprocity, he gave his friends to understand that it would be better not to act upon this measure. . . .
>
> President Arthur and his measures encountered the same embarassment which attends the policy of a defeated President, as his term draws to its close—the powerful opposition of the incoming Administration and the lukewarmness of his own party.[76]

The last treaty that was submitted by the outgoing administration and lost can be quickly dismissed because the decision of the Senate was obviously not influenced by partisanship or constitutional struggle with the President and because of the unimportance of the treaty. An extradition treaty with Mexico was signed on February 20, 1885, and was submitted to the Senate about two weeks later.[77] No action was taken by the Senate for more than a year. Then the treaty was approved with numerous amendments including several which seriously altered the provisions of the treaty as it had been negotiated,

[76] *Diplomatic Memoirs,* I, 259-260. Laughlin and Willis agree with this interpretation and add the opposition coming from the economic interests affected. *Reciprocity,* pp. 117, 124-125, 283.

[77] *Sen. Ex. Jour.,* XXIV, 493.

with the result that Mexico refused to exchange ratifications.[78] The amendments were adopted and the treaty was approved by unanimous votes. Consequently it may be inferred that politics was not involved.

Another extradition treaty was the next to fail, but it was of more importance since the other signatory power was Great Britain. Treaties with Great Britain, even on routine business, have frequently acquired special importance because of the presence of large groups of voters, particularly the Irish, whose antipathy to that country can be easily and profitably exploited by politicians. This fact and the crisis in the relations between the two countries produced during the years 1886-1889 by the disputes over the Newfoundland fisheries and over the fur-seal fisheries in Behring Sea, caused the extradition treaty, signed June 25, 1886, to receive much more attention than its provisions warranted.[79]

Nine days after it reached the Senate and within a month of its signature the treaty was reported from the Committee on Foreign Relations.[80] Then its speedy progress was halted and for over two years and a half it remained pending in the Senate but not neglected, for it was frequently debated. Although the terms of the treaty were not made public until April 5, 1888, when the injunction of secrecy was removed,[81] the knowledge that an extradition treaty had been made with Great Britain was enough to start a flood of protests to the Senate.[82] With rare exceptions these came from Irish clubs and societies, while the three petitions urging ratification came from bankers.[83] Two unsuccessful attempts were made to have the treaty considered in open session.[84] Finally, on February 1, 1889, after being amended in several unimportant particulars it was re-

[78] *Ibid.*, XXV, 483-484.

[79] The treaty and some diplomatic papers relating to it are in *Foreign Relations, 1888, Part II,* 1730-1744.

[80] *Sen. Ex. Jour.*, XXV, 539, 552.

[81] *Ibid.*, XXVI, 230.

[82] *Ibid.*, XXV, 729, 735, 747, 748, 752, 762; XXVI, 106, 420, 421, 435, 445.

[83] *Ibid.*, XXVI, 193, 256, 435.

[84] *Ibid.*, XXV, 576; XXVI, 161.

jected by a vote of fifteen to thirty-eight in favor of the resolution advising and consenting to its ratification.[85]

An analysis of the vote shows that party politics cannot be held responsible for the defeat of the treaty. Five Republicans and ten Democrats voted for the treaty and twenty-four Republicans, thirteen Democrats and one Readjuster voted against it. But, although a majority of both parties opposed this treaty negotiated by a Democratic administration, it is noticeable that the Republican opposition to it was much greater. Accordingly, politics may have affected the size of the vote. Certainly the treaty was used for political effect in the presidential election of 1888, when great efforts were made to detach the Irish vote from the Democratic party by picturing Cleveland as the subservient friend of Great Britain.[86]

The extradition treaty was greatly overshadowed in public interest and in importance by another treaty with Great Britain that was rejected while the former was still pending. This was the treaty of February 15, 1888, providing for a settlement of the questions relating to the northeastern fisheries. At intervals since 1783 these fisheries had given rise to disputes which were sometimes heated, but which had always been settled amicably by diplomatic negotiations. One such settlement expired in 1885 and in the following year some American boats were seized by the Canadian authorities. The resulting tension was greatly increased by the fact that the dispute over the seal fisheries in the Behring Sea had reached a crisis at the same time and Canadian boats were being seized there by officials of the United States. The situation was such that a war might have resulted. By an act of March 3, 1887, Congress authorized the President to adopt measures of retaliation, but instead of following that

[85] *Ibid.*, XXVI, 443-444, 446.

[86] "His enemies, especially in New York, were again appealing to the Irish vote in the plea that President Cleveland was a British tool 'employed by Ireland's cruel enemy to aid her work of enslavement.' To this end his extradition treaty was distorted into a scheme for placing all the machinery of the government in this country at the service of England for the suppression of defection in Ireland." Robert McElroy, *Grover Cleveland,* I, 294.

belligerent procedure he endeavored to settle the dispute by the exercise of the treaty-making power. The treaty of February 15, 1888, was the result.[87]

A few days later the treaty went to the Senate accompanied by a long message from the President in which he reviewed the history of the dispute and defended the settlement proposed.[88] In accordance with a suggestion of the President the treaty and his message were made public the following day. The proceedings in the Senate had hardly begun when an unprecedented step was taken. By a vote of twenty-one to nineteen the Senate resolved to consider the treaty in open executive session.[89] This was the first treaty to undergo the rigors of a public debate by the Senate. On a number of previous occasions attempts had been made to have a pending treaty considered in open session and in practically every case the motion to that effect was made by some opponent of the treaty, but it had always been defeated. In this instance when the motion was first made it was voted down almost unanimously, one of the leading speeches against it being made by a Republican member of the Committee on Foreign Relations. But at a caucus the Republicans decided to vote for an open session and to permit no amendments to the treaty.[90] The twenty-one senators who then voted for the motion, when again proposed, were all Republicans and their nineteen opponents were all Democrats. Thus by a strictly party vote there was established a precedent which, whether wise or not, would certainly have shocked the framers of the Constitution.

An open executive session means that the public is admitted to hear the debates and that the proceedings are published in full each day in the *Congressional Record.* Accordingly, from

[87] Good secondary accounts of the diplomatic history of the question are in Henderson, pp. 451-529. Moore, *American Diplomacy,* pp. 87-104. The more important diplomatic papers were inserted during the debates on the treaty in the *Congressional Record* of the *50th Cong., 1st sess.*

[88] *Sen. Ex. Jour.,* XXVI, 186-190.

[89] *Ibid.,* p. 268.

[90] *Congressional Record,* June 7, 1888, p. 4980.

May 28, 1888, until the final vote on the 21st of the following August, the arguments that were made for and against the treaty are available. The instances when treaties have been considered in open session have invariably shown that when a treaty is the subject of a contest in the Senate the constitutional distribution of the treaty-making power between President and Senate becomes involved and the treaty is certain to be attacked on the grounds that the prerogatives of the Senate are being invaded by the President. This time it was alleged, first in the majority report of the Committee on Foreign Relations and then repeatedly in the debates on the floor of the Senate, that the proceedings were irregular because the negotiators for the United States had not been appointed by and with the consent of the Senate.[91] So opprobrious did this failure to submit the names of the negotiators to the Senate appear to Senator Chandler that he denounced it as " a gross violation of the Constitution, wilfully, recklessly, and defiantly perpetrated; and the Senate might well have refused on this ground even to consider the terms of a treaty thus first introduced into its presence." [92] This attack was met and successfully answered by the Democratic minority of the Committee on Foreign Relations in its report by the insertion of a list of the persons employed by the United States in conducting negotiations since 1789, which showed that 438 had been appointed without the concurrence or advice of the Senate, while only 35 had received senatorial sanction.[93]

Most of the other arguments were equally insincere. The Republicans attacked the treaty as a base surrender of the rights of the United States, but they used their strongest terms in denouncing the Democratic administration that made it. In

[91] *Compilation of the Reports of the Committee on Foreign Relations,* VIII, 271.

[92] *Congressional Record,* July 16, 1888, p. 6355.

[93] *Compilation of the Reports of the Committee on Foreign Relations,* VIII, 332-333, 337-362. The unsoundness of the senatorial criticism has been thoroughly exposed in a recent study. Henry M. Wriston, *Executive Agents in American Foreign Relations.*

their enthusiasm for that task they gave ample proof of the fact that the Senate was not considering the treaty as the constitutional fathers had intended but were playing politics. Thus Senator Hoar in his long prepared speech on the treaty, a speech of which he was particularly proud,[94] said,

> Those were the days when the flag, beautiful as a flower to those who loved it, terrible as a meteor to those who hated it, floated everywhere in peaceful seas, and was honored everywhere in friendly ports. No petty British officer hauled it down from an American masthead. No Canadian minister of justice laughed in the face of an injured American citizen when Grant was in the White House.
>
> I confess that, much meditating on these things, I take little satisfaction when I think of Grover Cleveland. I do not like the policy which everywhere robs American citizenship of its glory. I do not like the methods of fraud and crime which have destroyed popular elections in so many Democratic States. I would have the box where the American freeman casts his ballot sacred as a sacramental vessel. I do not like this conspiracy between the old slave-holder and the English manufacturer, to strike down the wages of the American workman and the comfort of the American workman's home. I do not like your refusal to maintain the American Navy and to fortify and defend the American coast. And I like no better the present treaty. It leaves the American sailor to be bullied and insulted without redress, and abandons the American right to the fisheries, older than the nation itself which the valor of our fathers won for us and the wisdom our fathers preserved for us.[95]

Clearly the arguments were directed to the voters in the presidential election in progress and did not concern the merits of the question. That such was the case was noted in a private letter by Cecil Spring Rice, then Secretary of the British Legation in Washington, who, after commenting on the "purely party vote" of the Senate Committee, wrote, "The reasons

[94] *Autobiography of Seventy Years,* II, 145.

[95] *Congressional Record,* July 10, 1888, p. 6060. The Baltimore *Sun* of July 12, 1888, said of this speech, "It will be used as a campaign document, as will various of the speeches of other Republican Senators on the fisheries treaty. The crusade against the treaty inaugurated on the Republican side of the Senate is palpably dishonest. The evidences are thick that had it been negotiated by a Republican administration it would have been defended as solidly by them as it is now denounced."

given are addressed not to the Senate but to the more bigoted and disagreeable faction of the Republican party. The time is a hopeless one to have chosen, and every four years politics here become simply the lowest form of personal demagogue-ism." [96] From the moment it entered the Senate the treaty became a political issue and the votes on it followed party lines strictly. The majority report of the Committee on Foreign Relations opposing the treaty was signed by five Republicans, for the Republicans had a majority in the Senate, and the minority report favoring it was signed by four Democrats. The twenty-one senators who voted for considering the treaty in open session were all Republicans and their nineteen opponents all Democrats. On the last day of the debate a motion was made to send the treaty back to the Committee on Foreign Relations with instructions to report any amendments necessary to remove ambiguities or remedy defects, or to report a plan for arbitrating the dispute over the fisheries. This motion was defeated by a vote of twenty-nine to thirty-one, all the negative votes being Republican and the affirmative Democratic.[97] An attempt was then made to amend one of the articles so as to meet one of the objections that had been most strenuously urged. This, too, was voted down by a strictly party vote.[98] The treaty was then rejected with thirty Republican senators voting against and twenty-seven Democrats for it.[99]

Such a record renders it unnecessary to spend much time in proving the treaty was not considered on its merits but on its political possibilities. It was then and has since been generally recognized that it was made a political issue, not because of a real difference in policy between the two parties but merely

[96] Stephan Gwynn, *The Letters and Friendships of Sir Cecil Spring Rice,* I, 93.

[97] *Congressional Record,* Aug. 21, 1888, p. 7766.

[98] *Ibid.,* p. 7767.

[99] *Ibid.,* p. 7768. Senator Hoar in his *Autobiography of Seventy Years,* II, 149, says two Democrats, Palmer and Turpie, were against the treaty. But the record shows that Turpie was paired for the treaty, and the only Palmer then in the Senate was Thomas W. who was a Republican. John McAuley Palmer, the Democratic senator, did not enter the Senate until the next Congress.

because the treaty happened to be presented during a presidential campaign and one side saw an opportunity of securing some political advantage from it.[100] In fact, according to the account of the representative of the Canadian government in the negotiations a " leading Republican senator " was honest or indiscreet enough to admit this, for in defending his party's action he frankly asserted, "We cannot allow the Democrats to take credit for settling so important a dispute." [101] Nor was this action by the Republican senators totally unexpected by the British negotiators. One of them in a letter written to a friend five days before the treaty was signed had given proof of his prescience by stating, " Our treaty is really progressing but it is sure to be squashed in the Senate, not because the Senate disapproves of it, but because they disapprove of the present Government." [102]

The Democrats naturally accused the Republicans of playing politics, saying, " Had a Republican administration negotiated this treaty every Republican senator would have approved of it; and because it has been sent here by a Democratic President, they have determined in party caucus to vote against its ratification. The consideration of the treaty in open session was a mandate of a party caucus in order that their appeal to the prejudices of voters against England might have its full force

[100] Writers on diplomatic history either give no explanation of the Senate's action or agree with the conclusion expressed in the following terms by Dunning, *The British Empire and the United States,* p. 280, " The Senate of the United States refused to approve it, for reasons which so far as the public debate on the questions may be assumed to reveal them, related much more to President Cleveland's candidacy for re-election than to the merits of the fisheries question." Only one writer offering a different explanation has been discovered. Fish, *American Diplomacy,* p. 376, says, " American fisherman, however, were unwilling to admit equal competition, particularly, as fishing bounties had been discontinued in 1866; and their representatives in the Senate succeeded in defeating the treaty." This high tribute to the influence of the relatively small and unimportant fishing industry seems to be unwarranted. Senator Teller of Colorado was one of the leading opponents of the treaty and all the Republican senators from the Mississippi valley and the west voted against it.

[101] Sir Charles Tupper, *Recollections of Sixty Years,* p. 192.

[102] Gwynn, *Cecil Spring Rice,* I, 93.

and produce the effect desired."[103] To this the Republicans answered, "there is not a Democrat on that side of the Chamber who would have supported it if it had not come from a Democratic administration."[104] It is probable that if there had been a Republican administration and it had appeared politically profitable to defeat the treaty the Democrats in the Senate would have found reasons for voting against it. As it was, the Republicans assumed the responsibility of killing the treaty for political ends. The political advantages expected were obvious. In 1884 Cleveland had carried New York State by a very small majority, and if the Irish Democrats could be alienated from him by being persuaded that he was subservient or even friendly to Great Britain, that state and the election would be lost to the Democrats.[105] The risk of further complicating the already critical relations with Great Britain was disregarded for the hope of a political victory.[106]

Partisanship was in no way responsible for the loss of the next two defeated treaties. On March 12, 1888, a treaty had been signed with China which provided for the exclusion of Chinese laborers from the United States.[107] When it reached

[103] *Congressional Record,* July 27, 1888, p. 6900.

[104] *Ibid.,* July 21, 1888, p. 6611. This was Senator Teller who took the most active part on the Republican side, was always partisan, and frequently surpassed Senator Hoar's best efforts in making campaign speeches. See especially, *ibid.,* Aug. 15, 1888, p. 7562.

[105] Other evidence was used to convict Cleveland of being too friendly to Great Britain. The pending extradition treaty has already been mentioned in this connection. The most spectacular proof was the letter the British Minister, Lord Sackville West, was tricked into writing and which was made public on the eve of the election.

[106] Immediately after the rejection of the treaty Cleveland sent a message to Congress in which he asked that, as the Senate had refused to amend the treaty and had shown its unwillingness to have the dispute settled by diplomatic negotiations, Congress authorize him to take very severe measures of retaliation. This tended to help Cleveland politically by showing his willingness to be aggressive with Great Britain, but it was a step toward war. Fortunately Congress did not grant his request.

[107] The treaty and diplomatic correspondence concerning it are in *Foreign Relations, 1888,* Part I, 392-404.

the Senate, two amendments were made unanimously and then the treaty was approved without any opposition.[108] The Chinese government also wanted to make some amendments in the treaty and ultimately ratifications were not exchanged.[109]

The other treaty was a very unimportant one with Mexico, signed July 11, 1888, which provided for regulating the crossing and recrossing of the frontier by pasturing, estray or stolen cattle.[110] Two changes were made in the treaty by the Senate by unanimous votes and the treaty was unanimously approved.[111] Whether these amendments were responsible for the failure of Mexico to ratify the treaty does not appear, and is immaterial for present purposes as the unanimous votes show that no politics was involved and all the circumstances eliminate the possibility that the treaty suffered in any way from a constitutional struggle between Senate and President.

[108] *Sen. Ex. Jour.*, XXVI, 257.

[109] Although politics cannot be held directly responsible for the loss of the treaty, political maneuvers affected the treaty after it had left the Senate and was still pending. The votes of the Pacific states " seemed likely to be cast in favor of the presidential candidate whose party was most radical in its opposition to the Chinese. Under the spur of the exigencies of the campaign and the uncertainty of the ratification of the new treaty by the Chinese government, a law was hastily passed through Congress absolutely prohibiting the admittance of Chinese laborers into the United States. Although this legislation, known as the Scott Act, was in direct violation of treaty, President Cleveland allowed it to become a law, justifying his action by the failure of China to ratify the new treaty." Foster, *American Diplomacy in the Orient,* p. 301.

[110] *Foreign Relations, 1888,* Part II, 1296-1299. *Ibid., 1894,* p. 418. A multilateral protocol for the protection of industrial property had been signed on April 15, 1891. The Senate added a reservation stating that the cost to the United States was not to be increased without the previous consent of Congress and that certain provisions were not to go beyond the limits of American legislation. The action of the Senate was unanimous, a fact which eliminates the possibility of political motives. The character of the reservation shows a tendency to protect the powers of Congress as against the Executive. But the reservation was evidently not the cause of the failure of the other parties to accept the protocol since another protocol of the same date and to which the same reservation was added, was ratified. *Sen. Ex. Jour.*, XXVIII, 157, 170.

[111] *Sen. Ex. Jour.*, XXVI, 355.

It was four years later, when another presidential election was being held and another change of administration was about to take place, that the next treaties were lost. On March 25, 1892, after overcoming much inertia and some reluctance on the part of the French government, Whitelaw Reid, the Minister of the United States at Paris, succeeded in concluding an extradition treaty with that government.[112] It was a treaty of no importance and it is difficult to see that it had any political significance, yet the votes on it in the Senate show the influence of partisan spirit. Differences of opinion in regard to an extradition treaty, which involved no other questions of policy, would not follow party lines if they were considered solely on their merits.

The treaty went to the Senate in due course and after several minor amendments had been incorporated it was rejected by a tie vote.[113] The twenty-three affirmative votes were cast by twenty-two Republicans and one Democrat. The opposition was composed of twenty Democrats, one independent, and two Republicans, one of whom voted against the treaty so as to be in a position to move to reconsider the vote. He did so, and the treaty went over to the next session of the Senate. Then a further amendment was added, fixing a minimum amount of money for the embezzlement of which a criminal could be extradited, and the treaty was approved by a vote of forty to sixteen.[114] Twenty-eight Republicans, ten Democrats, and two Populist senators favored the treaty, and fifteen Democrats and one Republican opposed. Four Democrats, who had voted against the treaty when it was rejected, now voted for it. Possibly they were converted by the amendment regarding embezzlement, but no attempt had been made on the first occasion

[112] "For nearly two years I could get no satisfaction about the Extradition question. At last they have committed themselves to immediate negotiations which I have some reason to hope may be concluded within the next month or two." Reid to Harrison, Dec. 1, 1891. Royal Cortissoz, *The Life of Whitelaw Reid,* II, 166.

[113] *Sen. Ex. Jour.,* XXVIII, 237.

[114] *Ibid.,* pp. 375, 382.

to amend the treaty in that respect. The changes made by the Senate gave the French government a convenient excuse to refuse to ratify a treaty which it had not sought, and so the negotiations ended in failure.

A treaty providing for the annexation of Hawaii to the United States was signed in Washington on February 14, 1893, with the representatives of the revolutionary government which had secured control of the Hawaiian government during the previous month.[115] On the following day the treaty was transmitted to the Senate with a message from the President urging prompt and favorable action on it and stating that "the overthrow of the monarchy was not in any way promoted by this government." [116] Two days later the treaty was reported from the Committee on Foreign Relations, an unusual demonstration of speed on the part of that agency due to the fact that the Republican majority controlled the committee and due to the need for haste if the defeated Republican administration was to secure the credit for accomplishing annexation. But the Senate itself was not so easy to manage and the session expired with the treaty still pending.[117] A few days after he took office Cleveland withdrew the treaty from the Senate and sent an agent to Hawaii to investigate the circumstances attending the revolution.[118] The report of this agent confirmed the suspicions entertained by Cleveland and many others that the diplomatic representative and the armed forces of the United States had been partially responsible for the successful revolution.[119] For

[115] *Foreign Relations, 1894, Appendix,* II, 202-205.

[116] *Sen. Ex. Jour.,* XXVIII, 397-398.

[117] It had been considered only one day. *Ibid.,* p. 402. Realizing the hopelessness of trying to get a vote on the treaty the Republicans did not want to waste on it time that was needed for legislation and appointments.

[118] *Ibid.,* p. 410.

[119] The findings of the special agent are in *Foreign Relations, 1894, Appendix* II. A different conclusion was given in the majority report of the Committee on Foreign Relations. It, the minority report, and the testimony upon which both were supposed to be based are in *Compilation of the Reports of the Committee on Foreign Relatons,* VI, 363-1169.

that and other reasons the treaty was never resubmitted to the Senate.

Although no votes were taken on the treaty in the Senate it is clear that the reason it was not acted on was the opposition of Democratic senators. A number of them made their opposition known through the newspapers.[120] They were guided to some extent by the wishes of Cleveland, who, although he gave no public expression to his views, undoubtedly let the members of his party in the Senate know what he thought should be done. It is known that at a conference with his future Secretary of State and several other political leaders the Hawaiian treaty was discussed.[121] The Secretary of State who had signed the treaty and who was, of course, in a position to know the views of the Senate, has written that the treaty " seemed in a fair way to be acted upon promptly and favorably by that body, when Mr. John G. Carlisle, a former member of the Senate and the prospective Secretary of the Treasury, came to Washington and put himself in communication with his party associates in that chamber. Henceforth action on the treaty seemed blocked, and it was understood that Mr. Carlisle brought a message from the President-elect to have the annexation question postponed for the consideration of the new Administration." [122] Thus, either because of the desire to rob the Harrison administration of the glory of annexation, as the *Tribune* said, or because of Gresham's personal animosity to Harrison, as Foster said, or because of the desire to protect the honor of the United States from a violation of international morality, as Cleveland said,[123] or because of the natural feeling that all decisions on pending problems should be left for the incoming

[120] New York *Tribune,* Feb. 17, 20, 21, 25, 1893.

[121] Matilda Gresham, *Life of Walter Quintin Gresham,* II, 744, 807-808.

[122] John W. Foster, *Diplomatic Memoirs,* II, 168. Before completing the negotiations Foster had consulted prominent Democrats in the Senate and they had assured him no serious opposition to the treaty would be made on their side of the chamber. The New York *Tribune,* March 10, 1893, also stated that Cleveland asked the Democratic senators to postpone action.

[123] McElroy, II, 65-66.

administration, another important treaty was defeated in the Senate by partisan action.

Again an interval of four years passed without the loss of any treaties and then another defeated administration negotiated a treaty which remained in the Senate until the installation of the new administration, after which it was soon rejected. But on this occasion the incoming President advocated the treaty warmly and it was not defeated by opposition from one party alone, so that partisanship was clearly not responsible. That other potent destroyer of treaties, senatorial jealousy of its constitutional powers, was the rock on which this treaty was to be wrecked. The threatened rupture of friendly relations between the United States and Great Britain over the Venezuelan boundary question afforded an excellent demonstration of the wisdom of having machinery provided in advance to settle such disputes without resorting to force or improvising plans of arbitration while public opinion was excited. The lesson had been appreciated in both countries and on January 11, 1897, a treaty was signed by Secretary of State Olney and Sir Julian Pauncefote by which each country agreed to adjust their future disputes according to the several methods of arbitration provided in the treaty.[124]

Writing many years later Olney said this treaty "seemed to me more important than the Venezuelan affair," and by thoughtful persons not misled by the sensational features of the latter affair that judgment will be accepted.[125] Indeed the treaty merits a high ranking among the significant treaties negotiated by the United States, because it marks a definite turning point in the arbitration policy of the government. Previous to 1897 the claim to leadership in the substitution of arbitration for force as a means of settling international disputes, a claim proudly and frequently made by American speakers, was largely justified. Since 1897, despite many and vehement

[124] The treaty and diplomatic correspondence are in *Foreign Relations, 1896,* pp. 222-240. Also *Reports of the Committee on Foreign Relations,* VIII, 388-425.

[125] Olney to George W. Smalley, April 7, 1911. MS. Olney Papers.

assertions of devotion to that ideal, the record reveals that in action the United States has not only lagged behind the advancing practices of the rest of the civilized world but has even retrograded. The cause of this unfortunate showing is to be found not in any antipathy of the public to arbitration but in the fear of the Senate that it might lose some of its control over the conduct of foreign relations. Every attempt to create peaceful machinery for settling the disputes of the country with other nations has stimulated such a desperate defense by the Senate of its treaty-making power that beginning with that of 1897 every general arbitration treaty has either been emasculated or rejected.

First emasculation and then rejection was the fate of the treaty of 1897. Evidently apprehensive of amendments which would at least partially nullify the merits of the treaty the President, when submitting the treaty to the Senate on the same day it was signed, called the attention of his partner in the treaty-making power to the fact that "the provisions of the treaty are the result of long and patient deliberation and represent concessions made by each party for the sake of agreement upon the general scheme." [126] When the Senate did act it displayed its customary indifference to the necessity of a meeting of the minds in conducting diplomatic negotiations, but no action was taken until the next Congress. To the anxious eyes of the Secretary of State the delay was ominous and could be interpreted in only one way. "I fear," he wrote, "the statement that the Treaty is to be talked over to the next session is only too true . . . though I am not absolutely sure. Indeed the suggestion is made that it is not only to be talked over to the next session but is to be talked to death, the senatorial idea being that the interest in the question is subsiding and that the time will come when the Treaty can be rejected without any particular objection or remonstrance on the part of the public." [127]

[126] *Sen. Ex. Jour.,* XXX, 356.

[127] Olney to H. L. Nelson. Feb. 11, 1897. MS. Olney Papers. He went on to

The delay was clearly not due to Republican opposition to the treaty of a Democratic administration, for throughout its disastrous senatorial career the treaty received more Republican than Democratic support and the new President, McKinley, in his inaugural message urged its ratification in the strongest terms, saying, "I urge the early action of the Senate thereon, not merely as a matter of policy, but as a duty to mankind." [128] If the new President was correct when he claimed arbitration "as the leading feature of our foreign policy throughout our entire national history," the Senate proved its willingness to depart from traditional policy when, two months later, after sixteen amendments including several of vital importance had been adopted, the treaty failed by a few votes to receive the requisite two-thirds majority, forty-three senators favoring it and twenty-six opposing it.[129] On the next day with no discernible intention of irony a resolution was introduced in the Senate declaring "the United States favor the principle and practice of international arbitration." [130]

There is abundant evidence to justify the statement of the New York *Herald* on May 6, 1897, that the Senate rejected the treaty "in opposition to the will of the people of the United States." The negotiation of it had been in part the culmination of a widespread agitation for arbitration that began many years earlier in France, England and the United States.[131] The strength of the movement in the United States can perhaps be gauged by the numerous resolutions in favor of arbitration introduced into Congress, of which the most noteworthy was a concurrent resolution, passed by the Senate on February 14, 1890, requesting the President to negotiate arbitration treaties.

suggest the desirability of holding meetings to keep public opinion aroused. His correspondence contains numerous other appeals to leaders of public opinion to bring pressure to bear on the Senate.

[128] Richardson, *Messages and Papers of the Presidents,* XIII, 6242.

[129] *Sen. Ex. Jour.,* XXXI, 104.

[130] *Congressional Record,* May 6, 1897, p. 907.

[131] *Arbitration and the United States,* World Peace Foundation, Pamphlet Series, IX, 494-500.

The public, moreover, favored more than a vague general principle, for immediately upon the news of the signing of the Olney-Pauncefote treaty vigorous expressions of opinion in its favor began to reach the Senate. More petitions and memorials were received than on any preceding treaty. Several hundred are recorded in the *Executive Journal of the Senate*; most of those favoring ratification coming from church organizations, bar associations, colleges and business men's organizations; practically all of the dozen or more opposing the treaty coming from Irish clubs and societies.[132] Senators testified that their mail was loaded down with letters urging speedy, favorable action and a few, including Hoar and Lodge, resented such expressions of opinion as "meddling with important diplomacy."[133] The British Ambassador informed his Foreign Secretary that the treaty "was received with acclamation all over the country."[134]

In its defiance of such a decided public opinion the Senate could hardly be motivated by partisan considerations. Other evidence is positive that politics cannot explain the Senate's rejection of the treaty. Not only was it advocated as strongly by the Republican administration as it had been by the preceding Democratic administration that made it, but also the votes in the Senate did not follow party lines either on the amendments or on the question of approving the treaty as amended. The forty-three affirmative votes were cast by thirty Republicans and thirteen Democrats; the successful twenty-six negative votes were cast by ten Republicans, thirteen Democrats, two Populists and one independent.[135]

[132] More than two thousand despatches from newspapers, mayors of cities, chambers of commerce, and other organizations, all showing that public opinion favored the ratification of the treaty are published in *55th Cong., 1st sess., S. Doc.*, No. 63. The surveys of the *Literary Digest* of May 15 and May 29, 1897, indicate a similar newspaper opinion in favor of the treaty.

[133] *Congressional Record,* Jan. 22, 1897, pp. 1045-1047.

[134] R. B. Mowat, *The Life of Lord Pauncefote,* p. 169.

[135] This allocation of senators to parties is open to challenge for the Populist party had invaded the old organizations to such an extent that names were often

If not politics, what did cause the Senate's action? In a remarkable letter, surely one of the most remarkable private letters ever composed for the eyes of officials of another government, the Secretary of State who had negotiated the treaty analyzed the motives of the Senate and stated his conclusions. It was no momentary wave of desperation or rage at seeing the Senate wreck his work, such as has wrung so many denunciations of the Senate from both his predecessors and followers in office, for Olney, then over two months out of office, was by temperament a phlegmatic man and in this case his deliberation and motive are proven by an earlier letter of explanation. In this first letter addressed to Henry White, then attached to the United States Embassy in London, Olney wrote, "There are some of your English friends, . . . who will be greatly astonished at the unfortunate outcome and who will doubtless be calling upon you for explanations. For such I am thinking of writing you a note which, if you choose, I shall have no objection to your showing them. I do not want them to feel either that the American people are blind and insensate haters of England or that general arbitration between the two great English speaking countries is a lost cause."[136] Henry White correctly understood the reference to "English friends," for months later he requested a copy of Olney's letter and stated, "I have never succeeded in getting it back from the official circles in which it circulated and unfortunately I did not have it copied myself previously, the reason being that I showed the original to Arthur Balfour first and he asked me to let him circulate it among his colleagues without returning it to me."[137]

So it was with knowledge that he was writing for the eyes of another government that Olney addressed the following let-

meaningless. Several contemporary newspapers in publishing the results the day after the Senate acted, despite the rule for secrecy, printed different analyses but varying so slightly as not to invalidate the point made above.

[136] May 8, 1897. MS. Olney Papers.

[137] Henry White to Olney. Sept. 23, 1897. MS. *ibid.*

ter to White. After stating that " I feel bound to give you the best explanations I can offer of a calamity which seems to me to be not merely of national but of world wide proportions," and asserting that the American people did not prefer brutal methods nor hate England innately he wrote:

The causes of such rejection, the reasons that is, influencing the vote of each particular Senator, can not of course be exhaustively stated. 'Jingoism' pure and simple may have turned the scale in one instance . . . in another dislike of anything emanating from the Cleveland administration . . . in another undue influence may have been brought to bear by the ship-building interests which are said to deprecate the existence of the Treaty as tending to stop the increase of our navy. These, with other like considerations peculiar to individual Senators, should not be regarded as having any decisive effect upon the fate of the Treaty which was in my judgment really determined by the influences about to be stated.

In the first place, it must be borne in mind that the Senate is now engaged in asserting itself as the power in the national government. It is steadily encroaching, on the one hand on the executive branch of the government, and on the other on the House of Representatives. . . . This aggressive attitude of the Senate towards other departments of the government is largely responsible for the treatment it has given the General Arbitration Treaty. After long protracted and troublesome discussion and negotiation, a perfected Treaty was laid before the Senate by the executive branch of the government exercising therein an undoubted constitutional function. The Senate immediately assumed an hostile attitude. The Treaty, in getting itself made by the sole act of the executive, without leave of the Senate first had and obtained, had committed the unpardonable sin. It must be either altogether defeated or so altered as to bear an unmistakeable Senate stamp . . . and thus be the means both of humiliating the executive and of showing to the world the greatness of the Senate. Hence, the Treaty has been assailed from all quarters by Senators of all parties and although the present executive advocated its ratification no less warmly than his predecessor. The method of assault has been as insidious as it has been deadly. A single sound objection to the Treaty as signed has yet to be stated. Yet, awed by the universal public sentiment for the Treaty and feeling compelled to seem to defer to it while in reality plotting to defeat it, Senators have exhausted their ingenuity in devising amendments to the Treaty. Hence, before the Treaty came to a final vote, the Senate brand had been put upon every part of it and the original instrument had been mutilated and distorted beyond all possibility of recognition. The object of the

Senate in dealing with the Treaty . . . the assertion of its own predominance . . . was thus successfully accomplished and would have been even if the Treaty as amended had been ratified. Whether the responsibility of Senators for the result will also be successfully evaded remains to be seen. While we may admit with President Lincoln . . . that it is possible to fool all the people a part of the time . . . they will be blind indeed if they fail to perceive that the General Arbitration Treaty has been done to its death not by open enemies but by professed friends.

The second place among the causes of the General Arbitration Treaty's defeat must undoubtedly be assigned to 'silver' and the irritation of silver Senators against Great Britain as the most conspicuous and efficient supporter of the gold standard. This feeling is both more wide-spread and more deep-seated than would at first be imagined. [He describes the extent of the sentiment and to illustrate 'how Anglophobia even if not originating with silver seizes upon it as a pretext and justification' quotes from speeches of Senator Lodge].

Finally, it must be conceded that the career of our late Ambassador to Great Britain has been decidedly unpropitious in its operation upon the fate of the treaty. [Bayard's effusive speeches and comparisons unfavorable to Americans induced an unfavorable senatorial atmosphere].

It is quite improbable that a single Senator would assign for his vote against the Treaty the considerations above set forth. Indeed, if an anti-Treaty Senator were questioned and obliged to answer, the chances are that he would respond by plausible pretexts rather than by his real reasons. Nevertheless, I feel quite confident that the underlying chief causes of the Senate's rejection of the Treaty are those I have mentioned.[138]

Contemporary newspaper and periodical comments agreed largely with Olney's interpretation of the motives of the Senate.

[138] Olney to Henry White. May 14, 1897. MS. *ibid.* This letter is summarized in a few lines in Henry James, *Richard Olney,* p. 149, and in Allan Nevins, *Henry White,* pp. 125-126. Months later in another and this time purely personal letter to White, Olney said his former letter "was always faulty in one respect. In its enumeration of the causes of the failure of the General Arbitration treaty, it made no mention of Lord Russell's speech before the American Bar Association at Saratoga. The Arbitration treaty accomplished exactly what Lord Russell intimated was both impracticable and inexpedient and his speech was an arsenal from which the enemies of the treaty drew the most powerful weapons they used against it. No doubt Lord Russell did not mean it. But if he had held a brief for the destruction of the treaty, he could not have carried out his purpose more effectively." October 8, 1897. MS. Olney Papers.

Some placed greater weight on the influence of the Irish vote, a Boston paper saying, "Had Irish-Americanism anything to do with the failure of the English arbitration treaty? We trust so and believe so. We should be very much ashamed of our fellow citizens of Irish blood if they had not done their utmost to baffle the attempt to place this republic before the world as a mere colony of Great Britain." [139] But Sir Julian Pauncefote, like Olney and most of the papers, believed the constitutional fears of the Senate the decisive consideration. Writing to his government two days after the rejction he said, "But the Senate, in its jealousy of the Executive, absolutely disregarded public opinion. It determined to retain absolute control over every case of arbitration, and for that purpose to destroy the Treaty by amendments which reduce it to a mere agreement to arbitrate any dispute, provided it be with the consent of the Senate, and on such terms and on such conditions as the Senate might choose to prescribe." [140]

Better even than the opinions of both negotiators is another piece of evidence supporting the same conclusion. During the consideration of the treaty in the Senate one opposing Senator wrote to another a note which being private and personal gives one of the rare senatorial statements of genuine motives in acting on a treaty. He said, "The Committee this morning as is generally agreed did good work in amending the Treaty with Great Britain so as to (1) keep the Senate in Control of Arbitral Submissions, (2) to preserve its function as to the Confirmation of Arbitrators, (3) & in requiring two on each side

[139] *The Pilot* as quoted in the *Literary Digest* of May 29, 1897. The opinions of other papers are given in the same issue, also in that of May 15th and Feb. 20. See also D. F. Fleming, *The Treaty Veto of the American Senate,* pp. 80-83. With unconscious but colossal effrontery William Lyman, signing himself president of the Irish National Alliance, passed judgment on what constituted patriotism to the United States in a telegram to Senator John T. Morgan reading, "Accept heartiest congratulations on death of treaty. You and followers have saved the honor of America and are the only genuine Americans in the Senate." MS. Morgan Papers.

[140] Mowat, *The Life of Lord Pauncefote,* p. 169.

under Article III. . . . On the whole the Treaty is better in the wastebasket or the fire than anywhere else." [141]

Foremost among the amendments was one requiring that every agreement submitting any question to arbitration should be communicated by the President to the Senate and that it should be approved by two-thirds of the Senators present before it would become effective. In other words each was to be a treaty. The minority report of the Committee on Foreign Relations stated frankly that such a change was regarded by all the members of the Committee "as being necessary to preserve the constant and unembarrassed action of the Senate." [142] When the Senate adopted that amendment by an overwhelming majority it initiated a policy that has been consistently followed and that has nullified or killed every general arbitration treaty negotiated since then. The policy was not dictated by any inherent objection to arbitration but, as Senator Daniel put it, by the desire "to keep the Senate in Control," a desire born of the constitutional arrangement of the treaty-making power.

Another treaty with Great Britain made by the defeated Cleveland administration also failed to receive the advice and consent of the Senate. This treaty, signed on January 30, 1897, was of very minor importance, as it provided for the demarcation by a joint survey of so much of the 141st meridian as might be necessary for the determination of the boundary between Alaska and Canada.[143] The line had previously been surveyed by each government independently with the result that there were differences, sometimes of only a few feet, which it was now proposed to eliminate by a joint survey by representatives of the two governments.[144] The treaty went to the Sen-

[141] John W. Daniel to John T. Morgan. March 12 (22?), 1897. MS. Morgan Papers.

[142] *Compilation of the Reports of the Committee on Foreign Relations,* VIII, 410.

[143] The treaty is in *Proceedings of the Alaska Boundary Tribunal,* III, 371-373, published as *58th Cong., 2d sess., S. Doc.,* No. 162.

[144] *Foreign Relations, 1896,* pp. 291-293.

ate where it was still pending when the time for the exchange of ratifications expired.[145] There is no evidence that politics was in any way responsible for the failure of the Senate to act on the treaty. What little evidence there is suggests the contrary. The absence of comment, the insignificance of the treaty, and the fact that both the Democratic and Republican members of the Committee on Foreign Relations subscribed to the report of that committee recommending its acceptance with one unimportant amendment, are indications that party considerations were not present. The inaction of the Senate was probably due to their desire to leave this question to be settled with the others relating to the boundary between Alaska and Canada, about which negotiations were then in progress.

The last treaty to be defeated before the Spanish-American War was the second treaty for the annexation of Hawaii. Cleveland's treatment of the former treaty had put the Republican party on the defensive so that annexation was now desired not only for itself but also as a vindication of the party's earlier conduct. The revolutionary government of 1893 was still in control of Hawaii, a fact which tended to justify the earlier affair as it showed they did not require the support of the armed forces of the United States to stay in power, and immediately upon the return of the Republicans to control, a new treaty was negotiated. It was signed on June 16, 1897, and was sent to the Senate on the same day.[146]

As in so many other cases, the Senate never reached a vote on the treaty. In spite of the pressure applied by the President both in public messages and in personal interviews it became apparent that only a majority of less than two-thirds of the Senate would vote for the treaty.[147] The efforts made on behalf of the treaty were evident to Cleveland in his retirement and

[145] *Sen. Ex. Jour.*, XXX, 426; XXXI, 604; XXXII, 141.

[146] *Ibid.*, XXXI, 169.

[147] For a public message see Richardson, *Messages and Papers of the Presidents*, XIV, 6263-6264. Senator Hoar gives an interesting account of the way the President appealed to him in a private interview. *Autobiography of Seventy Years*, II, 307-308.

with grim satisfaction he wrote Olney, "All the influence of this administration appears unable thus far to bring to a successful issue the Hawaiian monstrosity." [148] Most of the opposition came from the Democrats in the Senate although a number of them refused to follow the majority of their party, just as several Republicans left their party and opposed the treaty. Finally, in the words of the man who drafted the document, "owing to the opposition of many of the Democratic Senators to the Hawaiian Treaty and the facility of obstruction and delay in that body, it was decided to attempt to bring about the annexation by joint resolution, following the precedent of the annexation of Texas." [149] This method of avoiding the use of the unwieldy treaty-making power was vigorously denounced by the opponents of annexation as a violation of the Constitution and was distasteful to some of those who felt themselves justified in resorting to it.[150] The war with Spain, which began during the month after the introduction of the joint resolution, made annexation a war measure and it passed both Houses by large majorities.[151]

[148] Feb. 16, 1898. MS. Olney Papers.

[149] Foster, *Diplomatic Memoirs,* II, 174.

[150] Foster goes on to say, " Such a course was repugnant to Senator Davis and Congressman Hitt, the chairmen of the two committees, as well as myself, because of its evasion of the constitutional provision and the creation of a bad precedent; but it was felt that the exigencies of the war justified this extreme measure." *Ibid.* For denunciations of it, see the speeches of Senator Bacon and Senator Allen, *Congressional Record,* June 20, 1898, p. 6148, July 4, 1898, p. 6634. McKinley was contemplating the use of a joint resolution for annexation in July 1897, according to a conversation reported by Schurz. *The Writings of Carl Schurz,* VI, 272. Cleveland's comment, again to Olney was, " Hawaii is ours. As I look back upon the first steps in this miserable business and as I contemplate the means used to complete the outrage, I am ashamed of the whole affair." July 8, 1898. MS. Olney Papers.

[151] It received exactly a two-thirds majority in the Senate. *Congressional Record,* July 6, 1898, p. 6712. The twenty-one negative votes were cast by sixteen Democrats, three Republicans and two Populists. The latter might be included with the Democrats as they were elected by a coalition of Democrats and Populists.

CHAPTER VIII

AN EXCEPTION, THE PEACE TREATY OF 1898

We are going to have trouble over the Treaty. How serious I do not know, but I confess I cannot think calmly of the rejection of that Treaty by a little more than one-third of the Senate. It would be a repudiation of the President and humiliation of the whole country in the eyes of the world, and would show we are unfit as a nation to enter into great questions of foreign policy. I cannot believe that the opposition which is of course composed of Southern Democrats can succeed.

HENRY CABOT LODGE.[1]

Our friends assure me votes enough were secured defeat treaty, but your advice shakes several—the two chief leaders against treaty tell me if you will acquiesce in your friends going with them as fixed matter settled, reply free.

ANDREW CARNEGIE.[2]

No account of the defeated treaties or of the part played in the making and unmaking of treaties by political motives in the Senate would be complete without meeting the question presented by the treaty of peace with Spain. If politics has had so baneful an effect why was this treaty saved when every circumstance connected with it pointed to its logical inclusion in the list of victims to party activity in the Senate? It came at a moment when no important treaty had been approved by the Senate for more than twenty-five years. It contained a radical departure from the traditional policy of the United States which the President requested the senators, of whom more than a third were political opponents, to approve. Thus, McKinley's peace treaty presents a striking parallel to the peace treaty Wilson was to submit to the Senate twenty years later. The new policy of each President had already been foreshadowed, although somewhat obscurely. McKinley's proposal to establish

[1] To Roosevelt, Dec. 7, 1898. H. C. Lodge, ed., *Selections from the Correspondence of Theodore Roosevelt and Henry Cabot Lodge,* I, 368.

[2] Telegram to W. J. Byran. Jan. 11, 1899. MS. Bryan Papers.

a colonial empire had been anticipated by the acquisition of Hawaii, while Wilson's proposal to abandon the isolation policy had been preceded by the participation of the United States in the Algeçiras Conference. Nevertheless, the American public and the Senate on both occasions understood that a fundamental and permanent departure from old policy was being proposed.

Since it is human nature to be interested chiefly in results, the fact that McKinley's policy and treaty were approved tends to obliterate the memory of the narrow and precarious margin by which that victory was won. The treaty of peace with Spain was signed on December 10, 1898, and was sent to the Senate on January 4, 1899.[3] Undoubtedly in the hope of promoting a favorable reception there, three senators, including one from the minority party, had been appointed members of the commission sent to Paris to negotiate peace. But even before the final signing of the document, it was apparent that, in spite of this wise maneuver, winning the constitutional approval of the Senate would be an arduous if not impossible task. Senator Lodge confessed to Roosevelt his mental excitement at the prospect of the rejection of the treaty by the Democratic minority, of course, and, not being able to foresee the role which he was to play twenty years later and by which he would be chiefly remembered in history, asserted that a rejection of the treaty would humiliate "the whole country in the eyes of the world, and would show we are unfit as a nation to enter into great questions of foreign policy."[4]

After the treaty was in the hands of the Senate its survival appeared improbable to contemporary observers both in and out of the Senate. Hope of saving it rose when a motion by the opposition to consider it in open session was voted down.[5] But such questions were decided by majority vote, while for ratification there would be needed the constitutional majority

[3] *Sen. Ex. Jour.*, XXXI, 1161.

[4] The entire paragraph is quoted at the head of this chapter.

[5] *Sen. Ex. Jour.*, XXXI, 1234.

of two-thirds of the senators present, a number that could be reached only with the assistance of Democratic votes. The improbability of securing these lasted till the very end. A senator supporting the treaty informed Bryan on January 20 that it was almost certainly doomed.[6] Four days later a senator opposing the treaty wrote that if the Republicans did not amend it so as to promise Philippine independence "I don't think there is much chance of their getting the treaty ratified." [7] About the same time Andrew Carnegie, who was in Washington to lend his aid in the fight against imperialism, rejoiced in its approaching defeat and wrote, "I told the President two weeks ago we should beat the Treaty & he was sure I was 'away off.' He knows now." [8]

The newspapers, like Bryan and Carnegie, learned what was happening in the Senate, despite the injunction of secrecy, and their reports cast additional light on the desperate and doubtful nature of the contest. On February 1 the New York *Journal*, a vehement supporter of the treaty, reported that the treaty was in great danger. The next day it said that McKinley had been informed that ratification would not be sanctioned unless a resolution promising independence to the Filipinos were adopted. On the 4th, because the adoption of such a resolution had been prevented by opponents of the treaty, the same paper confidently asserted that the treaty would not be ratified during that session. The following day, however, hope was again expressed and a list of the individual senators for and against the treaty showed that its fate depended on four doubtful senators. On the morning of the 6th, the day the vote was to be taken, the *Journal* announced that its poll showed that the treaty was safe, although it admitted that four senators were doubtful and were being "labored on." [9]

[6] H. M. Teller to W. J. Bryan. MS. Bryan Papers.

[7] James K. Jones to W. J. Bryan. MS. *ibid.*

[8] Andrew Carnegie to W. J. Bryan. Jan. 26, 1899. MS. *ibid.*

[9] The other papers gave reports on the daily fluctuations in the Senate similar to those of the *Journal* although varying in details. The New York *Herald*, for

This prediction was fulfilled that afternoon when the Senate gave its consent to the treaty without amendment by a vote of 57 to 27.[10] According to the detailed account of the proceedings written by Senator Lodge to Roosevelt, the issue was uncertain until five minutes before the final vote, when the second of the four doubtful senators was won over. No wonder he reported that as a result of the great nervous strain he felt "as if there was not an ounce more of exertion left in any muscle of my body," for it was, he said, "the closest, hardest fight I have ever known." [11]

It had been a desperate struggle and a shift of two votes would have reversed the result. Still, the treaty was saved and an examination of the causes of that surprising event is necessary. The arguments made in the executive sessions of the Senate could be reconstructed with a fair degree of accuracy from the debates in open session on resolutions concerning the constitutionality of acquiring the Philippine Islands, from the interviews with individual senators printed in the newspapers, and from the usual leaks to the papers in violation of the rules for secrecy, but senatorial like other debates seldom cast much light on the motives determining the votes that follow. Far more reliable evidence can be found in an analysis of the vote itself, a process which in this instance reveals that the votes for

example, on Feb. 1, stated that a harmless resolution was to be adopted to save the treaty; on Feb. 2, reported that the resolution would not pass because of presidential opposition and gave summaries of several speeches made in the secret session of the previous day; on Feb. 4, carried a list of the senators for and against the treaty and said that five were doubtful; on Feb. 5, reported more of the debates in the supposedly secret sessions of the Senate; and on the next day when the vote was to be taken asserted that ratification was assured. The list of doubtful senators given by the *Herald* on Feb. 4, differed from that which the *Journal* printed on Feb. 5, and from the more authoritative list which Lodge gave to Roosevelt, but two senators were included by all three.

[10] *Sen. Ex. Jour.*, XXXI, 1284. Pairs were announced, 4 senators in favor and 2 against the treaty.

[11] Lodge, *Selections*, I, 391-392. Demonstrating the foolishness of attempting to predict the future he goes on to say, "and probably we shall not see another [fight] in our time where there was so much at stake."

the treaty came from 40 Republicans, 10 Democrats, 2 Populists, 4 Silverites, and 1 independent; while the votes against the treaty were cast by 3 Republicans, 21 Democrats, 2 Populists and 1 Silver senator.[12] Although the fluid state of party lines makes exactitude in placing a few members of the Senate impossible, the vote shows that the vast majority of Republicans supported the treaty of the Republican President and two-thirds or more of the Democrats opposed it.

Such a division on an issue that had newly arisen, makes a strong presumptive case that partisan bias determined most of the votes. All the other contemporary evidence corroborates the presumption so exactly that it becomes almost a certainty. This is true despite the fact that the evidence will not support even an estimate of the number of Democrats who opposed the treaty because it was made by a Republican administration.[13] Similarly, there is not sufficient data on which to hazard a speculation as to how many Republican senators supported the treaty for political reasons and against their judgment of its merits. Certainly a few did. Senator Platt of New York, according to a letter written by Roosevelt, with whom he was then on very friendly terms, " really is against the Philippines, but he stands by the President." [14] There is evidence that other

[12] New York *Journal,* Feb. 7, 1899. Latané, *America As a World Power,* p. 77, gives the vote as yea, 40 Republicans, 10 Democrats, 3 Populists, 2 Silverites and 2 Independent; nay, 22 Democrats, 3 Republicans and 2 Populists. Peck, *Twenty Years of the Republic,* p. 612, gives the vote as for the treaty 42 Republicans, 10 Democrats, 3 Populists and 2 Silverites; against the treaty 2 Republicans, 24 Democrats, 2 Populists and 1 Silver senator. Classification is almost a hopeless task in the cases of some of the senators. How, for example, should H. M. Teller be placed in 1899 when his record shows he was elected to the Senate in 1891 as a Republican, in 1897 as a Silver Republican and in 1903 as a Democrat?

[13] In three long letters to Bryan, Senator James K. Jones explained his opposition to the treaty despite Bryan's support of it, and never once referred to the political effects of either ratification or rejection. Since the letters were private and the two were intimate friends and closely associated in politics such a reference would have been natural and the omission of it seems to justify the belief that Jones opposed the treaty on its merits. January 17, 24, 30, 1899. MSS. Bryan Papers.

[14] Roosevelt to Lodge, Jan. 23, 1899. Lodge, *Selections,* I, 388.

Republican senators also subordinated their opinions to political pressure, in some cases even after opposing the treaty in the Senate.[15]

Clearly the tendency to act on treaties for political reasons was present, but why it did not operate completely and kill the treaty has still to be explained. If an appreciable minority of the senatorial opponents of the President, on this occasion approximately one-third of the Democrats, could always or usually be trusted to abandon their party and form their decisions respecting a treaty solely on its merits, the constitutional requirement of a two-thirds majority might be more easily defended. However, voting contrary to the majority of the party proves neither the absence of political considerations nor the presence of disinterested zeal for the public good. Before the treaty with Spain can be cited as an exception to the usual rule the forces inducing the independent voting must be sought.

One factor that seemed both to later historians and to interested contemporary Americans to explain in part these nonpartisan votes that saved the administration's policy was the outbreak of fighting between the Filipinos and the American troops in Manila. It was believed that startling news of such a nature appearing in the headlines of the papers on the eve of the vote in the Senate would make opposition to the treaty appear unpatriotic and a surrender under duress. So Roosevelt wrote of his gratefulness "partly to the Senate, partly to Providence and partly to the Filipinos. They just pulled the treaty through for us."[16] In making the same point the New York *Journal* even put quotation marks around words stated to have been used by Senator McLaurin in the final secret session. He was reported as having stated that he had been opposed to the treaty but that in view of the new situation with the American army being attacked by the Filipinos he thought the treaty

[15] The names of several are given in a book written many years afterward by a man who had been in the Senate at the time. R. F. Pettigrew, *Imperial Washington,* p. 205.

[16] To Lodge, Feb. 7, 1899. Lodge, *Selections,* I, 390.

should be ratified.[17] But Lodge, replying to Roosevelt, denied that the beginning of hostilities had any material effect on the Senate. With the exception of the four doubtful senators, one of whom was McLaurin, Lodge said that everyone voted as he had indicated he would before the fighting began. "The line of opposition," he wrote, "' stood absolutely firm, to my great astonishment. I thought the news from Manila would have shattered it, but it did not, marvelous as it may seem."[18] Lodge, of course, was in a position to know the facts of the case and his testimony, corroborated by the other contemporary statements that only three or four senators were in doubt before the new war started, is sufficient to eliminate this factor as the real solution to the problem of why the seventeen Democrats, Populists and Silverites voted for the treaty. The answer to that question must be sought elsewhere.

As always in close fights, one force applied was the promise of patronage and other similar gifts in the power of the administration party. Apparently it was used extensively on behalf of the treaty. In the letter just quoted Senator Lodge, after explaining to Roosevelt that no gratitude was due Filipinos or Providence for the favorable vote, assigned the credit for victory to Aldrich, himself and others who had done the necessary managing and "hard fighting, which does not appear on the surface." The managing and hard fighting beneath the surface did not escape observation. A newspaper, whose vision was not colored by hostile prejudice since it advocated the speedy ratification of the treaty, reported that promises of good committee places in the new Senate were being offered in exchange for votes.[19] And Senator Pettigrew, if his memory and honesty can be trusted, was so outraged by what he saw that he privately complained to the chairman of the Committee on Foreign Relations of "the open purchase of votes to ratify this treaty right

[17] Feb. 7, 1899. The New York *Herald* of the same date also reported the McLaurin as having said this.

[18] Feb. 9, 1899. Lodge, *Selections,* I, 391.

[19] New York *Journal,* Feb. 4, 1899.

on the floor of the Senate before the eyes of the senators and all the world." [20]

The use of patronage to maintain party solidarity on an administration measure is so customary that political ethics sanctions the practice however remote it may be from the ideas of the framers of the Constitution when they fixed the treaty-making power. When, however, votes of political opponents are secured by the same means there seems to be a general recognition, certainly among those opposed to the measure in question, that some stigma attaches to the bargain. And in this "hard fighting" which did "not appear on the surface" some senators stated privately that opposition senators were offered not merely patronage but appointments for themselves and perhaps even money. Senator Morgan, a Democrat who supported the treaty ardently and with unquestioned sincerity, wrote several years later in a strictly confidential letter that a large bribe was offered in vain for the vote of the Populist Senator Heitfeld, who, according to both Lodge and the newspapers was one of the doubtful four. "This statement," wrote Morgan, "is made on the authority of what he said to Senators in the cloak room, while in a state of violent anger, soon after the offer was made by Pettigrew, then a member of the Senate. I did not hear it, but others, now here, heard it, and it was several times repeated by Senator Heitfeld. I also esteem him a thoroughly honest and reliable man." [21] Senator Hoar, the

[20] Pettigrew, p. 206. Among those he mentions specifically as being "purchased" is the vote of one of the Democratic senators who remained doubtful until the final session.

[21] John T. Morgan to Henry Watterson, Dec. 10, 1903. MSS. Morgan Papers. In this letter are listed a number of cases where bribes of money or appointments for themselves were offered to senators, the names and amounts being given in detail. The letter was written with deliberation and care, in fact so cautious was Senator Morgan that it was never mailed to Watterson, according to a notation of Morgan's on the envelope containing the letter. The revelations intended for Watterson were to be held in strictest confidence, yet Senator Morgan evidently feared their source might be divulged, for in another letter in the same envelope he asked his colleague, Senator Pettus, if it were safe to send the letter to

most prominent of the three Republicans opposing the treaty, believed one of his Democratic colleagues guilty of accepting a bribe, in the form of an appointment for himself, and the former Democratic Secretary of State evidently shared his belief. Olney wrote to Cleveland that

> Hoar also told me what may be known to you but what I had not heard of before as regards Senator Gray. I expressed some astonishment at the latter's attitude on the Philippine business. He replied that it was perfectly awful. I asked him what he meant. Thereupon he said that not long before the signing of the Treaty of Paris Gray sent over an eloquent telegram to the President protesting against the cession of the Philippines to the United States in the strongest manner on the grounds of principle and policy and expediency. McKinley made no other reply than by a curt direction 'Sign the treaty.' 'He did it,' Hoar proceeded, 'comes home, champions the treaty in the Senate, and now comes out Judge of the Circuit Court of the United States.' [22]

Admitting the probability that these questionable methods may have secured several votes for the treaty, it can nevertheless be asserted with relative certainty that they fail to account for most of the essential ten Democratic or seven Populist and Silver votes.

In fact neither Olney nor Hoar believed that patronage and bribes were chiefly responsible but agreed in attributing the determining influence to William Jennings Bryan. Certainly this is the explanation of the independent votes now generally

Watterson saying, "I am informed by some of his closest friends, that he is scrupulously honorable in matters entrusted to his confidence, but they say that when he is in his cups, he forgets and spills over." These facts substantiate what Morgan wrote in his letter to Watterson, namely that he was not idly or irresponsibly gossiping but was expressing his deliberate indignation at what he believed to be true.

[22] Olney to Cleveland, March 22, 1899. MS. Olney Papers. Gray's first and ad interim appointment was dated March 29, so that when Olney wrote this letter it was not publicly known that he was to be appointed. In his book, *Autobiography of Seventy Years,* II, 313-315, Senator Hoar quotes Gray's cablegram in full and says that Gray afterward supported the treaty but makes no reference to his appointment. Despite his indignation expressed to Olney, Senator Hoar deferred to senatorial tradition and made no opposition to Gray's confirmation as Judge of the Circuit Court. *Sen. Ex. Jour.,* XXXII, 279.

accepted.[23] The evidence available to justify the belief that Bryan decided the fate of the treaty seems ample and trustworthy. Olney accepted it as conclusive, for writing to Cleveland the month after the treaty was ratified he said, "I had a talk with Senator Hoar the other evening. He asserted with much warmth—what I suppose to be true—that but for Bryan and his influence with Democratic senators, the treaty would not have been ratified." [24] Senator Hoar's public statement to the same effect, upon which most subsequent writers have relied, was published in 1903 without meeting a denial from Bryan or being challenged by any one.[25] Another member of the Senate has written of the way in which Bryan, after appealing to several others, came to him and advanced a number of arguments, though chiefly that of political expediency, in a fruitless effort to persuade him to vote for ratification.[26]

Andrew Carnegie, who was in Washington during the month preceding the vote and in daily contact with members of the Senate, stated in his autobiography that "Bryan had it in his

[23] Every secondary account examined held Bryan chiefly or at least partially responsible. All of the inadequate biographies of Bryan agree on this, the best of them saying, "Bryan went to Washington and cajoled and dragooned seventeen Democrats and Populists in the Senate into approving the Spanish treaty." Paxton Hibben, *The Peerless Leader,* p. 222. Following the published account of Senator Hoar, most of the writers make Bryan appear dramatically during the crisis of the contest in the Senate and save the treaty. His correspondence, however, contains letters from Carnegie and others written from Washington as early as January 10, 1899, and continuing till the day before the vote. Since the treaty went to the Senate on Jan. 4, it is clear Bryan did not make his personal appeal to his senatorial followers in the final tense moments but very early in the proceedings.

[24] March 22, 1899. MS. Olney Papers.

[25] *Autobiography of Seventy Years,* II, 322-323.

[26] Pettigrew, pp. 270-271. This participant whom Senator Morgan named a corruptionist in the letter quoted above, insisted that corruption not Bryan saved the treaty. He concludes, "I do not believe Mr. Bryan's visit changed the result, although several Democrats, who made speeches against it, voted for the treaty. The only effect of his visit was to give an excuse for Democrats, for a cash consideration, to sell out to Aldrich and vote for the treaty."

power at one time to defeat in the Senate this feature of the Treaty," that "there were seven staunch Bryan men anxious to vote against Philippine annexation," and that "one word from Mr. Bryan would have saved the country from disaster." [27] This account written some years later is supported by the letters and telegrams which Carnegie sent to Bryan during the critical month of January 1899, and which were based on information given him by the senators who were waging the fight against the treaty. His certainty of Bryan's power to decide the contest, his intimate knowledge of the situation in the Senate, and his nervous tensity are all revealed in the following letter:

My Dear Col. Bryan

Friends here who know tell me the Treaty can be defeated with 2 or 3 votes to spare. Your advocacy of ratification has disorganized matters. . . . Several are now shaky against defeating it. . . .

I wish you were here to be satisfied that you have the power to defeat the Treaty thus giving the Country time to reflect—I am certain that only time & discussion is needed to save us—Mason of Illinois made a great speech today—took highest ground—*Liberty* Independence Philippines same as Cuba Senate impressed.[28] Hoar made deep impression yesterday—Our friends say situation looks better but the two leaders separately said to me today we were all right until Bryan came & somewhat disorganized us—wish he could be here to see the situation. There seems little hope of doing anything in this House or Senate upon equal vote—our chance is the Treaty 2/3s—I hope you can see your way to wire your friends that if they can defeat the treaty you will do so.

Of course I have no game of party politics to play. . . .[29]

Bryan himself agreed that his opinions were influencing some senators. In his reply to the above letter he wrote, "I fully realize the responsibility that rests upon anyone who can influence a vote at such an important crisis as this." [30] And in a telegram replying to the one from Carnegie quoted at the head of this chapter, he admitted, "Have tried to convince others but

[27] *Autobiography of Andrew Carnegie,* p. 364.

[28] Nevertheless, Mason, a Republican, voted for the treaty.

[29] January 10, 1899. MS. Bryan Papers.

[30] Jan. 13, 1899. MS. *ibid.*

have not tried to control them." [31] Arguments from so preeminent a political leader as Bryan was between 1896 and 1900 are fairly certain to be so convincing to a considerable portion of his party followers that "controlling" them is unnecessary. Although most of the seventeen independent voters who gave the senatorial sanction to McKinley's treaty were conspicuously devoted followers of Bryan, not all of them were. Senator Gray of Delaware was of the eastern anti-Bryan wing of the party. Moreover, in several other cases the votes were cast not only independently of party but also of Bryan. Senator Morgan's record as a frequent wanderer from his party's lines and as a consistent expansionist would warrant the opinion that his vote for the treaty was the result solely of the dictates of his own mind and emotions, even without Senator Hoar's comment to that effect. But in the light of evidence such as the above the conclusion is inescapable that it was Bryan's influence that accounted for most of the seventeen senators who were not blind party followers. The treaty was saved because of one man's unusual character and ideas, or lack of them.

Why Bryan exerted himself to same McKinley's measure, embodying a policy he honestly believed to be disastrous for the country, is a puzzle that does not have to be solved here. Whether he was sacrificing principles on the altar of political expendiency, as Hoar, Carnegie, Pettigrew and others have asserted; [32] whether he was displaying a monumental fidelity

[31] Jan. 11, 1899. MS. *ibid.*

[32] In the selections cited above. Carnegie frequently insinuated in his letters to Bryan that the latter was playing politics with this great issue by such sentences as these: "Of course I have no game of party politics to play" (Jan. 10, 1899), and "It isnt so good for your party that the Administration should be driven back to safe American policy but I know you prefer the Country's good to your party's. *So do I.*" (Jan. 26, 1899) MSS. Bryan Papers. And Pettigrew, if he can be believed, told Bryan when he was soliciting Pettigrew's vote that "he had no business in Washington on such an errand; that his stand reflected on his character and reputation as a man, and indicated a lack of knowledge of human affairs which must make his friends feel that he was not a suitable person to be President of the United States." p. 271.

to the idea of majority rather than minority rule, as he maintained to Carnegie;[33] whether he was stampeded by a pacifist desire to end the war at the earliest possible moment, as some have said;[34] or whether he was blindly obeying his fate to lose on all his major issues, are alike immaterial. His motives were not those of the Senate.

What is important is the fact that the senators who voted at his request and against their judgment were voting for political reasons fully as much as the majority of the Republican senators who stood by the administration and the majority of the Democrats who opposed it. Accordingly the action of the Senate on the treaty of peace with Spain is not an exception to the rule of political votes in such cases. That the result was no vindication of the constitutional treaty-making machinery was only too apparent to the Secretary of State, who wrote to an intimate friend:

> You know I told you long years ago that there would never be another Treaty, of any significance, ratified by the Senate. The truth of this becomes clearer to me every hour. You may say I am contradicted by the ratification of the Treaty of Peace. But I hold that this is a most striking confirmation of my theory. A treaty of peace, in any normal state of things, ought to be ratified with unanimity in twenty-four hours. They wasted six weeks in wrangling over this one, and ratified it with one vote to spare. We have five or six matters now demanding settlement; I can settle them all, honorably, and advantageously to our own side; and I am assured by leading men in the Senate that not one of the Treaties, if negotiated will pass the Senate. I would have a majority in every case, but a malcontent third would certainly dish every one of them. To such disastrous shape has the original mistake in the Constitution grown in the evolution of our politics.[35]

---

[33] "If people are with us we can declare policy by resolution. If people are against us minority of senate cannot save us." Telegram Jan. 11, 1899. "My plan cannot fail if the people are with us and we ought not to succeed unless we do have the people with us." Letter Jan. 13, 1899. MSS. Bryan Papers. He expressed similar views in an article in the New York *Journal* of Jan. 9, 1899.

[34] Charles S. Olcott, *The Life of William McKinley,* II, 139.

[35] John Hay to Henry Adams, Aug. 5, 1899. *Letters of John Hay and Extracts from Diary,* III, 156.

CHAPTER IX

BITTER CONTESTS WITH STRONG PRESIDENTS, 1899-1919

Now the irreparable mistake of our Constitution puts it into the power of one-third + 1 of the Senate to meet with a categorical veto any treaty negotiated by the President, even though it may have the approval of nine tenths of the people of the nation. JOHN HAY.[1]

. . . the Democrats held a caucus Saturday, and expect . . . to line their men against the treaty, or to exclude some of them from Democratic society. It is a sinister and ugly thing to begin to caucus on foreign relations. SENATOR JOHN C. SPOONER.[2]

The individual Senators evidently consider the prerogative of the Senate as far more important than the welfare of the country.

THEODORE ROOSEVELT.[3]

The United States emerged from the war with Spain with a growing consciousness of its position as a world power and with colonial possessions crowded with subject peoples of a different race. The war, therefore, marks a natural dividing line in the history of the country and especially in the history of its foreign relations. Whether the change will prove as epochal in the history of the United States as the acquisition of the first overseas possession and subject people did in the history of the Roman Republic cannot be told as yet, but the events of the twenty-five years following the war with Spain at least justify the confident statement that a new direction was given to the current of American history.[4] Little of that could, of course, be

[1] To Joseph H. Choate, Aug. 18, 1899. Thayer, II, 219.

[2] To Senator Shelby M. Cullom, Feb. 5, 1906. MS. Spooner Papers.

[3] To Silas McBee, Feb. 16, 1905. MS. Letterbook. Roosevelt Papers.

[4] Those who enjoy the tempting, futile game of drawing historical parallels can find ample material in the striking but superficial similarities in the circumstances attending the transitions of Rome and of the United States into empires. In its early expansion over contiguous territory Rome, like the United States in

appreciated by the American public of 1899, despite the dire predictions of the anti-imperialists like Carnegie, Carl Schurz, Senator Hoar, or Bryan, whose maladroit opposition had done so much to commit the country to the policy he opposed.

Neither did anyone interpret the successful ratification of the important treaty of peace as an indication of any change on the part of the Senate in its attitude toward treaties or toward its partner in the treaty making power. In fact the Senate began the new era by manifesting a more domineering spirit than it previously had shown. When Senator Lodge maintained in an interview that a treaty sent to the Senate is not properly a treaty but merely a project, the Secretary of State wrote to a friend that this meant "that if France and the United States make a treaty, after careful study and negotiation, it is nothing more, when sent to the Senate, than a petition from the two nations to that body to make a real treaty for them. The attitude of the Senate toward public affairs makes all serious negotiation impossible."[5] If John Hay was unduly critical and sensitive it must be remembered that just when the Senate was in its most

its westward expansion across the continent, expected the ultimate admission of the people in the added areas to full citizenship on terms of equality with those in the older sections. This policy was ended and the rule of subject peoples was begun when Rome became involved in a war with Carthage over the neighboring island of Sicily and emerged with Sicily as her first overseas possession. By substituting Cuba for Sicily and Spain for Carthage the description approximates the circumstances by which the United States acquired its first colony of subject people and became an empire. More then that, not long after becoming an empire Rome intervened decisively in the then old center of civilization and withdrew to the surprise of many without taking any territory for herself and without accepting any obligations to maintain the settlement effected. Then followed a period when Roman policy was the subject of a contest between the citizens who wanted to assume the rôle of world power with all its implications and the group who preferred the traditional isolationist policy in order to shed no Roman blood for old world quarrels and to expose no Roman youths to the corrupting influence of a decaying civilization. Those who want to can find a parallel for Roman intervention in the east in the American participation in the World War, and for Cato's attitude and words in the positions taken by men like Senators Reed and Borah.

[5] John Hay to Henry White. Allan Nevins, *Henry White,* p. 154.

assertive period it was he who was forced to negotiate simultaneously with foreign governments on one side and with the Senate on the other, and that it was he who had to endure the dictation of the Senate. His immediate successors in office were in a better position because of the reassertion of executive leadership and power by Roosevelt and Wilson; earlier Secretaries of State did not have to confront a Senate that had grown accustomed to dominating in such matters by the experience of fifty years. Hay knew that the Senate not only insisted on its well-established constitutional right to amend or rewrite treaties but was beginning to display a disposition to go much farther and to supplant the State Department and President completely by dealing directly with foreign governments. No such encroachment was frankly avowed, but under the guise of collecting information at least one effort was made to establish direct and official contact between the Senate and a foreign government in order to discuss or conduct a pending negotiation. This remarkable proposal was contained in a letter to Hay from Senator Morgan, then chairman of the Committee on Interoceanic Canals. The Senator wrote, under date of January 22, 1902,

> I have the honor to request that you will learn from his Excellency, the Minister of Colombia, if he is willing to confer with the Senate Committee, on the subject of any offer his Government proposes to make for the concession to the United States of the right to construct, complete and own and control, in perpetuity, a ship canal. . . .
>
> * * * * * * *
>
> Of course it is understood that the Senate Committee has no authority or disposition, to enter upon any negotiation with the Government of Colombia, or its minister touching this subject. Its object and duty, is to ascertain and report to the Senate such facts, connected with this subject, as will enable Congress to act intelligently and advisedly with reference to any proposition Colombia is prepared to make to the United States in respect of such concession, its terms and conditions, and the length of time it will require to complete the governmental action of Colombia, so as to make such concession perfect under the laws of Colombia.
>
> This request is made subject, of course, to your preference as to making these inquiries in your right as Secretary of State.

The great urgency of the general public demand for a ship canal through the American Isthmus, requires the Senate to move with all proper energy in the enactment of measures to accomplish this great object; and this inquiry has been ordered to ascertain the true situation.

* * * * * * *

I repeat that the Senate Committee on Interoceanic Canals has no disposition to interfere, in any way, with the diplomatic functions of the President, but our duty to the Senate requires the Committee to ascertain the facts upon which legislation may proceed wisely, advisedly, and with due regard to the necessity for prompt action which the country is so earnestly demanding.[6]

Obviously the Senator was protesting too much and the inevitable result of such a conference with a foreign minister would be " to interfere with the diplomatic functions of the President." But the domination over the Executive which the Senate had established almost without opposition during the preceding quarter of a century was now to be challenged. The accident of an assasin's bullet ended the succession of mild or mediocre Presidents that had followed Lincoln and brought to power a man who delighted in using it. Roosevelt won for himself a distinguished place in the history of the presidency by

[6] MS. Morgan Papers. On Jan. 18, 1905, Senator Morgan wrote to Senator Spooner suggesting that the Belgian Minister be invited to testify before a Senate Committee on conditions in the Congo, as he was reported to be willing to do. Morgan went on to say that the Committee would not, of course, try the case of Leopold in the Congo, but it should collect information for the Senate. MS. Spooner Papers. Only two instances of official contact between the Senate and a foreign government have been discovered. The first was the appearance of the Danish Minister of War, General Raasloff, before the Committee on Foreign Relations in a vain effort to secure the ratification of the treaty of 1867. This contact, however, was made after the treaty had been negotiated. The other case occurred in 1914 when the diplomatic representative of Nicaragua on the invitation of the Committee on Foreign Relations appeared before it and discussed a proposed treaty. *Congressional Record,* June 27, 1914, p. 11225. Innumerable instances of unofficial contacts, that is social intercourse with senators as individuals, and not official relations with the Senate as a body, are recorded. Many a foreign diplomat has entertained, flattered and conciliated members of the Senate in the hope of facilitating the consummation of a pending negotiation or the ratification of a completed negotiation.

a vigorous leadership which raised that office to a position of supremacy in the government such as only Lincoln and Jackson among his predecessors had attained. The Senate, of course, did not submit meekly to presidential control; nor was the President always successful in the numerous contests, some of which were over questions of foreign policy and treaties. When Taft succeeded Roosevelt the balance of power was restored in favor of the Senate. But this recovery proved to be only temporary, since Wilson, even before the war brought him dictatorial powers, realized the potentialities for leadership in the presidency and exercised a control over Congress greater even than that Roosevelt had enjoyed. The entry of the United States into the war magnified the supremacy of the Executive and the subordination of the legislature. Naturally Congress and especially the Senate resented this situation and, after the armistice had freed them from the restraints imposed by the war, eagerly seized the first opportunity to resume the eternal contest with the President for domination in the government. Almost inevitably the treaty of peace served as the battle ground and the constitutional treaty-making power of the Senate as the most effective weapon to be used against the President. The victory won by the Senate shifted the balance of power again and, exploited skillfully in the decade since then, has led to a more effective senatorial control over foreign policy than that body had ever before enjoyed in the history of the country.

These events make the period from the Spanish American War to 1920 the classic one for the study of the struggle between President and Senate over foreign policy and the treaty-making power. Yet, unfortunately the records necessary for a full understanding of the period are not available. The course of the major conflicts and even of many of the minor skirmishes can be traced with reasonable accuracy and completeness, but the parts played by individuals, the various plans considered, the decisions taken, and the reasons for them are as yet only partially revealed. Not only are many of the private papers of participants inaccessible, but even some vital official records are still kept secret. The *Executive Journal of the Senate,* the official source necessary for essential details of the action of the Senate on treaties, has been made public only to March 9, 1901. The proceedings in the Senate on a few of the defeated treaties since that date are known, as several of them were considered in open session and in some other cases, after the injunction of secrecy was removed, the votes on the final question, at least, have been published.[7] In all the other cases either the details are lacking or nothing is known. This situation, curious in a country that prides itself on the absence of secret diplomacy, would be incomprehensible did not the experience of the past make it safe to assume that no important treaties have been signed and submitted to the Senate without knowledge of that fact becoming public despite the rules for secrecy.[8]

[7] Since about 1918 it has been customary to print the proceedings in the *Congressional Record* when the injunction of secrecy is removed. But an examination of the *Record* shows that before that time there were numerous instances where the injunction of secrecy was removed but the proceedings were not published. This statement taken from the *Record* is typical: "The injunction of secrecy was removed from the following convention, which was ratified by the Senate May 16, 1902." P. 5563. The bare recital of the fact of the Senate's favorable action casts no light on the question whether amendments were adopted or proposed or on the vote by which the action was taken. Many other similar instances can be cited. See *ibid.,* Mar. 14, 1902, p. 2792 and Aug. 29,1916, p. 13348.

[8] Since 1932, when the State Department published the *List of Treaties Submitted to the Senate, 1789-1931, Which Have Not Gone into Force,* it has been possible to ascertain what treaties were signed and whether the Senate rejected, amended or neglected them. Further information is still lacking in some cases. Of course, the rules of the Senate are not binding on the President and the latter is under no obligation to keep secret the fact that he has negotiated a treaty, or, for that matter, the provisions of it. But such a defiance of the Senate and such a failure to cooperate might easily arouse sufficient hostility to bring about the rejection of the treaty. Usually the Executive is careful not to offend the sensibilities of the Senate, and in one case went to the ridiculous limit of observing the senatorial injunction of secrecy regarding the provisions of a treaty which had been published three years earlier by an international bureau, maintained in part by the United States, and which had subsequently been registered with the League of Nations. Manley O. Hudson, "The 'Injunction of Secrecy' with

In the case of the first treaty defeated by the Senate in the early days of this new era, there was not a well-defined contest testing the relative strength of President and Senate. The Senate exercised its deadly power without opposition from the weak and amiable McKinley, whose inactivity was unprecedented. The treaty slain in this curious fashion without protest was the first Hay-Pauncefote treaty, signed on February 5, 1900. The Spanish war had made the demand for the construction of a canal between the Atlantic and Pacific oceans insistent, and had intensified the desire to remove the restrictions of the Clayton-Bulwer treaty. Negotiations were speedily begun with Great Britain and they led to this treaty, which authorized the United States to construct and manage a canal either directly or through a private company but which retained the principle of neutralization and the prohibition of fortifications.[9] In none of the voluminous published material is there the slightest evidence suggesting that the President interviewed a senator, or used his powers as party leader, or appealed to the public, or in any way raised a hand on behalf of the treaty. It was then, and has since been considered the personal affair of the Secretary of State. Apparently Hay himself shared this belief in his personal responsibility, for, when the Senate rewrote the treaty, he attempted to resign. McKinley then accepted his full share of the condemnation of the negotiations; in fact he had never disowned the treaty, but had merely been indifferent to its fate. Lacking the active support of the head of the administration, who alone had power to combat the Senate, the treaty succumbed easily and John Hay could only give vent to his impotent rage in letters to his friends.

To the surprise of the Administration it was soon clear that the agreement Hay had made did not go far enough to meet the views of the Senate.[10] Three amendments so drastic as to con-

Respect to American Treaties," *American Journal of International Law,* XXIII, 329-335.

[9] *57th Cong., 1st sess., S. Doc.,* No. 85. *Foreign Relations, 1901,* pp. 241-243.

[10] In writing to his government Sir Julian Pauncefote remarked on the sur-

stitute the substitution of a new agreement were made by that body. The first declared that the Clayton-Bulwer treaty was superseded; the second provided that the regulations governing the use of the canal should not apply to measures taken by the United States for its own defense or for the maintenance of public order; and the third struck out the article providing for the adherence of other powers to the treaty. The first and third amendments were adopted by unanimous votes,[11] and the second by a majority of sixty-five to seventeen.[12] The revised treaty then received the advice and consent of the Senate by a vote of fifty-five to eighteen.[13] Great Britain refused to accept the treaty in this form, the chief objection being that the Clayton-Bulwer convention was "an international compact of unquestionable validity [and] could not be abrogated or modified save with the consent of both parties to the contract." [14]

The unanimous votes on the amendments furnish sufficient proof that the treaty was not defeated in the Senate because it became an issue between the political parties. And yet political considerations were not absent. On the final question the Democratic votes cast were divided almost equally; twelve favoring the treaty and ten opposing it, and it was the Republican vote of forty-three to eight that produced the necessary two-thirds majority.[15] Stronger traces of partisan influence were

prise of the President and his Cabinet at the senatorial opposition. Mowat, *Lord Pauncefote,* p. 283.

[11] *Sen. Ex. Jour.,* XXXII, 620.

[12] *Ibid.,* p. 598.

[13] *Ibid.,* p. 624.

[14] *Parliamentary Papers,* 1902, CXXX, *United States,* No. 1, p. 3. The essential parts of this despatch are quoted in Moore, *Digest of International Law,* III, 212-216. Senator Lodge in an article in *Scribner's* of January, 1902, read the British Government, and the State Department a lesson in the American conduct of foreign relations. It was here he asserted that a treaty submitted to the Senate is "a mere project for a treaty" or as John Hay said in the letter quoted above "a petition from the two nations . . . to make a real treaty for them."

[15] Again exact analysis of the vote by parties is rendered well-nigh impossible because of the recent political confusion, although the general trend is clear. The New York *Tribune,* of December 21, 1900, stated that the eighteen negative

revealed in some of the proceedings, since a number of other amendments, which would have made the treaty still more objectionable to Great Britain, were proposed and supported chiefly by the Democrats in the Senate and were successfully opposed by the Republican majority.[16] The Secretary of State had anticipated attempts by the Democrats to squeeze what political advantage they could from his negotiations with Great Britain. Writing to the American Ambassador in London some six months before the convention was signed he said, "The Democratic press evidently thinks there is some political capital to be made by denouncing any arrangement with England, and they, in common with a large number of German newspapers, are ready to attack any treaty with England, no matter how advantageous to us, as a hostile act towards Ireland and Germany."[17]

What Hay did not anticipate, and what helps to explain the failure of the treaty to become an issue between the parties, was that the Republican senators also were aware of the political potentialities of a treaty with England especially when the traditional hostility of certain sections of the public was intensified by the Boer war. With only slight hesitation the more politically-minded Republicans became frightened at the use to which Hay's treaty might be put and easily reached the conclusion that the American public demanded a fortified and an exclusively American canal. Although favoring Hay's diplomatic policy, Carnegie, in a letter to an unnamed prominent Republican that found its way into the papers, predicted that to accept the treaty "is to commit political suicide for the forthcoming campaign."[18]

Senator Lodge, in defending his action, which Hay privately denounced as cowardice, had no doubts as to what the American

votes were cast by eleven Democrats, three Populists, two Silverites, and two Republicans.

[16] *Sen. Ex. Jour.*, XXXII, 598-599, 609, 620-623.

[17] Thayer, II, 218-219.

[18] New York *Tribune*, Feb. 27, 1900.

people thought. "The plain facts of the case," he wrote, "are these: The American people will never consent to building a canal at their own expense, which they shall guard and protect for the benefit of the world's commerce, unless they have virtually complete control. There is no use arguing about the wisdom of this attitude. This is what the American people and the American press, without a dissenting voice, demand, and it is that sentiment which the Senate is representing." [19] That so ardent a nationalist as Roosevelt should have objected to Hay's treaty was not surprising, but it was remarkable that he should abandon the natural field for his activities as governor of New York State and lead an attack in the papers on the Republican administration's foreign policy. Was patriotism solely responsible or was something else mixed with it? The fact that his manifesto was given to the press immediately after an important conference of friends to discuss his political future suggests that perhaps it was one of those happy occasions when both patriotism and personal advancement could be promoted by taking a stand for what it was believed the people wanted.[20] And it is certain that the Roosevelt of 1900 was politically sensitive and desperately eager to place himself before any strong current of public opinion.

Yet the unconscious tribute paid by historians to the ability of the politicians in and out of the Senate to hear and understand the voice of the people may not be deserved.[21] Thus far

[19] To Henry White, Dec. 18, 1900. Nevins, *Henry White,* pp. 154-155.

[20] The political implications of Roosevelt's criticism of the treaty were clear to at least one of his observers. The New York *Tribune* on Feb. 13, 1900, said, "The strong intimation of his purpose not to be forced or persuaded into accepting the Republican nomination for Vice-President which was conveyed yesterday morning in Governor Roosevelt's announcement of his hostility to the isthmian canal treaty in its present form—the form which the Administration believes it should and must retain—was confirmed yesterday afternoon by the Governor's formal declaration. . . ." The later and much-quoted criticism of the treaty which he sent privately to Hay is in Thayer, II, 339-341. A letter mentioning the conference preceding the public attack on the treaty can be found in Nathaniel W. Stephenson, *Nelson W. Aldrich,* p. 449, n. 7.

[21] "Unquestionably the Senate had correctly interpreted the majority opinion

no student has ever analyzed the comments of the newspapers, the first and chief resort of the historian in seeking the elusive and perhaps non-existing thing called public opinion. The briefest of glances at this type of data is sufficient to raise grave doubts as to the correctness of identifying the *vox Senatus* with the *vox populi.* The New York *Tribune* not only asserted that "the vast majority of the people of the United States" approved the treaty,[22] but also confirmed the many statements of John Hay that at first the members of the Senate Committee on Foreign Relations favored it, as "closer study . . . has convinced all but a few irreconcilables in the Senate that every consideration of true American policy is satisfied." [23] The same paper published, on February 15, a survey of press comments on the treaty in which more than half of the fifty papers quoted expressed themselves in favor of the treaty as it stood. The quotations published in *Public Opinion* give the same impression of public or editorial opinion, eight papers supporting the treaty and opposing amendments to permit fortifications or to abrogate the Clayton-Bulwer treaty, while five denounced the treaty because of those points.[24] Even a year later after the critics of the treaty had had time to arouse the public and had succeeded in the Senate, newspaper opinion was still nearly equally divided.[25] Perhaps the senators were mistaken in believing that an aroused public opinion demanded a revision of the treaty. Perhaps they were stampeded into their position by the vigorous attacks of a vociferous minority.

Such was the judgment of John Hay who, though strongly prejudiced, was nevertheless anxiously noting the effect of newspaper comments on his treaty. In a letter to Henry White

in the United States. . . ." Nevins, *Henry White,* p. 155. This statement, like the many others of which it is typical, is not supported by adequate evidence or by even the motions of scholarship.

[22] Feb. 6, 1900.

[23] Feb. 7, 1900. For the favorable attitude of the Senate Committee, see the *Tribune* of Feb. 9, 1900, and the New York *Times* of Feb. 11, 1900.

[24] *Public Opinion*, XXVIII, 198-199. Feb. 15, 1900.

[25] *Ibid.,* XXIX, 806. Dec. 27, 1900; XXX, 355-356. Mar. 21, 1901.

he gave his account of the influence of the Boer war on public opinion and thus indirectly on the pending treaty:

> The Irish and the Germans, for the first time in my knowledge, seem to have joined their several lunacies in one common attack against England and incidentally against the Administration for being too friendly to England. I do not imagine that this coalition can survive many months, but for the moment it lifts all our light-weight politicians off their feet. You would hardly believe, if I told you, how it has affected, not only men habitually timid, like Lodge and ———, but men like Davis and Cullom, who are anxious about their home vote, and men like ——— who are mad for popularity, and shout always with what seems the voice of the crowd.
>
> . . . nearly every member of the Foreign Relations committee approved the treaty and promised his support—but the *Sun* and the *Journal* began their furious attack which met with so much response from the papers in Chicago, who are cross with the President for personal reasons, that it frightened the weak sisters out of their wits. Lodge was the first to flop—then Cullom, who is a candidate for reelection, and in great danger of failing. They have worked on Davis, who is too indolent to make a strong fight. Wolcott, who is all right, is most of the time in New York, and was of no use.[26]

Political cowardice on the part of Republican senators facing the noisy opposition of a minority was also the explanation Hay sent to the American Ambassador to Great Britain. "The two men," he wrote, "who gave me the heartiest assurances of support . . . were Davis and Lodge; a few newspaper articles changed their minds entirely, or if not their minds, their action. Many Senators tell me that of course it is important to preserve honorable and even friendly relations with England; but not a man Jack of them will say it in the Senate now that Wolcott's gone. I do not know that I can blame them; the breath of their lives is popularity, and it is always, for the moment, amusing to blather away at England." [27] To his more intimate friend,

[26] Nevins, *Henry White,* pp. 151-152.

[27] A. L. P. Dennis, "John Hay," *The American Secretaries of State and Their Diplomacy,* IX, 159. In a letter to John W. Foster at about the same time Hay stated that the same factors were hampering American policy in the Far East. The passage has been often quoted but is worth repeating here. "There is such

Henry White, Hay was especially bitter in his denunciation of what he called the cowardice of Senator Lodge, also a friend of long standing. "You will be sorry to learn that Lodge, after accepting and applauding the treaty, has suddenly lost his nerve and wants it rejected." [28] And still later he wrote that the treaty could have been ratified intact "if our people had any pluck, or if Lodge had acted squarely." [29] Even when writing to a comparative stranger, like the Democratic editor, Henry Watterson, he could not refrain from aiming a jibe at Lodge: "Of course, that ["as we damn please"] is just what we are going to do—but why say it when we are going through the motions of ordinary civility? A man doesn't say 'Please pass me the butter—if you don't I'll take it anyway and slit your damn weazand if you wink.' Yet Mr. Lodge, bred at Harvard, says that is the proper, honest and honorable way to ask for butter. Even when the other side is perfectly willing to pass it along." [30]

But the eagerness of some senators to arouse and exploit popular hatred of England and the supine surrender of other senators to the fear of possible political consequences were not the only factors explaining the action of the Senate. Inevitably, personal, petty and entirely irrelevant considerations were present. Whitelaw Reid, wrote Henry White, "Intimated that the real cause of Davis's action was an aggrieved feeling at not

a mad-dog hatred of England prevalent among newspapers and politicians that anything we should now do in China to take care of our imperiled interests, would be set down to 'subservience to Great Britain' . . . every Senator I see says, 'For God's sake, don't let it appear we have any understanding with England.' How can I make bricks without straw? That we should be compelled to refuse the assistance of the greatest power in the world, *in carrying out our own policy,* because all Irishmen are Democrats and some Germans are fools—is enough to drive a man mad." Thayer, II, 234-235.

[28] Nevins, *Henry White,* p. 151.

[29] *Ibid.,* p. 154. None of this animosity toward Lodge is revealed in the letters published in Thayer's life of Hay, perhaps because, as there is reason to believe, the contents of this book were submitted to Roosevelt's editing before publication.

[30] Jan. 11, 1901. MS. Watterson Papers, Vol. III, letter No. 1504. This note was given to me by a friend who had access to this collection.

having been consulted beforehand; I mean before the Treaty was sent in if not actually before it was negotiated."[31] Hay was only too keenly aware of such improper motives on the part of senators. His often-quoted letters on the subject were wrung from the rage of a sensitive, frustrated man and as such would not be worth quoting again were it not that they throw some light, however oblique, on the reasons entering into the decisions of the Senate. During these months when his canal treaty was suffering mutilation his anguish produced the following bitter comments:

Every day some statesman comes up and asks me the true inwardness of Clayton-Bulwer, meaning that if I give him a Consul or two, he will vote for my Treaty next winter.[32]

The worst of all is the uncertainty about what the Senate may do in any given case. You may work for months over a treaty, and at last get everything satisfactorily arranged, and send it into the Senate, when it is met by every man who wants to get a political advantage or to satisfy a personal grudge, everyone who has asked for an office and not got it, everyone whose wife may think mine has not been attentive enough—and if they can muster one third of their Senate and one, your treaty is lost without any reference to its merits.[33]

The fact that a treaty gives to this country a great, lasting advantage, seems to weigh nothing whatever in the minds of about half the Senators. Personal interests, personal spites, and a contingent chance of a petty political advantage are the only motives that cut any ice at present.[34]

. . . and in the Senate a minority of one-third is able to bring to nought in a moment of spite or partisan malice the result of a year of unselfish work.[35]

The thing that has aged me and broken me up has been the attitude of the minority of the Senate. . . . We must get everything and give nothing,—and even then some malignant Senator or newspaper will

[31] To Hay, May 16, 1900. Nevins, *Henry White,* p. 153. Senator Davis was Chairman of the Committee on Foreign Relations.

[32] To Henry Adams, June 15, 1900. *Letters and Diary,* III, 178.

[33] To Henry White. Aug. 11, 1899. *Ibid.,* pp. 160-161.

[34] To Richard Watson Gilder. Apr. 24, 1900. *Ibid.,* p. 177.

[35] To E. A. Abbey. Jan. 24, 1900. *Ibid.,* p. 173.

attack the deal, and say we have surrendered everything,—and that scares our cowardly friends out of their wits.[36]

First there is the constitutional mistake of giving the absolute veto to one-third of that body, and secondly the habit which has grown up of late years, of the introduction of trivial Amendments involving matters which have been thoroughly considered in the negotiations and rejected; then the practice of endless delay which gives the newspapers the chance to find subjects of attack, of which they will avail themselves with imperfect knowledge of the matter in question, till the parties divide, and all hope of a two-thirds vote is gone.[37]

It is a painful and humiliating state of things, but I see no escape from it, since the Fathers in their wisdom chose to assume that one-third of the Senate in opposition would always be right, and the President and the majority generally wrong.[38]

It is a curious state of things. The howling lunatics, like Mason and Allen and Pettigrew, are always on hand, while our friends are cumbered with other cares and most of the time away. 'W' has been divorcing his wife; Morgan is fighting for his life in Alabama; Cullom, ditto in Illinois; even when Providence takes a hand in the game, our folks are restrained, by 'Senatorial Courtesy,' 'from accepting His favors.' Last week 'X' had *delirium tremens*; Bacon broke his ribs; Pettigrew had the grippe, and Hale ran off to New York on 'private business,' and the whole Senate stopped work until they got around again. I have never struck a subject so full of psychological interest as the official mind of a Senator.[39]

Corroboration for these jaundiced accusations of Hay came from the most authoritative sources possible—from Lodge and Roosevelt, one the leader and the other the staunchest defender of the senatorial attack on the treaty. It is clear from their later words and actions that neither believed that the votes had been cast because of the issues involved. When the second Hay-Pauncefote treaty was in the Senate, Roosevelt, as President, used weapons which confirmed Hay's comments on the low motives animating senators. Since the new treaty included

[36] To John G. Nicolay. Aug. 21, 1900. *Ibid.,* p. 185.

[37] To John J. McCook. April 22, 1900. *Ibid.,* p. 175.

[38] To President McKinley. Aug. 19, 1899. A. L. P. Dennis, *Adventures in American Diplomacy,* p. 151.

[39] To Joseph H. Choate. March 7, 1900. Thayer, II, 226.

either by express stipulation or by implication all the Senate's amendments to the first treaty, no special activity would have been necessary had the treaty been considered on its merits alone. The type of thing Roosevelt did can be learned from advice which Senator Lodge gave him, and which damns Lodge's colleagues as completely as even Hay would have wished. Lodge urged that "*all* questions of patronage must be kept in abeyance and must wait until the English treaty . . . is out of the way. Such an attitude will help the treaty I know. I hope Morgan proved amenable. Your seeing all these Senators and especially asking them to lunch is most wise and effective." [40] While evidence of the use of patronage is never easy to find there is plenty to prove that Roosevelt was exerting unusual pressure on the Senate. Hay, who must have marvelled at the contrast between McKinley's passive indifference and Roosevelt's energetic fighting, wrote gleefully but doubtfully, "It is amusing to see how enthusiastic the President is in favor of the treaty. He gave Billy Mason a drastic calling-down the other day. . . . But I wish we could see this treaty through before he begins to take the Senate by the collar." [41] Hay himself played to the petty vanity of members of the Senate and assiduously consulted many of them privately during the negotiations so that they could not feel neglected and resentful as Davis was said to have been on the former occasion.[42] But this policy was not without disadvantages, for news of the contemplated surrender by Great Britain leaked out to the papers and stimulated references to "our triumph," so that Hay feared the British government might break off the negotiations. It was an annoying dilemma, said Hay. "If we keep negotiations secret from leading Senators, we incur their ill will and opposi-

[40] Lodge, *Selections,* I, 507. The time element benefited the second treaty since it reached the Senate a year after a presidential election and not just before one as the first treaty had.

[41] Nevins, *Henry White,* p. 159.

[42] Dennis, "John Hay," *The American Secretaries of State and Their Diplomacy,* IX, 158-159.

tion. If we tell them confidentially what we are doing and thus secure their co-operation—their vanity leads them to blab everything to some newspaper, to show that they are 'in it.' "[43]

If history were a science like chemistry it would be possible to ascertain how many parts of politics, of petty spite and of personal interests were contained in the resulting act of the Senate. An exact analysis would also disclose the accurate weight to be attributed solely to an honest difference of opinion on the merits of the treaty. It seems logical to assume that more than the usual amount of sincere opposition was present, since the policy was one to which rational objection could be so easily made and against which the powerful appeals of the Monroe doctrine and national defense could be plausibly raised. Yet the extent to which reasonable arguments, or political considerations, or other factors entered the mind of each senator as he decided how to vote is manifestly impossible to determine. John Hay did not see any except improper motives; the senators would admit the existence of none but proper motives. The historian looking behind the words of the actors can find evidence of the former and must assume the presence of the latter.

Whatever the motives dominating the Senate, its action won public vindication when the second Hay-Pauncefote treaty, which included by stipulation or by implication the Senate's amendments to the first treaty, was successfully negotiated. But the applause so frequently given to the Senate for securing the additional concessions from Great Britain in the second agreement was properly earned only if the gains justified the risks run and if the Senate had calculated correctly the chances of success. Since the risks involved in defeating the first Hay-Pauncefote treaty failed to materialize, they have seldom been considered; but they were real to Roosevelt, who became President in the interim, to Hay still Secretary of State, and to Senator Lodge, who felt his personal responsibility for them. All three believed that the next American Congress would certainly

[43] Dennis, *Adventures in American Diplomacy,* p. 164.

authorize a canal irrespective of the treaty rights of Great Britain and they contemplated with apprehension the possibility of war. Roosevelt approved the prospective refusal to abide by the Clayton-Bulwer treaty, but warned that before making it "we want to be sure of the position we intend taking should Germany and England combine against us. Of course, such a combination would be one of the utmost folly for England, because she is certain to have her paws burned, while the nuts would go to Germany. But the last two years have shown that British statesmen are capable of committing the wildest follies."[44] Senator Lodge agreed on the danger from English stupidity, but failed to see on what grounds Germany could join in the war.[45] Ironically, it was the German government, which Roosevelt feared in a possible combination with England, that was chiefly responsible for the speedy acquiescence of the British to the further American demands. If the senators had based their decision on an appreciation of the benefit to be gained from the rising German threat to Great Britain, the senatorial position might justly be applauded as sound and realistic diplomacy, but there is no evidence that any of them understood the European situation and its opportunities for the United States.

Some striking similarities and some curious contrasts to the case of the Hay-Pauncefote treaties appeared as a group of treaties died in the Senate during the same period. The result in each instance was a victory for the Senate, yet in neither case was it a clear victory over the Executive, since the man who happened to be President at the crisis offered no resistance. This time the rôles were reversed and it was McKinley who was fighting for the treaties while it was the new President, Roosevelt, who permitted them to expire undefended. As before, the relationship between President McKinley and his Secretary of State was peculiar, but on this occasion it was the President who assumed personal responsibility, while Hay showed no

[44] Lodge, *Selections,* I, 485.

[45] *Ibid.,* pp. 486-488. See also Nevins, *Henry White,* pp. 155-158.

interest at all in the success of the treaties. In fact, Hay probably did not regard the negotiations as the work of his Department. He washed his hands of them so completely that in none of his extensive published correspondence is there so much as a single comment on the Senate's attitude toward the treaties. Usually he needed slight provocation on that subject.

The treaties provided for commercial reciprocity and were known as the Kasson treaties from the name of the special agent of the Department of State who negotiated them. Eleven of them were signed within a short period and, as they involved the same principles, aroused the same opposition and met the same fate, they can be considered together. Five were with Great Britain; one (signed June 16, 1899) provided for commercial reciprocity with Barbadoes, one (signed July 18, 1899) provided for reciprocity with British Guiana, one (signed July 21, 1899) provided for reciprocity with the colony of Turks and Caicos Islands, one (signed the following day) provided for reciprocity with Jamaica, and the fifth (signed on July 24, 1899) provided for reciprocity with Bermuda. The other treaties were with Argentina, July 10, 1899; France, July 24, 1899; Nicaragua, October 20, 1899; Denmark for the island of St. Croix, June 5, 1900; the Dominican Republic, June 25, 1900; Ecuador, July 10, 1900.[46]

All were designed to comply with section four of the Dingley Tariff Act of 1897, which said that without further action by Congress the tariffs levied by that law could be changed by not to exceed twenty per cent and for a period of not more than five years by reciprocity treaties if made within two years of the passage of the act.[47] This section of the tariff bill was a concession to the moderate tariff or reform group in the Re-

[46] The treaties are printed in *56th Cong., 1st sess., S. Doc.,* No. 20, 21, 22, and 225. See also Laughlin and Willis, *Reciprocity, Appendix II.* On January 31, 1903, an additional agreement with France was signed, in which the terms of the treaty of July 24, 1899 were extended to Porto Rico. *Foreign Relations, 1908*, p. 289.

[47] *U. S. Statutes at Large,* XXX, 204.

publican party through which they could be reconciled to accepting the high rates provided elsewhere in the bill. But reciprocity in principle and reciprocity in the form of treaties lowering specific tariff rates were two distinct things. The bargain, if one had been made and not merely implied, was easily repudiated after McKinley was assassinated. As soon as opposition to the reciprocity policy developed, McKinley, who had become deeply committed to tariff reform, had shown he was not going to surrender on this issue without a struggle. An appeal to public opinion is one of the weapons in the presidential armory and McKinley resorted to it. His last public address, made in Buffalo the night before his assassination, was devoted to a defense of the Kasson treaties not only with economic arguments but also on the grounds that reciprocity would remove dangerous international irritations.[48]

Although Roosevelt had been speaking in much the same vein as McKinley, he soon abandoned reciprocity and deserted the treaties he had inherited from his fromer chief. Throughout his entire career as President, Roosevelt proved his political sagacity and agility by resisting all pressure to revise the tariff.[49] The resolute opposition to reciprocity that he quickly encountered in the high protectionist wing of his party led him to evade the issue.[50] In his first annual message to Congress, after solemnly stating some generalities on the subject of reciprocity, he concluded with a single damning reference to the treaties: "I ask the attention of the Senate to the reciprocity treaties laid before it by my predecessor." [51] With these cold words he

[48] Olcott, II, 311-312.

[49] In a penetrating analysis of Roosevelt's attitude toward the tariff, he is pictured as dropping his early ideas of revision on the insistence of the conservative Speaker Cannon who warned him of the political dangers involved. Henry F. Pringle, *Theodore Roosevelt,* pp. 414-415.

[50] Stephenson, *Aldrich,* pp. 176-180. The evidence submitted in this account, by far the best for the maneuvers of the leaders during the contest over reciprocity, seems conclusive that Roosevelt's final position was due to the firm stand of Aldrich, but the importance of the latter is so exaggerated throughout the book that doubts inevitably arise.

[51] Richardson, *Messages and Papers of the Presidents,* XIV, 6653. The pre-

signified his desertion of the treaties. For them there was to be no "calling down" of Billy Mason, no luncheon invitations, no delicate withholding of patronage.

Cast adrift by the Executive, the treaties succumbed readily to the opposition of the ultra-protectionists among the Republicans, added to that of the Democrats, for the latter, as usual, generally opposed the policy of reciprocity even though some of them were willing to accept any reduction of duty that could be obtained.[52] These groups were aided by the vociferous protests which came from the representatives of the industries that might be adversely affected, and the appeals and pressure used during the framing of a tariff bill were now used against the treaties.[53] A guess as to how much each of these factors counted in the defeat of the treaties cannot be hazarded, for no votes were even taken in the Senate on any of them.[54] Plain-

ceding paragraphs were full of such weaseling statements as "Subject to this proviso of the proper protection necessary to our industrial well-being at home, the principle of reciprocity must command our hearty support."

[52] "This third failure to carry into successful operation a permanent system of reciprocity demonstrates that there are radical elements of opposition to it. . . . The Democratic Party has generally been arrayed against it, although it has received the hearty support of some prominent members of that party. . . . A considerable element of the Republican Party has not given it hearty support, because of the fear that it might injuriously affect some of the protected industries of the country." Foster, *Diplomatic Memoirs,* II, 18.

[53] For a description and analysis of this opposition, see Laughlin and Willis, *Reciprocity,* pp. 335-350. Letters and statements opposing the French reciprocity treaty are given in the *Compilation of the Reports of the Committee on Foreign Relations,* VIII, 606-635. The opposition came from the Senate Finance Committee and not the Committee on Foreign Relations. The following newspaper comment is significant: "It is understood that the Administration realizes the mistake it has made in keeping everything connected with this treaty secret, and denying even to members of the Finance Committee access to the data and correspondence upon which the treaty is based. An effort is to be made by him [Kasson] to win over the antagonistic members of the Finance Committee by taking them into his confidence." New York *Tribune,* Feb. 8, 1900.

[54] Additional articles and separate conventions extending the time for the exchange of ratifications were negotiated. Two of the separate conventions for this purpose were approved unanimously by the Senate. *Sen. Ex. Jour.,* XXXII, 570, 615, and 571, 614. But no action was taken on the reciprocity treaties within the extended period.

tively the Chairman of the Commit
later wrote, "I pressed them as best
rich, Senator Hanna, and other adv
were so bitterly opposed to them—n
from myself seeming to have much i
were dropped and allowed to expir
Political opposition was certainly
responsible. Again the diplomatic
had ended in failure because of the
Senate. But, it must be repeated, th
power of the Senate was only a
tive since the new Presi
made by the admini
Notwith

ttee on Foreign Relations
I could, but Senator Ald-
ocates of high protection,
o one in the Senate aside
terest in them—that they
e by their own terms." [55]
present and was partially
negotiations of a President
treaty-making power of the
e successful assertion of the
partial victory over the Execu-
ad not fought for the treaties
which he had been a minor part.
pathy to the policy of general
stration negotiated two recipro-
eived the sanction of the Senate
of the argument that the peculiar
try to the United States obligated
h exceptional commercial rela-
d treaty providing for reciprocity
nd Newfoundland, fell a victim
aties. The treaty went to the Sen-
a November 8, 1902.[56] Two years
d then Roosevelt appealed to Sena-
rstanding with Senator Crane, also
ubject of amendments and to report
Committee on Foreign Relations.
objections to the treaty," wrote Roose-
, but show a real purpose of trying to get it." [57]

[55] Shelby M. Cullom, *Fifty Years of Public Service,* p. 374.

[56] During the attempt to secure reciprocity with Canada in 1911, many earlier documents were reprinted in *S. Doc.,* No. 80, *62d Cong., 1st sess.* In Part 2, pp. 1589-1592, is the Hay-Bond treaty, and on pp. 1592-1617 are protests against it from various New England fishing interests together with a number of contemporary newspaper comments.

[57] Lodge, *Selections,* II, 110.

Stimulated by this promp
1905, when the treaty w
raised by New England fis
to the treaty since the an
advantages of the bargai
sided had the treaty beco
American would have the
to accept it." [58]

In assigning responsibilit
the treaty it is clear that the
small group in New England
wished to exclude the one poss
The President attributed entire resp
which constitutes an amazing comm
minority to block a treaty. After the S
treaty to death the government of New
against the New England fishermen on it
indignation Senator Lodge wrote Roosevelt u
be sent to the area to protect American righ
reply was that sending a warship would be provoc
forbearance was desirable since the failure of the n
had given deep and natural offense to Newfoundland
course of his explanation there occurred this statement:

> The essential fact is that in view of Gloucester's attitude, which
> dered it absolutely impossible to negotiate any treaty which Newfoun
> land would accept, it was most unwise to enter into the negotiations a
> all, and all of us who advised or acquiesced in those negotiations being
> begun, share the responsibility. If we had never gone into the negotia-
> tions at all this trouble would not have arisen, and the prime fault was
> going into them. No consultation with Gloucester, no change in the
> course of procedure either by the administration or in the Senate, would
> have availed anything, because the facts were that our fishermen would

pting the Senate acted in February
as amended to met the objections
hing interests. The process was fatal
mendments eliminated nearly all the
l to Newfoundland. Indeed so one-
me that one journal asserted, "No
effrontery to ask Sir Robert Bond
y for the amendments whi
major share mus
who en

[58] Boston *Evening Transcript,* Feb. 9, 1905. In this same article the amendments, apparently not yet published in any official record, are summarized. Similar comments on the nature and cause of the Senate's action can be found in the *Outlook,* LXXIX, 408-409 (Feb. 18, 1905). *Nation,* LXXX, 238-239 (Mar. 30, 1905). *Review of Reviews,* XXXI, 400 (April 1905).

not accept any treaty which we could negotiate, and therefore there should have been no attempt made to negotiate the treaty at all.[59]

To infer that Roosevelt meant that the great treaty-making power of the United States could always be controlled and rendered impotent by so small a minority as the fishermen of Gloucester, Massachusetts, would manifestly be improper. But his matter-of-course acquiescence is eloquent testimony of the frequency of the occurrence. Not only the two-thirds provision but the procedure and customs of the Senate multiply many times the obstructive force of a minority. When conditions are favorable, as was the case in this instance, a microscopic group can offer a successful resistance.[60] The circumstances favoring the Gloucester fishermen were first the widespread antipathy to all reciprocity, already noted in connection with the earlier reciprocity treaties, and second, the failure of anyone to fight for the treaty. The benefits to be gained from reciprocity with Newfoundland were too slight to induce other business interests to campaign for the proposal. Even the President did nothing on behalf of the negotiations begun under his own auspices. He had never been interested in reciprocity *per se* and, as his letters to Lodge prove, he readily admitted upon the first appearance of opposition the mistake of attempting this

[59] Lodge *Selections,* II, 175. Lodge's letter asking for the warship is on the preceding page.

[60] Further proof of the powers of a small group to obstruct a treaty was supplied by another example originating in Roosevelt's administration. On July 2, 1903, a treaty with Cuba was signed, in which the United States recognized the sovereignty of Cuba over the Isle of Pines. Before the Senate acted the time fixed for the exchange of ratifications had lapsed, but a new treaty was signed on March 2, 1904, with exactly the same provisions except that no date for ratification was set. The exception proved to be a wise one as the protests of the few United States citizens who had invested money in the island were sufficient to block action in the Senate for twenty-one years. Although the period of inaction was so long that the original document was temporarily lost the treaty was technically still pending before the Senate and it received the consent of that body on March 13, 1925. *Foreign Relations, 1904,* p. 240. New York *Times,* January 25, March 13, 14, 1925.

particular reciprocity treaty. The President had not lost in a battle with the Senate for he had surrendered his treaty without a fight.

During the very month that the Newfoundland reciprocity treaty quietly joined the large number already in the senatorial graveyard for treaties, the President and the Senate were battling for mastery over the fate of a number of other international agrements. These struggles received a large measure of attention from the contemporary American public, and deserve more from the student of treaty-making under the American Constitution, for the episodes were among the most significant in the long contest between President and Senate. To understand them it is necessary to appreciate the general situation which furnished their milieu. The Roosevelt of 1905 was a vastly different man from the timid President who had permitted McKinley's reciprocity treaties to die without a struggle. In the interim he had been elected by a tremendous majority to the high office he had attained through accident. The vote constituted a personal tribute expressing the approval of a delighted people. Only two or three political leaders in the history of the country have had a personal following comparable to his. No satisfactory explanation of his hold on the imagination of the people can be found in the records of things accomplished. Indeed it is a commonplace to point out that much more progressive legislation was passed during Taft's administration than while Roosevelt was President. And an examination of the evidence shows that behind all the clamor and excitement Roosevelt was not only willing but anxious to compromise in order to avert the alienation of either the conservative or progressive wing of his party. What endeared Roosevelt to his public, what brought him prestige and power were his enthusiasm, his intense activity, his rashness, his combativeness, his joy in battle. He was, as some one said of him, "pure action." To the newspapers he was a constant source of scintillating copy, and better than anyone in his generation he realized the advantage to himself of utilizing to the utmost the publicity value of the White House.[61]

More and more Roosevelt assumed in his own eyes and in those of the public the rôle of the champion of the common man against organized wealth and "big business." It was a rôle demanded by the times and one which Roosevelt found particularly delightful, as well as politically profitable. He entered upon it with keen zest and renewed energy as soon as possible after his election in 1904. The first and greatest battle was over the proposal to have the Interstate Commerce Commission fix railroad rates. In prompt response to Roosevelt's recommendations the House of Representatives, on February 9, 1905, passed the Esch-Townsend bill, but the conservative group in the Senate led by members of Roosevelt's own party successfully blocked all legislation until March 1906. The Hepburn act, which then became law, represented a compromise in which Roosevelt surrendered much that he had demanded. Thus the two antagonists were the President and the Senate, with the former widely hailed as a tribune of the people and with the latter as frequently denounced as a club of millionaires and of corporation lawyers.[62]

[61] There is an account of Roosevelt's relations with the newspapers and newspapermen by one of the latter in Mark Sullivan, *Our Times,* III, 69-97. After pointing out (p. 76) that "a cartoonist, going to his office in the late afternoon, need hardly worry about finding a topic for his cartoon, Roosevelt would have been sure to have done something or said something," Sullivan states, "Nine times out of ten the cartoon was Roosevelt in combat; always, almost without exception, it was Roosevelt in action. . . . I venture to say that not among the literally myriads of Roosevelt cartoons are half a dozen in which he sleeps, or even rests. Once, seeking to symbolize his retirement from the Presidency, I worked for days with an artist to devise a picture in which Roosevelt, his labors over, should enjoy repose. We gave it up. The thing could not be done, was contrary no less to art than to nature." Pp. 78-79.

[62] History was called upon to furnish parallels. "But as Gracchus's real struggle was with the Roman Senate, so will Roosevelt's real struggle be with the American Senate. And as in the Roman Senate there was a powerful party which bitterly opposed the Tribune, so it is evident that in the American Senate there is a party, hardly less powerful, which is determined earnestly to oppose

It was in the heat of this remarkable struggle, while the President was stimulating virulent newspaper attacks on the Senate, that a group of treaties supplied the means by which the Senate could assert its powers decisively against even so popular and dynamic a President as Roosevelt. They were ten identical general arbitration treaties signed with France (Nov. 1, 1904), Switzerland (Nov. 21, 1904), Germany (Nov. 22, 1904), Portugal (Nov. 23, 1904), Great Britain (Dec. 12, 1904), Italy (Dec. 14, 1904), Spain (Dec. 31, 1904), Austria-Hungary (Jan. 6, 1905), Mexico (Jan. 18, 1905), and Norway and Sweden (Jan. 20, 1905).[63] Similar negotiations were in progress with other countries and more treaties would have resulted, in fact one with Japan had already been signed, when the Senate showed its unwillingness to accept any of them.

The hostile action of the Senate was not due to a fear that the United States might be bound too rigidly by these agreements, for, in truth, they were feeble instruments for preserving international peace. They provided for the obligatory arbitration only of differences of a legal nature and those relating to the interpretation of treaties, and even from that restricted group there were specifically excepted questions affecting the vital interests, independence, or honor of the contracting parties. What aroused the antagonism of the Senate was a further provision stating that before appealing to the Hague Court the two powers were to conclude a "special agreement" defining the issue in dispute, the scope of the arbitrator's powers and the procedure to be followed. By a vote of fifty to nine the Senate amended the treaty with France so as to substitute the word "treaty" for the word "agreement."[64] The effect of

the President. History shows that it is in the upper branch of parliamentary bodies that the conservative interests of a State manifest their chief strength. It is in the Senate that Mr. Roosevelt will find some of his strongest antagonists." Charles S. Dana, "Theodore Roosevelt and Tiberius Gracchus," *North American Review,* CLXXX, 334 (March 1905).

[63] *Congressional Record,* Jan. 13, 1905, p. 805; Feb. 11, 1905, p. 2402.

[64] *Ibid.,* Feb. 13, 1905, p. 2477.

this amendment was to require a new treaty to be made in each instance before a dispute could be submitted to arbitration.

The nature of the amendment correctly indicated the reason for it. Certainly party politics was not responsible because the fifty votes were cast by twenty-eight Republicans and twenty-two Democrats. Perhaps partisanship accounts for the fact that all nine votes in favor of keeping the treaty in the form acceptable to Roosevelt came from Republicans. But, if so, it was immaterial since the great majority irrespective of party insisted on changing the treaty in order to prevent any possible infringement of the prerogatives of the Senate. In so doing they were obeying the same instinctive motive that had led Maclay to guard the Senate's powers jealousy on that memorable occasion when Washington visited the Senate to secure its advice and consent. And they were following exactly the precedent established when Olney's general arbitration treaty of 1897 had reached the Senate. As on that occasion the minority report of the Committee on Foreign Relations contained the explanation of the Senate's action, when it stated:

> The firm grasp upon our relations with foreign governments, placed in the hands of a minority of one-third of the Senate by the Constitution, whereby entangling alliances and wars have often been prevented, and our national independence and individuality have been preserved, is being relaxed and the people are losing the power of self-protection. It is silently passing from the hands of their representatives, who are charged with the two-fold duty of giving advice to the President, and of giving or refusing their consent to his agreements with foreign powers into the sole and exclusive power of the President.
>
> * * * * * * *
>
> Such is the effect that must result from the conventions now before the Senate and, so far as can be seen, that is one of the real intents and purposes intended to be accomplished by their ratification.
>
> * * * * * * *
>
> These conventions furnish that opportunity to the President, and there is neither reason nor safety in accepting this new and dangerous departure. Once the power is yielded to the President to arbitrate questions, great or small, with foreign powers, by diplomatic agreements with foreign powers, without consulting the Senate, it will never be reclaimed, and the Executive department will become entirely inde-

pendent of all other departments in the establishment of the supreme law of the United States.[65]

While the Republican members of the Senate would, of course, not subscribe to these accusations and insinuations of an attempt on the part of the Republican President to establish an autocracy there can be no doubt that they agreed on the necessity of doing something to protect the powers of the Senate. As the Chairman of the Committee on Foreign Relations, staunch Republican though he was, expressed it, "Nothing remained for the Senate to do but to assert and uphold its rights as a part of the treaty-making power." [66] All the testimony available is to the same effect.[67] Some contemporary observers commented that instead of defending its powers the Senate was extending them so as "to make the Secretary of State a mere

[65] *58th Cong., 3d sess., S. Doc.,* No. 155, pp. 11, 19. Roosevelt wrote that "the text of all these treaties, to which the Senate Foreign affairs Committee [sic] now objects, was submitted in advance to each member of the Committee a year ago, and no member save Morgan raised any objection, or expressed anything save approval." To Ernest Hamlin Abbott. Feb. 6, 1905. MS. Letterbook. Roosevelt Papers.

[66] Cullom, p. 399.

[67] Senator Lodge said, "The Senate was not of opinion that this power which was undoubtedly theirs ought to be taken from them in this way. . . ." *The Senate of the United States,* p. 27. Senator Platt of Connecticut, one of the nine voting for the treaty as drafted, wrote to a former senator, "But it does not do the Senate or the country any good to be continually looking to see if in some unimportant particular the Executive has not gone too far. I have known people so jealous of their own rights, and so fearful of interference therewith that they made their whole lives miserable, forfeiting the respect of everyone who knew them. I feel that the Senate is acting like such individuals." Louis A. Coolidge, *An Old-Fashioned Senator, Orville H. Platt,* p. 481. John Hay noted the event in his diary with more weariness than bitterness. "There was a loud clamor that the rights of the Senate were invaded—but every individual Senator felt that his precious privilege of casting two votes in opposition to every treaty must be safeguarded. And then, the President's majority was too big—they wanted to teach him that he wasn't *it.*" Thayer, II, 392-393. Roosevelt wrote that the trouble was "owing to the idiotic jealousy of the Executive which tends to make the Senate try to reduce the Executive to impotency." To J. St. Loe Strachey. Jan. 9, 1905. MS. Letterbook. Roosevelt Papers.

clerk of the Senate Committee on Foreign Relations." [68] Be that as it may, the motive of the Senate was clear and in the light of what had happened in 1897, and what was to happen to Taft's arbitration treaties of 1911, was to have been expected. The simultaneous struggle with the President over other questions and Roosevelt's contemporaneous attempt to disregard the Senate in his dealings with the Dominican Republic made the fate of the arbitration treaties inevitable.[69]

That the amendment made by the Senate would kill the treaties was clearly understood at the time. On the day before the Senate acted Roosevelt had written the Chairman of the Foreign Relations Committee a letter in which he had pointed out that such an amendment would make the treaties meaningless and that he would not attempt to secure the consent of other nations to an " expression of barren intention." [70] Much earlier, when he first learned of the Senate's attitude, Roosevelt had stated the same ideas in more blunt and unambiguous lan-

[68] *The Nation,* LXXX, 21 (Jan. 12, 1905). *Ibid.,* p. 44 (Jan. 19, 1905). In an article concluding a series of five on the subject of the Senate and the arbitration treaties, *The Outlook* summarized its position by saying, " It has been well said by one familiar not only with the political history of the United States but with the interior history of the United States Senate, that the Senate is a body of gentlemen whose chief concern is to enlarge their individual prerogatives and privileges." LXXIX, 727 (Mar. 25, 1905). These articles were undoubtedly written at Roosevelt's suggestion, yet the views expressed were widely held, for all the journals of opinion I have examined as well as the vast majority of the letters written to them join in denouncing the Senate's position. Indeed the Senate's resolute stand and *esprit de corps* in the face of an aroused public both on this occasion and in 1897 compels admiration.

[69] As hostile a critic as *The Nation,* which said the Senate would defeat the treaties " to glut its greed for power," had to admit that Roosevelt's Dominican policy gave the Senate great provocation. LXXX, 21, 126.

[70] Cullom, pp. 400-401. Roosevelt gave his letter to the newspapers and it was generally printed on the next day, Feb. 11, 1905. According to the Washington *Star,* of that date, the reading of Roosevelt's letter in executive session led to a debate in which Senator Morgan criticized Executive interference with the Senate when performing its part in the making of treaties and spoke of the letter as further evidence of the President's tendency toward the usurpation of the Senate's prerogative.

guage in private letters to two of his closest friends in the Senate. To Spooner he wrote:

The more I have thought over the matter the more I have become convinced that while the amendment proposed by the Southerners in reference to their states is objectionable, it is not as objectionable as the amendment you say was proposed by Lodge to the effect that the Senate must ratify any agreement hereafter arrived at between this and one of the foreign Powers concerned in reference to something to be arbitrated. It seems to me to put in such a provision makes these arbitration treaties an absurdity. We say that now we conclude an arbitration treaty to the effect that whenever we hereafter choose we shall conclude another arbitration treaty on any subject which we regard as fit. If each of these arbitration treaties is to have no possible effect until the other arbitration treaties are concluded—and this is what the amendment in question amounts to—then why have these arbitration treaties at all. It seems to me that the proposed amendment converts the whole business into a sham, and I think it neither wise nor proper for us to take part in a sham. I went into the work of getting these arbitration treaties publicly and with the belief that I had the sentiment of my party and of the country behind me, nor would I have gone into the effort to get these treaties if they were to be shams. . . . At any rate it seems to me nonsense to try to have a general arbitration treaty which shall amount to a meaningless manifesto to the effect that we intend, if the need arises, hereafter to have special arbitration treaties; but that the general arbitration treaty itself shall be wholly ineffective. This is just precisely what the proposed amendment does.

I have not made up my mind what my course ought to be in the matter and shall not until I have had a chance of speaking to you and Lodge and some others, but my present feeling is that it would be better for me to withdraw the treaties and state that in my opinion the proposed amendments made them shams, rather than to have them amended in the fashion suggested. If the people of this country are sincere in saying they wish to take a short but a real step toward increasing the chance for peaceful settlement of differences between them and foreign nations, then the people of this country will want these treaties passed; but I certainly cannot take part in what in my judgment would become an insincere pretense of doing what was really not done.[71]

[71] Jan. 6, 1905. MS. Spooner Papers. On the same day he wrote to Lodge often using the same words as in the Spooner letter. Lodge, *Selections,* II, 110-112. Lodge's position can be found in a letter to Taft, which the latter sent to the President. Taft to Roosevelt. Feb. 11, 1905. MS. Roosevelt Papers.

The power of the Senate had again been vindicated and its victory was clear. It was apparently this experience that led John Hay to give his famous description of the operation of the treaty-making power. "A treaty entering the Senate," he wrote, "is like a bull going into the arena: no one can say just how or when the blow will fall—but one thing is certain—it will never leave the arena alive." [72] But before the result can be taken as an accurate guage of the relative strength of the two partners in the making of treaties a troublesome doubt as to whether or not Roosevelt had fought to the fullest extent of his ability must be considered. That he had made some efforts is evident from the letters to Spooner, Lodge, and Cullom; and from newspaper reports of interviews with other senators on behalf of the treaties.[73] Evidently Roosevelt believed at first that his direct appeals would prove effective and he wrote confidently, "I think I have dragooned the Senators on the subject of the arbitration treaties." [74] It was not long, however, before he realized that further pressure was necessary at least on the Democrats, and the following letter to Lyman Abbott of *The Outlook* shows how he hoped to secure it.

I wish we could have the men who believe in international arbitration start a backfire on Senator Bacon, Senator Morgan, Senator Martin and the other men who are really holding up these treaties. I do not have to point out to you that to amend these treaties is to vote against them. We have got the foreign governments to accept this minimum, and if we now put in absurd and meaningless amendments we put ourselves into a humiliating position and expose ourselves to the risk of having foreign Powers treat us as insincere. Bacon is a man of meticulous mind, a violent partisan, with no real public spirit, and he and his followers are engaged in trying to beat the treaties with the unworthy

[72] Thayer, II, 393.

[73] Washington *Star,* Jan. 14, 16, and Feb. 3, 1905. When it appeared that Southern senators were going to insist upon an amendment excluding the repudiated debts of their states from the possible subjects to be arbitrated he wrote Cullom a letter on that subject, and to Cullom's evident annoyance the letter, which was marked personal, appeared in the newspapers almost before it was received. Cullom, p. 397.

[74] To Lyman Abbott. Jan. 11, 1905. MS. Letterbook. Roosevelt Papers.

purpose of preventing the administration getting whatever credit may attach to helping in the effort to serve the country. As you know, I dealt with the Republican Senators on my own hook and have them substantially straightened out. It is a shame if the Democratic Senators beat the treaties now. They ought to receive a sharp lesson.[75]

When Roosevelt finally understood that the Republican senators were as determined as their Democratic colleagues in their insistence on the proposed amendment he abandoned further efforts and wrote *The Outlook* not in order to stimulate greater pressure but " simply that you may know what the situation at the moment is." [76]

Although it is clear that Roosevelt fought for his treaties, the evidence is not incompatible with the belief that Roosevelt made only a partial use of his presidential weapons on behalf of a policy which he had adopted "publicly," as he wrote Spooner, but for which he did not choose to exert himself to the utmost. Roosevelt was no ardent advocate of arbitration. Several years before this time he had written of the "futile sentimentalists of the international arbitration type" and several years later he was to amaze Taft by attacking the latter's arbitration treaties with similar contemptuous language.[77] Apparently the treaties Roosevelt had negotiated in 1904 were a gesture for the benefit of the large group in the country who had continued and intensified the active campaign for arbitration and the peaceful settlement of international disputes, notwithstanding the setback in 1897. Certainly the treaties

[75] Jan. 28, 1905. MS. *ibid.* Three days later he wrote to Lawrence F. Abbott, " There is one change I would suggest in the letter. Bacon, Morgan and *Money,* not Martin, are holding the treaties up in committee. Both Daniel and Martin have been in effect against them, but it was Money, not Martin, who acted against them in committee, as I understand Martin is not on that committee. But it would be a very important thing if we could get Daniel and Martin active for them. Could your letter be changed along these lines? . . ." MS. *ibid.*

[76] To Ernest Hamlin Abbott. Feb. 6, 1905. MS. *ibid.*

[77] Lodge, *Selections,* I, 218; II, 404-414. Pringle, pp. 168, 551. Consistency was never a bugbear to Roosevelt's mind so he was able when receiving his Nobel Prize in Christiania on May 5, 1910, to give an emphatic endorsement to arbitration.

were used in the presidential election of 1904, for Roosevelt himself, in his letter to Lodge, stated that "During the campaign last summer I announced, and Hay announced that we were negotiating these treaties with the various countries concerned. Our party speakers on the stump made a great deal of it . . ."[78]

But the most accurate index to Roosevelt's attitude toward these treaties was his conduct when the next presidential election drew near and the temptation to capitalize the peace movement politically was again present. Then, despite his previous belief that it would be "neither wise nor proper for us to take part in a sham," despite his indignant refusal to "take part in what . . . would become an insincere pretense of doing what was really not done," despite his statement that it would represent "not a step forward but a slight step backward, as regards the question of international arbitration," he surrendered completely to the Senate and sponsored arbitration treaties with the Senate amendment of 1905. Beginning with the one signed with France on February 10, 1908, a series of twenty-five were negotiated and, like all gestures for peace, received wide approbation in the press.[79] Each of these specified that the special agreement governing an arbitration must be made by and with the advice and consent of the Senate. This result was, as Roosevelt had stated, a backward step that made arbitration more difficult since it had been the practice prior to 1908 to refer pecuniary claims of citizens against foreign governments to arbitration under simple executive agreements. After the treaties of 1908 that procedure was no longer possible and each time there had to be a separate treaty with all the formality and delay incident to the successful completion of such an agreement.[80] A sincere proponent of arbitration, who saw the situa-

[78] Lodge, *Selections,* II, 111-112.

[79] The most convenient account of them and their provisions is in a pamphlet published by the World Peace Foundation entitled, "Arbitration and the United States," pp. 521-523. Three failed to be completed but not because of the American Senate.

[80] John Bassett Moore, *International Law and Some Current Illusions,* pp. 86-89.

tion as clearly as Roosevelt did, would hardly have accepted the responsibility for these later treaties. The statement that the new arbitration treaties were considered by Roosevelt as a political and not a sincerely pacific move is supported not only by the circumstances and the chronology of the negotiations but also by Roosevelt's own admission to that effect. Writing some years later to an intimate friend he said, "I was lukewarm about those treaties. I only went into them because the general feeling of the country demanded it." [81] Consequently the belief that Roosevelt did not fight seriously for the treaties of 1904 is strengthened, as is the suspicion that in making public his letters on behalf of the treaties he was concerned not so much in saving the treaties as in discrediting the Senate as an obstructive body.

The completeness of the senatorial victory on the arbitration treaties is more curious and more dubious when contrasted with the events attending the agreements Roosevelt made with the Dominican Republic during the same months. The same furious contests over domestic economic issues again furnished the background for the fight between President and Senate. The same anxiety to protect its treaty-making power was prominent in the Senate. The parallel was more striking when the first Dominican treaty to reach the Senate was also defeated. But on this occasion Roosevelt was willing to go to great lengths in fighting for his policy and when the second treaty was finally ratified victory lay with the President and not with the Senate.

The wisdom of Roosevelt's Dominican policy and the events preceding or attending its application are subjects lying outside the scope of this study. It is essential, however, to emphasize its great significance. When Roosevelt decided to prevent European debt-collecting expeditions by having the United States assume a financial supervision over the Dominican Republic he made one of the most notable additions to that elastic group of ideas known as the Monroe doctrine and established a new policy for the United States in its relations with Caribbean

[81] Gwynn, *The Letters and Friendships of Sir Cecil Spring Rice,* II, 185.

countries. Notwithstanding the importance of the step and in spite of the fact that it involved an agreement with the Dominican Republic there is reason to believe that the administration hoped to manage without requesting the advice and consent of the Senate. Certainly the minor officials who represented the United States in the negotiations did not expect that the constitutional sanction of the Senate would be sought. The first agreement in which the United States, among other things, guaranteed the territorial integrity of the Dominican Republic, promised to adjust the foreign and domestic debt of the Dominican government and undertook to collect and distribute the customs receipts of that country, provided that it was to take effect on February 1, 1905, or eleven days after it was signed.[82] Obviously the Senate was not to be consulted for it could not have been expected to act in so brief an interval. Moreover, the State Department had been informed of this date before the agreement was signed so that it could have insisted upon a change had it desired one.[83] Later the State Department referred to this agreement as "a memorandum of a proposed agreement" but the language of the document nowhere gives a hint that it was not, as it purported to be, a final, completed negotiation.[84] When further negotiations were necessary and a provision requiring the Senate's approval was being inserted, the American Minister stated that "if the protocol must be submitted to the American Senate, it must also be submitted to the Dominican House of Congress." [85] From those words it is evident that he had not expected the original agreement would have gone to the Senate.

To what extent Roosevelt also shared the belief that it would be possible to sign an agreement of this nature with a foreign

[82] *Foreign Relations, 1905*, pp. 311-312. The second agreement which was the protocol submitted to the Senate and a large and unusually frank collection of diplomatic notes are published in this volume of *Foreign Relations*, pp. 298-391.

[83] *Ibid.*, p. 306.

[84] *The Nation*, LXXX, 103 (Feb. 9, 1905).

[85] Dawson to the Secretary of State. Feb. 13, 1905. *Foreign Relations, 1905*, p. 320.

power, and to put it into effect without securing the Senate's consent, cannot be stated with any degree of certainty. Later he wrote that "The whole Santo Domingo policy was carried on under direct supervision of John Hay, acting under my direction. Not a movement was taken save on our initiative." [86] Although the records available do not justify so sweeping a statement they do make it seem probable that Roosevelt had hoped to avoid the danger of having his policy defeated in the Senate. A letter he wrote to the Secretary of State shows that he had contemplated the possibility of ignoring the Senate. In it he stated with obvious regret, "I suppose we should submit this agreement in the form of a protocol." [87] Whatever doubts he still had were ended during the same day, for the State Department wired its representative in the Dominican Republic that in order to insure approval certain alterations would have to be made in the agreement and among the several required changes was the insertion of a provision stating that the agreement was to take effect after its approval by the United States Senate.[88] By the next day Roosevelt was writing to the editor of a journal, through which he frequently stated his views to the public, as if he had never even considered for a moment the suggestion to forget that the Constitution had given him a partner in the treaty-making power. "What I am doing with San Domingo [*sic*]," he wrote, "is to negotiate a protocol or treaty, preferably the former, which I shall then lay before the Senate. If the Senate approves, it will then become part of the policy of the country. If it does not, we shall have to look on and see chaos develop for a few months or years until

[86] To Robert Bridges. Mar. 21, 1905. MS. Letterbook. Roosevelt Papers. Hay was sick at home during the critical days in January. In fact he was already eliminated by the illness from which he was to die a few months later so that Roosevelt was his own Secretary of State. Hay, in an official and hence less trustworthy letter, written several months after the event to explain away embarrassing facts, denied that the State Department knew anything about the agreement until it was signed. Cullom, pp. 387-388.

[87] Jan. 25, 1905. MS. Letterbook. Roosevelt Papers.

[88] *Foreign Relations, 1905*, pp. 313-314.

our hand is forced. The only difference between this negotiation and any other kind of negotiation is that with a country like San Domingo, where revolutions are threatened continually and where very sinister influences are at work, we have to be prepared to support the existing government in its proposal until the Senate has a chance to act upon it. . . . If Senator Teller is honest he has had a pipe dream." [89]

Others besides Senator Teller had been having "pipe dreams" and their number and vociferous denunciations offer the best explanation of the administration's conversion to the idea of consulting the Senate. The terms of the agreement that had been signed with the Dominican Republic on January 20, were promptly disclosed to the Dominican press and by that means reached some American newspapers as early as Saturday evening, January 21. Immediately the Senate accepted the challenge to its constitutional powers, which it saw in this attempt to make an international agreement without its consent. Naturally the lead in the public attack was taken by the Democrats who undoubtedly were glad to find additional material to support their accusations of autocratic and unconstitutional conduct on the part of the President. Early on Monday Senator Teller interrupted the regular business of the Senate by inserting in the *Record* a newspaper article about the agreement. In the course of his remarks he raised the cry of Executive usurpation. "I deny," he said, "the right of the executive department of the Government to make any contract, any treaty, any proto-

[89] To Albert F. Baldwin of *The Outlook,* Jan. 26, 1905. MS. Letterbook. Roosevelt Papers. Roosevelt, in his private letters, shared the public ignorance of the name of the Dominican Republic. The use of the word "protocol" may be significant. Some authorities have endeavored to distinguish between a treaty and a protocol by saying that the latter is used for unimportant and informal agreements but in practice the distinction breaks down. Certainly in the present case the terms of the agreement were of great and lasting importance. Inevitably the suspicion arises that Roosevelt and the State Department were using the term because of the precedent in the case of the "protocol" after the Boxer uprising in China. That international agreement was signed by the United States but was not submitted to the Senate, apparently on the theory that it did not obligate the United States to do anything except receive money.

col, or anything of that character which will bind the United States. . . . The President has no more right and no more authority to bind the people of the United States by such an agreement than I have as a member of this body." [90] The organized Democratic attack was initiated on the same day in the form of a resolution which recited the newspaper accounts and called upon the President for information.[91] Under the rules of the Senate the resolution "went over" to the next day when Senator Lodge moved that it be referred to the Committee on Foreign Relations and a general discussion occurred. The keynote of the Democratic comments was sounded by Senator Bacon, who had introduced the resolution, when he said, "I do not think there can be any more important question than that which involves the consideration of the powers of the President to make a treaty which shall virtually take over the affairs of another government and seek to administer them by this Government, without submitting that question to the consideration and judgment of the Senate." [92]

The position of the Republican senators was decidedly embarrassing and those who participated in the debate revealed the stress of their conflicting loyalties to the Senate as a body and to the President as their party leader. In general they supported Lodge's motion to refer the resolution to the Committee on Foreign Relations where their majority could, and did, safely bury it. At the same time several eased their senatorial consciences, and incidentally warned the President, by professing to believe that the newspaper accounts were false. Thus Senator Foraker asserted, "I do not imagine the President has undertaken to exercise the treaty-making power without consulting the Senate of the United States." [93] In secret session

[90] *Congressional Record,* Jan. 23, 1905, p. 1227.

[91] *Ibid.,* p. 1244.

[92] *Ibid.,* Jan. 24, 1905, p. 1281. For other Democratic resolutions, see *ibid.,* Jan. 25, 1905, p. 1330 and Feb. 13, 1905, p. 2451.

[93] *Ibid.,* Jan. 24, 1905, p. 1284. The consternation of the Chairman of the Committee on Foreign Relations is apparent from his account of his visit to the State Department for enlightenment. Cullom, p. 387.

they could criticize the President frankly without the same political risks and Senator Spooner, who was to be the leading defender of Roosevelt's later actions, did so in unambiguous words, "I do not know," he said, "who informed the correspondent that I had, in secret session, resented the Dillingham-Sanchez protocol, which guaranteed the territorial integrity of Santo Domingo, without any reference to ratification, and to take effect in so short a time as to preclude, considering the distance between the two countries, an intention to submit it to the Senate; but whoever told it told the truth, because I am frank to say I regarded it as an attempt to do a thing which the Executive Department or its agents had no power to do, it being, in my opinion, clearly a treaty matter."[94]

Such sentiment even among the administration's supporters seemed to be effective, for it was on the day following the public debate mentioned that the State Department instructed its representative to have the agreement changed so as to provide for its submission to the Senate. In doing this Roosevelt was deferring to public as well as to senatorial opinion. On this occasion more conspicuously than on any of the other conflicts between the President and the Senate the newspapers were generally opposing Roosevelt. Like the debate in the Senate the journalistic comments were devoted chiefly to the constitutional relations of the President and the Senate and not to the wisdom of this new application of the Monroe doctrine. Even the New York *Times,* which at first went to the length of saying, "If it appears that the President has seen his way to doing, without consulting the Senate, a patriotic and needful work, which there is every reason to believe the Senate would have obstructed if it had had the opportunity, the people will rejoice," later reversed its position and spoke of "serious violation of law and Constitution" and of the obligation of the Senate to take notice of it.[95]

[94] *Congressional Record,* Jan. 23, 1906, p. 1426.

[95] New York *Times,* Jan. 28, Feb. 4 and 12, 1905. For typical criticisms of the administration policy see the Boston *Transcript,* Feb. 9 and 13, 1905; the

The new protocol, signed on February 7, 1905, which provided it was not to go into effect until approved by the Senate, included several other changes to make it more acceptable to the Senate and the public. The important alterations were the substitution of a promise to respect the territorial integrity of the Dominican Republic in place of the former guarantee of its integrity; the change in the provision by which the United States had agreed " to undertake the adjustment " of all the Dominican debt to the less binding agreement to " attempt the adjustment " of them; and the insertion in the preamble of a sentence explaining that the United States was acting because it would view " any attempt on the part of the governments outside of this hemisphere to oppress or control the destiny of the Dominican Republic as a manifestation of an unfriendly disposition toward the United States." [96] On February 15, Roosevelt sent this protocol, as he still called it, to the Senate with a vigorous message in which he based his policy on the necessity of upholding the Monroe doctrine.[97] The submission of the treaty to the Senate constituted, as a contemporary newspaper remarked, " a distinct triumph for that body in the contest it was forced to undertake for the maintenance of its Constitutional rights." [98]

Once the treaty was in the hands of the Senate Roosevelt's struggle with the Senate over his Dominican policy entered upon its second phase. In the first battle of the new contest the President's senatorial opponents were again to be victorious, but Roosevelt outmaneuvered them and ultimately won. It could hardly be expected that the Senate would reach a decision on so far-reaching a proposal as the Dominican treaty in the last two weeks of an expiring Congress. But Roosevelt immediately called the Senate into special session to confirm some appointments and to consider the treaty. From March 4 until it ad-

Denver *News*, Feb. 4, 1905; the Chicago *Tribune*, Mar. 4, 1905. See also, *The Literary Digest*, XXX, 157 (Feb. 4, 1905).

[96] *Foreign Relations, 1905*, pp. 342-343.

[97] *Ibid.*, pp. 334-342.

[98] New York *Times*, Feb. 18, 1905.

journed on March 18, the Senate devoted itself almost exclusively to the Dominican agreement. Because its sessions were secret and because the *Executive Journal* has not yet been published exact and detailed knowledge of what was done is impossible, but from other sources the main outline of events can easily be established. On March 10, the Committee on Foreign Relations, by what was reported to be a strictly party vote, recommended that the treaty be approved with a number of amendments.[99] "On the 15th," a well informed journal stated, "the Republican leaders told Mr. Roosevelt that the treaty would be rejected if it should be pressed to a vote. He was not disposed to withdraw it, but preferred postponement until the regular session. He reluctantly agreed with his advisers that the vote should be deferred; rejection, in his judgment, would seem to give notice to European creditors that we decline to take measures for the settlement of Dominican debts and would open the way for action by them."[100] This policy was adopted and the Senate adjourned without taking a vote on the treaty.

There can be no doubt that political opposition was responsible for the failure to muster a two-thirds vote in favor of the treaty. The suggestion, made by at least one newspaper, that the hostility to the treaty arose from the administration's attempt to ignore the Senate in the first agreement, was supported by a Democratic senator who asserted that "the views of the President regarding the Senate as a factor in the treaty-making power might well deter us from the acceptance of his policy."[101] But the affront influenced only the Democrats and

[99] Cullom, p. 391. *The Outlook,* LXXIX, 668 (Mar. 18, 1905), said one of the amendments omitted the reference in the preamble to the Monroe doctrine, which had been inserted at the suggestion of the State Department to secure additional support for the treaty. See also the Boston *Transcript* of March 11, and the Baltimore *Sun* of Mar. 11 and 19, 1905.

[100] *The Independent,* LVIII, 632 (Mar. 23, 1905).

[101] New York *Times,* Mar. 17, 1905. Francis G. Newlands, "The San Domingo Question," *North American Review,* CLXXX, 887 (June 1905).

accordingly political motives must be considered the dominant ones. On this last point the evidence is overwhelming. The newspapers and periodicals agreed that the Senate was divided on party lines. As one explained the situation, "With three seats vacant and two Senators disabled by indictment, 57 votes were required, and the Republicans could supply only 54. It had been expected that at least three Democrats would stand by the treaty, but in the course of the debate it was ascertained that the Democrats would oppose it without a break in their ranks." [102] Evidence from senatorial sources is to the same effect.[103] Roosevelt, who naturally knew the exact situation in the Senate, testified with great and bitter emphasis that partisanship was responsible. Through Congressman Babcock he informed the public of his indignation at the "drawing of party lines" in dealing with a treaty.[104] During the period when the arbitration treaties were being emasculated in the Senate Roosevelt had written to Hay, "I am getting to take your view of the Senate." [105] He was now to equal Hay's extreme denunciation in a letter to Joseph Bucklin Bishop. After asserting that "the worst thing the Senate did this year—the failure to confirm the Santo Domingo treaty—was due to the fact that the

[102] *The Independent,* LVIII, 632 (Mar. 23, 1905). Chicago *Tribune,* Mar. 16, 1905. St. Louis *Globe-Democrat,* Mar. 11, 20, 1905. The Portland *Oregonian* thought that "It would be interesting to know just what the Democrats would have done if the Santo Domingo treaty had been proposed by a Democratic President." Mar. 16, 1905.

[103] The best evidence is, of course, the subsequent caucus on this treaty and the official vote on the third Dominican agreement two years later. In 1905 it was evident in the open debates over resolutions seeking information and defending the Senate against "Executive usurpation" that the Democrats were opposing the treaty. See also Coolidge, *Orville H. Platt,* pp. 578-579. Senator Depew was quoted in the New York *Times* as saying, "The Democrats killed the treaties." Mar. 26, 1905.

[104] *The Nation,* LXXX, 237 (Mar. 30, 1905).

[105] Jan. 28, 1905. MS. Letterbook. Roosevelt Papers. To W. C. Tiffany he wrote, "It will indeed be an infamy if a minority of the Senate, from purely partisan reasons," rejects the treaty. Mar. 14, 1905. MS. *ibid.*

Democratic party as such went solidly against us," he continued in terms which reveal the full extent of his anger:

There is of course additional friction for which the Republican members cannot be held guiltless. Their attitude on the arbitration treaties represented the overwhelming feeling of the Senate, a feeling which is unjustifiable, but which is encouraged by men like Wayne MacVeagh and others and not rebuked with any emphasis by the outside public. This feeling is in effect that the Senate should exercise the chief part in dealing with foreign affairs. Now, as a matter of fact the Senate is wholly incompetent to take such part. Creatures like Bacon, Morgan, et cetera, backed by the average yahoo among the Democratic Senators, are wholly indifferent to national honor or national welfare. They are primarily concerned in getting a little cheap reputation among ignorant people, and in addition it is but fair to say that they are perhaps themselves too ignorant and too silly to realize the damage they are doing. Unfortunately, they often receive aid and comfort from men like Spooner and Hale—one of whom invariably uses his ingenuous mind to put in meticulous and usually slightly improper amendments to every treaty, and the other is very apt to criticize all the important steps of the administration. Both ultimately support the administration, but meanwhile they stir up opposition to it and give to Bacon, Carmack and their kind, arguments which they are too witless to develop for themselves. The result is what we see in the San Domingan matter. After infinite thought and worry and labor, with Root, Taft and Hay as my chief advisers, I negotiated a treaty which would secure a really satisfactory settlement from every standpoint of the San Domingan matter. Hale sneers at it in a speech. Spooner, with the aid of Foraker, puts in amendments which seem to justify the Democratic criticisms and which make it look as if they were adopting an apologetic attitude on the part of the administration. Mischievous monkeys like Wayne MacVeagh go about wagging their heads and furnishing arguments to the dull, silly, professional Democratic journals like the New York *World* and most of the southern papers. The result is that by a narrow margin we find ourselves without the necessary two-thirds vote in the Senate for confirming the treaties. The Senate adjourns. I am left to shoulder all the responsibility due to their failure. Bacon, Morgan, Carmack and company go off, hoping that disaster will come to the country because the Republican administration will thereby be discredited. Spooner and Foraker go away entirely self-satisfied, not feeling any sense of responsibility, and indeed not thinking about the matter at all; although they have been yelling that the Senate is part of the treaty-making power. Meanwhile I have to take all the steps and have to spend an industrious summer engaged in the pleasant task of making diplomatic bricks without straw. The Senate ought to feel that its action on the treaty-making power should be much like that of the President's veto over legislation. In other words, it should be rarely used, and the presumption should always be against every amendment. A man of Spooner's mind or of Hale's mind is a curse from the standpoint of getting things accomplished in matters affecting foreign affairs; but at the same time we must not forget that the Bacon, Morgan, Carmack type is a thousand-fold worse.[106]

A partisan minority in the Senate had apparently defeated another treaty. It is true that by not allowing a vote to be taken the Republican leaders had prevented an absolute rejection and thus had kept the treaty alive. Yet the spark of life in it was dim and flickering, for postponement under the circumstances seemed to be the equivalent of rejection. So it appeared to Senator Cullom who subsequently wrote, "It was thought that nothing more would be heard of the Santo Domingo protocol." [107]

Then followed an amazing event. Like many others Senator Cullom underestimated Roosevelt's resourcefulness and perseverance when fighting for a policy close to his heart. He defied the Senate a second time and put into effect at once a new agreement with the Dominican Republic. The new agreement, this time called a *modus vivendi,* was to be temporary, ending when the United States Senate should act on the protocol of February 1905. Under it the United States was not to take charge of the Dominican customs, but that service was to be rendered by men nominated by the President of the United States and appointed by the President of the Dominican Republic. The portion of the revenue intended for the creditors of the Dominican government was to remain in a New York

[106] Mar. 23, 1905. MS. *ibid.* The first portion of this letter, not quoted above, is printed by Bishop in his *Theodore Roosevelt and His Time,* I, 432-433. Inevitably one wonders why this letter was written. Was it merely an expression of natural bitterness, or was it another of those letters to "history" which Roosevelt left to influence the opinion of posterity? Was it an attempt to reach the public through the editor of the New York *Globe?*

[107] Cullom, p. 391.

bank until the Senate's decision on the treaty would permit its distribution or force its return to the Dominican Republic.[108] Essentially, the new *modus vivendi* contained the same policy and the same objectives as those in the treaty which the Senate had not yet approved. Roosevelt later acknowledged the identity of the two agreements, in fact he rather boasted of it. In his Autobiography he described his action by saying, " I went ahead and administered the proposed treaty anyhow, considering it as a simple agreement on the part of the Executive which would be converted into a treaty whenever the Senate acted." [109]

No hint of these later claims was given at the time. Then the President attempted to make his action appear as unlike defiance of the Senate as possible. In official statements Roosevelt explained that his arrangement was necessary, " pending the action of the United States Senate upon the treaty, to the end that in the meantime no change shall take place in the situation which would render useless its consummation or bring complications into its enforcement." [110] In other words foreign intervention or, as was more probable, a revolution in the Dominican Republic might make it impossible to execute the treaty even if the Senate should finally consent to it. This reasoning was based on the assumption that the Senate had not had time in which to reach a decision or at least had refused to render a decision.[111] The assumption had no validity in fact. If the Senate had failed to give its verdict, it did so not because of lack of time but because the Republican leaders, in consulta-

[108] *Foreign Relations, 1905*, pp. 360-366.

[109] P. 511. To an English friend he wrote in 1908, " In Santo Domingo, after two years delay I got the Senate to ratify the treaty I had made (and under which, incidentally, I have been acting for two years)." Bishop, II, 130.

[110] *Foreign Relations, 1905*, p. 360. This letter to the Acting Secretary of State was not for his information but for that of the public, and was immediately given to the newspapers. New York *Times*, Mar. 29, 1905.

[111] In his annual message of December 5, 1905, Roosevelt reiterated the idea. " In the meantime a temporary arrangement has been made which will last until the Senate has had time to take action upon the treaty." *Congressional Record*, Dec. 5, 1905, p. 98.

tion with Roosevelt, decided to prevent a vote which they knew would be contrary to their wishes. On the theory Roosevelt advanced it would be possible to put a treaty into effect for years while a majority of less than two-thirds prevented an adverse vote. Roosevelt's conduct was made more vulnerable to hostile criticism by his use of the navy to keep in office the Dominican government which had negotiated the treaty. Any doubts of his constitutional power to do such a thing were easily brushed aside. " I intend," he wrote, " to keep the island in *statu quo* until the Senate has had time to act on the treaty, and I shall treat any revolutionary movement as an effort to upset the *modus vivendi.* That this is ethically right, I am dead sure, even though there may be some technical or red tape difficulty." [112] Others were not so sure of the ethics involved and interpreted Roosevelt's action as proof of his intention to put his policy into effect despite the Senate. In fact his own Secretary of the Navy, who should have been indoctrinated with the official explanation, so interpreted events, for in a letter urging the recall of one naval vessel, he said, ". . . both ships were allowed to remain so as to satisfy the native statesmen that the failure of Congress to ratify the treaty would not lead the government to abandon its interest in the island." [113]

Naturally Roosevelt understood that his acts, however disguised by soothing explanations, would arouse a storm of protest from the Democrats who had opposed the treaty. Intimations of a great storm were given in interviews with them and in editorial comments, when the *modus vivendi* was announced.[114] Yet when the storm broke in the Congress that met

[112] Bishop, I, 434.

[113] Charles J. Bonaparte to Roosevelt. Aug. 7, 1906. MS. Letterbook. Bonaparte Papers. He went on to say, " This conviction has unquestionably been impressed on the intelligent minds of these eminent, though dusky, personages by this time, and there seems to be no good reason why the *Yankee* should not come home." Roosevelt later modified his attitude on this point. Howard C. Hill, *Roosevelt and the Caribbean,* pp. 165-166.

[114] Among the more vigorous statements was that of Senator Morgan who said, " This so-called modus vivendi seems to be a soft euphemism to ease the Presi-

in the following December it was a comparatively mild affair. So much time had elapsed that the issue was smouldering instead of burning fiercely. Also, the success of the temporary arrangement was undeniable. The President was, of course, denounced for violating the Constitution and usurping authority, but all the denunciation came from Democrats and it lacked fire. The Republican senators professed to see no invasion of the Senate's powers in the President's action and defended his course with more vigor than his critics employed in their attack. The previous division on the treaty had made the Dominican problem a party matter. Moreover, Roosevelt had made sure of Republican support before he concluded the *modus vivendi.* That he was uneasy about even staunch Republicans, when the powers of the Senate were at issue, is shown by his comments in a letter to Hay. "There has been," he wrote, "a rather comic development in the Santo Domingo case. . . . I decided to do so, but first of all consulted Spooner, Foraker, Lodge and Knox. All heartily agreed that it was necessary for me to take this action. Rather to my horror Taft genially chaffed them about going back on their principles as to the 'usurpation of the executive.' But they evidently took the view that it was not a time to be over-particular about trifles." [115]

The lead in defending the President was taken by Senator Spooner, whose "ingenuous mind" and "meticulous" amendments had angered Roosevelt during the previous session. His several speeches and the opposing speech of Senator Bacon of Georgia constitute one of the most thorough and fundamental considerations ever given to the constitutional relations of President and Senate in the conduct of foreign relations. Spooner's attempt to deny that the unratified treaty was being executed through the *modus vivendi* was hardly worthy of the occasion and now appears absurd because of Roosevelt's words

dent into execution of his illegal purposes until the Senate can decide to ratify all that he has done. . . ." Baltimore *Sun,* Mar. 30, 1905. For a typical editorial warning of the storm to come see the Boston *Transcript* of April 1, 1905.

[115] Bishop, I, 433.

to the contrary, but on the theoretical constitutional question his argument was a scholarly presentation of the dominant view. In this he was supported by Senator Lodge who insisted on "the absolute power of the President to initiate and carry on all negotiations." "There is no doubt," the latter continued with reckless disregard for the future, "that the Senate can by resolution advise the President to enter upon a negotiation, or advise the President to refrain from a negotiation; but those resolutions have no binding force whatsoever, and the action of the Senate becomes operative and actually effective only when a treaty is actually submitted to it. We have no possible right to break suddenly into the middle of a negotiation and demand from the President what instructions he has given to his representative. That part of treaty making is no concern of ours." [116]

Constitutional debates of even the highest type do not always affect the voting and the Democrats maintained their lines against the treaty. When signs of wavering appeared they held a party caucus on the subject and adopted a resolution stating that "the Senate ought not to advise and consent to the treaty," and that "if two-thirds of this caucus shall vote in favor of the foregoing resolution, it shall be the duty of every Democratic Senator to vote against the ratification of the said treaty." [117] The adoption of that resolution in a party caucus

[116] *Congressional Record,* Jan. 24, 1906, p. 1470. Bacon's main speech of Feb. 6, can be found on pp. 2125-2148, and Spooner's on pp. 1417-1431. See also debates of Dec. 15, 1905, pp. 433-436 and on Jan. 17, 1906, pp. 1173-1180. Spooner's efforts won him the following note from Roosevelt. "That was a magnificent speech of yours. I congratulate you upon it and thank you for it. Do let me see you soon." Jan. 24, 1905. MS. Letterbook. Roosevelt Papers. Roosevelt's own constitutional views were extraordinary. "The Constitution did not explicitly give me power to bring about the necessary agreement with Santo Domingo. But the Constitution did not forbid my doing what I did." *Autobiography,* p. 510.

[117] *Congressional Record,* Feb. 5, 1906, p. 2054. The fact that a caucus had been held and the terms of the resolution it adopted were made public through the revolt of Senator Patterson. His criticism of his fellow Democrats and the verbal discipline he received at the hands of the Democratic leader, Senator Bailey, make amusing reading. *Ibid.,* Feb. 7, 1906, pp. 2207-2219.

makes unnecessary further proof that the treaty was meeting with political opposition. Spooner, forgetting the past record of his own party, was properly indignant at this introduction of politics into the consideration of a treaty. Writing to Senator Cullom he said, "As you will have read, Patterson made a speech in favor of the Santo Domingo treaty. The Democrats are very angry. Morgan has indicated a disposition to vote for it; I am told that Rayner has, Foster, Clarke, and perhaps one or two others, but the Democrats held a caucus Saturday, and expect through the two-thirds rule which they adopted at the last session, and claim now to be still in force, to line their men against the treaty, or to exclude some of them from Democratic society. It is a sinister and ugly thing to caucus on foreign relations. . . ." [118]

The President also revealed a short memory. He had turned to his usual channels for guiding public opinion and for bringing pressure to bear on the senatorial opposition. To Lyman Abbott he had previously suggested the desirability of pointing out that the Democrats were opposing the treaty "simply because I happen to be a Republican President," and because they "think they can score a point against the administration." [119] The news of the Democratic caucus produced an angrier letter to a leading "muckraker," then at the height of his influence. "There has been," Roosevelt wrote

> no more striking betrayal of the people in Congress since I have been President than the action just taken by the Democratic caucus in the Senate about the Santo Domingo treaty. All honor is due to the two or three Democratic Senators who have stood by their convictions and the interests of the nation in this matter; and no condemnation can be too severe for those who, under the lead of Messrs. Bacon, Bailey, Tillman and Company, without a particle of conviction, but in a spirit of the narrowest factional partisanship, and with not merely a willingness but an eagerness to sacrifice the interests of the public to the favored interests of a faction, have voted to reject the treaty.[120]

---

[118] Feb. 5, 1906. MS. Spooner Papers.

[119] Dec. 14, 1905. MS. Letterbook. Roosevelt Papers.

[120] To Lincoln Steffens. Feb. 6, 1905. MS. *ibid.*

Roosevelt made no further special efforts to get this treaty ratified. His policy was already in effect because of the *modus vivendi* and the best strategy was to rely on its success and on time. Indeed, in the face of the Democratic opposition there was nothing else he could do. The treaty never was voted on and thus joined the number that had fallen in political battle.

The treaty, not Roosevelt, was defeated. On Feb. 8, 1907, a new agreement with the Dominican Republic was signed. It contained some significant changes from the former treaty. All references to the Monroe doctrine were omitted. It included no promise to respect the territorial integrity of the Dominican Republic, a clause open to the objection that " respect " might be interpreted as " guarantee." It did not obligate the United States to assist in preserving order, or to interfere in domestic affairs except for the collection of the customs. Nor did it pledge the United States to undertake the adjustment of the Dominican debt.[121] Although these significant provisions were missing, the new treaty still embodied the essentials of Roosevelt's program. Nevertheless, the Senate accepted it with startling alacrity. Just seventeen days after the signatures had been affixed the Senate gave its approval to the new treaty.

An analysis of the vote reveals that it was the willingness of three Democratic senators to break party ranks that saved the treaty. Two of them joined with forty-one Republicans to cast the forty-three votes in favor of the treaty, while the third united with the seventeen Republicans who were paired for the treaty. Nineteen Democrats voted against the treaty and nine were paired against it.[122] The Republican majority was so large that the addition of the three Democrats sufficed to secure the

[121] *Foreign Relations, 1907*, pp. 307-309.

[122] The injunction of secrecy was removed from the proceedings and the vote was published in the *Congressional Record,* Feb. 25, 1907, p. 3917. Through a mistake on Senator Beveridge's part he did not respect his pair with the Democratic Senator Clark of Montana who was listed as not voting. But for this error the vote would have been still closer. Clark and Beveridge later made a public explanation. *Ibid.,* Mar. 3, 1907, pp. 4571-4572.

necessary two-thirds majority. Even so the other Democrats could easily have prevented a vote in that session, which ended only a week later, but it was evident that their earlier ardor for this fight was gone. It may have been that several of them with political fences needing repair feared the effects of an extra session.[123] More plausible as an explanation of their conduct was the successful operation of the *modus vivendi* and the acquiescence of the public in that policy. Roosevelt repeatedly asserted that the public was indifferent to the whole affair, despite its importance, and cited that fact as the reason it took him two years to win the Senate's consent.[124] That same public indifference may well have induced the same attitude in the Democratic senators by convincing them that no political capital was to be gained in continuing their opposition.

Whatever the explanation, the episode remains a remarkable triumph for the President. It is true that he had been forced to abandon hastily the original plan to make an agreement without consulting the Senate. It is true that the first treaty to reach the Senate died there. It is true that the final treaty was radically modified because of senatorial criticism. Nevertheless, the ratification of that treaty, containing a new and important foreign policy, was a triumph and under the circumstances was remarkable. In his first agreement and in his *modus vivendi* Roosevelt had defied the treaty-making power of the Senate and had trampled on senatorial susceptibilities in a way that would normally have resulted in the most irreconcilable opposition. Yet he not only managed to secure and keep the support of senators of his own party but he even broke the resistance of his political opponents.

With this victory Roosevelt's struggles with the Senate over the treaty-making power were ended.[125] The presidency he

[123] Stephenson, *Aldrich,* p. 324.

[124] See letters to Taft, Aug. 21, 1907, to J. St. Loe Strachey, Feb. 12, 1906. MSS, Letterbook. Roosevelt Papers. The same point is made in a letter to Lodge. Lodge, *Selections,* II, 123.

[125] A number of other treaties negotiated by Roosevelt's administration failed

turned over to Taft had been greatly enhanced in power and prestige. In spite of his stronger initial position Taft met with misfortune and rebuffs where Roosevelt had found only success and popularity. Nevertheless, his experience with defeated treaties curiously paralleled Roosevelt's. The general arbitration treaties he sponsored were blocked by the Senate as those of his predecessor had been. The treaties providing for financial supervision over Caribbean countries were defeated by the Senate yet in the most important instance he contrived to put the policy into effect as Roosevelt had done in the case of the Dominican Republic.

On August 3, 1911, identical arbitration treaties with Great Britain and France were signed by the United States. In standing sponsor for these treaties, which were to be the models for agreements with other governments, Taft was both consummating his own desire to substitute judicial process for war and responding to a widespread public demand. The participants in the peace movement who had supported Olney's general arbitration treaty in 1897 and who had applauded and stimulated the efforts of Roosevelt, had not been dismayed by meager results. They rallied enthusiastically on behalf of Taft's treaties so that it was evident that the articulate part of the public hoped to see them speedily ratified. Newspapers, periodicals, and

to be ratified. These were multilateral treaties relating to codes of international law (Jan. 27, 1902), the learned professions (Jan. 27, 1902), extradition (Jan. 28, 1902), patents (Aug. 23, 1906), international prize court (Oct. 18, 1907 and Sept. 19, 1910), and copyright (Nov. 13, 1908). The Senate took no action on any of these except that on the subject of a prize court, which was approved with an amendment. The amendment, however, had nothing to do with the subsequent failure of the treaty to be ratified. Several other multilateral treaties failed during the period covered by this chapter. They dealt with obscene publications (May 4, 1910), the international time association (Oct. 25, 1913), and the protection of nature (Nov. 19, 1913). The first two of these were approved with amendments. The third was never acted on. Clearly in some of these cases, and perhaps in all of them, the action or non-action of the Senate was not responsible for the ultimate failure of the treaties. Certainly neither political considerations nor the constitutional struggle with the President was involved.

senators, whose hostility made them reluctant but trustworthy witnesses, all gave testimony of that fact.[126]

The treaties deserved in some respects the public approval they evoked, for they proposed a wider and more effective use of arbitration than had been suggested in earlier attempts. Disregarding the practice of eliminating from the subjects to be arbitrated such inclusive and vague disputes as those affecting national honor, these treaties provided for the arbitration of all differences "justiciable in their nature by reason of being susceptible of decision by the application of the principles of law or equity."[127] Moreover, they provided for a Joint High Commission of Inquiry to make advisory reports on non-justiciable disputes and to decide whether or not disputes were justiciable. In cases where the two parties could not agree as to the applicability of judicial processes to the dispute the Commission was

[126] Senatorial admissions of the popularity of the treaties can be found in the *Congressional Record,* Feb. 8, 1912, p. 1835; Feb. 29, 1912, p. 2598; Mar. 6, 1912, p. 2865; Mar. 7, 1912, p. 2944. See also Lodge's letter to Roosevelt. Lodge, *Selections,* II, 419. Roosevelt assumed the leadership in attacking the treaties outside of the Senate. *The Outlook,* XCIX, 66-70 (Sept. 9, 1911). The editor of *The Outlook* disagreed with his contributing editor and remained loyal to the Roosevelt policy of 1905. The battle between the editors in the columns of *The Outlook* occcasioned many comments in the newspapers and judging by them the editor believed that "the country overwhelmingly supports the treaty in question." *Ibid.,* p. 148 (Sept. 23, 1911). Editorial comments taken from the *Literary Digest* and *Current Literature* can be found in Fleming, pp. 99-101. The optimism of some of the leaders in the peace movement makes ludicrous reading now. For instance in his opening address at the Lake Mohonk Conference on International Arbitration in 1911, Nicholas Murray Butler said, "Never before has the mind of the world been so occupied with the problems of substituting law for war, peace with righteousness for triumph after slaughter, the victories of right and reasonableness for those of might and brute force. . . . The long years of patient argument and exhortation and of painstaking instruction of public opinion in this and other countries are bearing fruit in full measure." *International Conciliation,* Document No. 43, p. 3. The American Association for International Conciliation, which published this pamphlet, printed and distributed others while the treaties were pending.

[127] The two treaties were printed as *62d Cong., 1st sess., S. Doc.,* Nos. 91 and 92.

to consider it and if five of the six members—three having been appointed by each country—should decide it was a justiciable question, then it was to be referred to arbitration. No matter by whom the decision to arbitrate was made there was to be a special agreement in each case defining the powers of the arbitrators, the questions at issue and other matters of procedure and these special agreements had to receive the advice and consent of the Senate. This last provision, which meant that the treaty was an agreement to make a second treaty, represented a surrender to the senatorial position in the hope that apprehension about constitutional prerogatives would not block this move for the peaceful settlement of disputes.

The precaution proved to be futile, however, since the Senate found a threat to its treaty-making power in the provision giving the Commission authority to decide whether or not a dispute was justiciable. The majority report from the Committee on Foreign Relations stated the argument clearly: "A special agreement, coming to the Senate after the joint commission had decided the question involved to be justiciable, could not be amended or rejected by the Senate on the ground that in their opinion the question was not justiciable. . . . By this clause the constitutional powers of the Senate are taken away *pro tanto* and are transferred to a commission, upon the composition of which the Senate has no control whatever. . . . To take from the Senate, in any degree or by any means, the power of saying whether a given question is one for arbitration or not is to destroy the power of the Senate on the most important point to be decided in connection with differences arising with any other nation. Even if it were constitutional, to deprive the Senate to this extent of their share in the treaty-making power would be most unwise and most perilous." [128] Accordingly the report recommended that the provision be eliminated from the treaty. It was on this point that the attack of the Committee on Foreign Relations centered.

[128] *62d Cong., 1st sess., S. Doc.,* No. 98. The minority reports of Senators Root and Cullom, Republicans, of Burton, also a Republican, and of the Democratic Senator Rayner are in this same document.

Taft answered this argument in the speeches he made while touring the country to arouse public sentiment for his treaties.[129] However successful he may have been with the public, his reasoning did not persuade the Senate and it was the danger to the power of the Senate that one senator after another stressed as the major objection to the treaties. The arguments used are readily available since the treaty was considered in open executive session, the second to be so considered and the first since the defeated fisheries treaty of 1888. Consequently the debates were printed in full in the *Congressional Record* and they show that the defense of the Senate's prerogatives was the central theme of the discussion.[130] The publicity of the proceedings afforded opportunities for speeches of the type that have been used for political ends. Thus the Democratic Senator Hitchcock and the Republican Senator Heyburn found it advisable to denounce the entangling alliance with Great Britain which they saw lurking in the treaty.[131] But no political capital was to be gained by defending the Senate's powers against a popular measure so that the frequent reiteration of that thought was almost certainly an expression of the sincere views of the speakers.

Although the overwhelming majority of the Senate agreed on the necessity of altering the treaties to preserve the Senate's complete freedom of action, there was a difference of opinion as to the most desirable means to that end. The Committee on Foreign Relations had recommended the elimination of the offensive provision. Deferring to the wishes of some of the Republican senators, Lodge abandoned the Committee's recommendation and urged that the treaty be amended indirectly by a

[129] He spoke in Boston on Aug. 3, in Ocean Grove, N. J., on Aug. 15, in Rochester on Aug. 23, in Hartford on Sept. 7. The newspapers of those or the following dates reported his speeches. His article, "The Dawn of World Peace," in the *Woman's Home Companion* of November, 1911, was a clear statement of the conflict with the Senate and a strong appeal to the women of America.

[130] *Congressional Record, 62d Cong., 2d sess.,* pp. 646, 1062, 2602, 2820, 2829, 2866, 2949, 2951.

[131] *Ibid.,* pp. 647, 2824, 2943.

ratifying resolution which would state, as he wrote Roosevelt, "that we understand it to mean what it does not mean."[132] To Lodge the method used was a matter of detail, although he warned the Senate that the more drastic process of striking out portions of the treaties would be more likely to prevent their ratification.[133] This consideration had little influence, for when the vote was taken the direct amendment of the Committee was adopted and the provision was dropped by the small majority of forty-two to forty.[134] Political affiliations determined the views of the senators, since an analysis of the vote shows that the majority was composed of thirty-six Democrats and six Republicans and that the minority consisted of thirty-seven Republicans and three Democrats. Politics was also the decisive factor in reaching another important decision, this time on an issue of policy and not merely of means to a desired end. By a vote of forty-six to thirty-six an amendment was added that excluded from the field of arbitration all questions concerning the admission of aliens into the United States, or the admission of aliens to educational institutions, or the territorial integrity of the States and of the United States, or the alleged indebtedness of any state, or the Monroe doctrine or other purely governmental policy. Thirty-nine Democrats and seven Republicans voted for this amendment. All of the thirty-six votes against it were cast by Republican senators. To what was left the Senate gave its advice and consent by a vote of seventy-six to three.[135]

As had been predicted Taft, seeing in the amended treaties retrogression rather than progress toward the peaceful settlement of international disputes, refused to renew the negotiations with Great Britain and France on the terms dictated by the Senate.

The speaking tour to arouse public opinion and thus to bring

[132] Lodge, *Selections,* II, 419-421. The resolution can be found in the *Congressional Record, 62d Cong., 2d sess.,* p. 943.

[133] *Ibid.,* p. 2883.

[134] *Ibid.,* p. 2953.

[135] *Ibid.,* pp. 2954-2955.

pressure to bear on the Senate had constituted the President's chief effort on behalf of the treaties. By nature not a forceful leader, Taft was further handicapped in his relations with the Senate by the split in his party and by the general atmosphere of failure attending his administration. Consequently the success of the Senate was easily won. After a mellowing lapse of time Taft described his experience good-naturedly. When the treaties reached the Senate, he wrote, " that august body truncated them and amended them and qualified them in such a way that their own father could not recognize them. . . . And since the treaties had really been framed as models, when they came back thus crippled and maimed, they were not very useful. So I put them on the shelf and let the dust accumulate on them in the hope that the Senators might change their minds, or that the people might change the Senate; instead of which they changed me." [136]

To the student of the operation of the treaty-making power the victory of the Senate over the President is illuminating. It revealed the deep and persistent hostility of the Senate to all general arbitration treaties because of the fear that its constitutional control over treaties might be restricted in some way. It showed again that the Senate was willing to disregard a strong wave of public opinion in the defense of its prerogatives. It demonstrated once more that on arbitration systems, which can only be established by means of treaties, the Senate would have the final word. It offered further proof of the tendency to partisan action in the Senate on treaties.

Because Taft's Caribbean policy could be partially applied without a formal international agreement, it met with greater success although the three treaties he made to further it were blocked by the Senate. The obscurity often surrounding recent events makes an investigation of the Senate's motives in this episode more than ever like groping in the dark for a black object. The other aspects of the transaction are reasonably clear.

[136] T. Marburg and H. C. Flack, editors, *Taft Papers on the League of Nations*, pp. 178-179.

One of the treaties was with Honduras and the other two were with Nicaragua. All were continuations of Roosevelt's Dominican policy, a policy of financial supervision and intervention which Taft's critics named "dollar diplomacy," but which his supporters claimed was essential for the prevention of chaos and for the preservation of the Monroe doctrine. The same policy continued by the Wilson administration in the case of Nicaragua led to a tentative agreement which the Senate refused to approve and finally to a treaty which was accepted although it contained approximately the same provisions as those of the second treaty Taft had negotiated.

The first of these treaties to reach the Senate was that signed with Honduras on January 10, 1911. In the course of time the debt of Honduras had accumulated to a face value of some $125,000,000, an amount which was uncollectable and on which interest was not being paid. Through the efforts of the Department of State an American banking house agreed to lend Honduras $10,000,000 which, because of the willingness of the bondholders to accept a fraction of the face value of their holdings, would have retired all the debt, paid all claims and provided $2,500,000 for needed internal improvements. The loan, however, was conditional upon the existence of a treaty between Honduras and the United States embodying safeguards regarded by the bankers as indispensable. Accordingly a treaty was negotiated providing that the loan was to be secured upon the customs of Honduras, that the tariff was not to be changed without the consent of the United States, that the customs were to be under the control of an official appointed by the government of Honduras from a list presented by the fiscal agent of the loan and approved by the President of the United States, and that this collector-general of the customs was to be protected in the performance of his duties first by Honduras and secondly by the United States at its discretion.[187]

[187] *Foreign Relations, 1912*, pp. 560-562. Taft's long message of transmittal expounding the relations of the agreement to the Caribbean policy of the United States and the further statement by the Secretary of State are in the same volume, pp. 555-560, 568-572.

Such were the terms of the treaty which, the President assured the Senate, would restore order in a region vital to the interests of the United States and would forestall foreign intervention. The likelihood of achieving these ends was diminished materially a few days after Taft informed the Senate of his negotiations because the Honduran Congress rejected the convention by an overwhelming majority.[138] Notwithstanding this action and the assertions of its finality by the Honduran government, the Taft administration again and again entreated the Senate in the name of the Monroe doctrine to approve the treaty.[139] The appeals fell on deaf ears. Although the Committee on Foreign Relations twice reported the treaty favorably, a member of the Committee predicted its rejection because of the "party conviction" of the Democratic senators that the whole policy of guaranteeing debts should be abandoned and because of the reluctance of some Progressive Republican senators to grant favors "to Wall St." [140] Whatever the explanation, no action was ever taken on the treaty by the Senate. While it was still pending in the Senate, its fate had become merged with that of the more important loan convention made with Nicaragua.

The loan convention with Nicaragua, containing the identical provisions of the Honduran treaty, was signed on June 6, 1911.[141] During the previous year a revolution had been unsuccessful because the United States had established a "neutral zone" protecting the government and steps had been taken to eliminate the chief temptation to revolution and to restore financial stability by placing the customs under the control of the United States. A group of American bankers agreed to advance the $15,000,000 requested if the guarantees of the

[138] *Ibid.*, p. 562.

[139] *Ibid.*, pp. 573, 581, 583, 608, 610, 611, 1073, 1078, 1082.

[140] New York *Times*, June 10, 1911. No official records of the Senate are available but letters of the Secretary of State to members of the Committee on Foreign Relations stated that favorable reports had been made. *Foreign Relations, 1912*, pp. 581, 608, 610.

[141] *Ibid.*, pp. 1074-1075.

Honduran treaty were extended to them. When submitting this treaty to the Senate the President again explained the Caribbean policy of the United States and again invoked the name of the Monroe doctrine.[142]

The repetition of these arguments, urgent appeals from the Secretary of State and the speedy ratification of the convention by Nicaragua stimulated no response from the Senate and any favorable effect may have been counterbalanced by the news that the administration, the bankers and Nicaragua had initiated their program without waiting for the sanction of the Senate.[143] The administration had approved the appointment of the citizen of the United States who became collector-general of the customs, exactly as it would have done under the terms of the treaty, and had participated in the transaction in several other ways. This anticipatory execution of the treaty did not create a friendly atmosphere in the Senate where one was badly needed. In May 1912, a motion to report the Nicaraguan and Honduran treaties from the Committee on Foreign Relations failed by a tie vote, a result which a newspaper said meant the death of the treaties since it precluded any hope of getting a favorable two-thirds vote in the Senate.[144] The State Department refused to abandon hope so easily and a year later spoke of the treaties as still pending before the Senate.[145] But the journalist had interpreted the situation correctly. No action was ever taken by the Senate and the treaties were lost.

Before all hope of saving the Nicaraguan loan convention had been given up but after its defeat appeared probable, the Taft administration attempted to promote the Caribbean policy of the United States and to solve the most pressing of Nicaragua's financial problems by means of another treaty. The new bargain resulted from the peculiarly close relations that had been established with the government of Nicaragua. A revolution that had broken out in 1912 had been crushed by the land-

[142] *Ibid.*, pp. 1072-1074.

[143] *Ibid.*, pp. 1076-1092.

[144] New York *Times*, May 9, 1912.

[145] *Foreign Relations, 1913*, p. 1040.

ing of several thousand United States marines and other troops. The protection of the lives and property of United States citizens was not the only cause of this military intervention, as the State Department frankly informed the revolutionists that it would " discountenance any revival of Zelayaism and lend its strong moral support to the cause of legally constituted good government for the benefit of the people of Nicaragua." [146] The " legally constituted good government " thus kept in power by the United States naturally was on intimate terms with its protector. These led to the signing of a new treaty on February 8, 1913, by which the United States was to pay $3,000,000 for an option to construct a canal across Nicaragua, for the right to establish a naval base of the Gulf of Fonseca and for a ninety-nine year lease of Great and Little Corn Islands in the Caribbean.[147] Since this treaty reached the Senate in the last weeks of the Taft administration its chances of surviving were slight. Aside from the usual rush of business during the closing days of a Congress, the Democratic senators would insist that the whole question be kept open for the incoming Democratic administration. Ultimately the treaty shared the fate of the Nicaraguan and Honduran loan conventions, for the Senate never acted on it.

The evidence available for determining the nature of the successful senatorial hostility to these three treaties is slight in quantity and sometimes poor in quality, yet it all points to one conclusion. Senator Bacon, the senior Democratic member of the Committee on Foreign Relations, attacked the administration because of the military intervention in Nicaragua and because of the way in which the State Department had anticipated the ratification of the loan convention.[148] But the military

[146] *Foreign Relations, 1912*, p. 1043.

[147] Apparently the text of this treaty has never been officially published. There is a summary of it by George T. Weitzel, who signed it as the United States Minister to Nicaragua, in *64th Cong., 1st sess., S. Doc.*, No. 334, p. 10. See also *Foreign Relations, 1914*, p. 953.

[148] *Congressional Record*, Aug. 21, 1912, pp. 11430-11432.

intervention occurred more than a year after the first two treaties had reached the Senate and several months after the tie vote of the Committee on Foreign Relations, so that it could not have been responsible for the hostility of the Senate. According to contemporary newspaper and periodical comments the Senate refused to accept the treaties because of the objection of many of its members to "dollar diplomacy," which would make the United States government a partner of the lending bankers and the United States army and navy an agency for the collection of debts. However, the objection was felt only by Taft's political opponents. Without exception the journals agreed that the senators blocking the treaties were the Democrats and the Progressive Republicans who, in 1911 and 1912, were equally political opponents of Taft.[149] More authoritative evidence that the Democratic senators were primarily responsible can be found in a letter written by the new Secretary of State in 1913. Referring to the loan convention which in theory was still before the Senate Bryan wrote, "Senator Bacon tells me that the Democrats are nearly unanimous in opposing this treaty because they think it provides for an interference on our part in Nicaraguan affairs."[150] Accordingly the three treaties may properly be added to the list of those defeated by political divisions in the Senate.

Moreover, events were soon to demonstrate that party considerations determined the attitude of the Democratic senators, since they approved for the Democratic administration a treaty containing the same policy which they had successfully opposed when advocated by a Republican administration. In other ways, too, the subsequent efforts of the Wilson administration to continue the Taft Nicaraguan policy produced illuminating results. They first led to the rejection by the Senate of a draft treaty, for on this occasion the Senate was consulted before the proposed convention was signed. The senatorial veto of the

[149] For typical statements, see *The Outlook,* XCVIII, 857 (Aug. 19, 1911). New York *Times,* June 10, 1911; Dec. 3, 1911; May 9, 1912.

[150] Bryan to Woodrow Wilson. May 24, 1913. MS. Letterbook. Bryan Papers.

draft was equivalent to the defeat of a treaty, as the willingness of Nicaragua to make the agreement was certain. Indeed the important innovation, making this proposal different from the Taft canal treaty of February 1913, had been added at the request of the Nicaraguan government. It was not remarkable that the President of Nicaragua whose political life, and perhaps physical life as well, had been saved by the military intervention of the United States should have desired to incorporate the terms of the Platt Amendment in a treaty with the United States.[151] It was truly remarkable that the Secretary of State who accepted the suggestion to extend the control of the United States over an alien people should be Bryan, the anti-imperialistic crusader. This extraordinary development evoked comments of amazement from both foreign and domestic journalists.[152] They would have been even more astonished if they could have read a letter from Bryan to the President in which the Great Commoner revealed himself as a proponent of the practice of *realpolitik*. "While the Platt amendment provision," he wrote, "is asked for by the Nicaraguan government, and is intended for the benefit of that government, still I think that it is of advantage to us, in that it will give us the right to do that which we might be called upon to do anyhow. We cannot escape the responsibilities of our position, and this is an opportune time for us to secure the necessary treaty provision, as we can secure it at their request." [153]

[151] *Foreign Relations, 1911*, p. 670. *Ibid., 1914*, p. 953. The Platt Amendment, which would have made Nicaragua as much a protectorate of the United States as Cuba, provided among other things that the United States could intervene at its discretion to maintain a government adequate for the protection of life, property, and individual liberty.

[152] The New York *Times* of July 24, 1913, quoted the comment of the Paris *Temps* on Bryan's changed attitude. See also *The Outlook,* CIV, 725 (Aug. 2, 1913).

[153] Bryan to Wilson. June 12, 1914. MS. Letterbook. Bryan Papers. Astonishment would have turned to incredulity if they could have seen another letter of Bryan's to Wilson, for in it he rivaled Knox's solicitude for the interests of the bankers who had advanced money to Nicaragua in anticipation of the ratification

Appropriately the heartiest applause for Bryan came from the conservative Republican senators.[154] They and the Progressive Republicans remained for and against the policy as they had been during the previous administration. But the Democratic senators exhibited no dull and unchanging devotion to the position they had previously taken and for which they had advanced good reasons. The shift was not an easy one to accomplish and the Democrats who had successfully opposed the mild program proposed by Taft were placed in an embarrassing position when the new Democratic administration became more orthodox than the Papacy. In fact they refused to follow Bryan the full length of his strange path and thus compelled the abandonment of the proposed treaty. They had been given the opportunity to express their views without being forced into open rebellion against the administration, for Bryan had submitted his draft of the treaty to the Committee on Foreign Relations before signing the document.[155] Frequent conferences with the committee convinced the Secretary that the Platt Amendment provisions would not be accepted and he returned

of the treaty. Bryan to Wilson. Jan. 22, 1915. MS. *ibid.* It is apparent from Bryan's letters to Wilson that the Nicaraguan problem and policy were decided by the Secretary of State. Nevertheless, the President concurred, for in a letter to Bryan he wrote that "the proposed Nicaragua treaty [with the Platt Amendment] has my entire approval." June 19, 1913. MS. *ibid.* Wilson's official biographer offers the following explanation: "It is a significant commentary upon the implacable nature of the forces which, under the existing social and economic order, determine the foreign policies of states that both Bryan and the President, although opposed to everything that savoured of 'dollar diplomacy,' were thus irresistably forced into arrangements that did not differ greatly, in aggravated cases like that of Nicaragua, from those of Taft and Knox." Ray Stannard Baker, *Woodrow Wilson: Life and Letters,* IV, 438.

[154] New York *Times,* July 22, 1913.

[155] Bryan to Wilson, July 31, 1913; Jan. 23, 1914. MSS. Letterbook. Bryan Papers. Several secondary accounts state that a treaty, or an additional article was signed. These letters of the Secretary of State not only disclose the aversion of the Democratic senators to the Platt Amendment but also corroborate his official statement that no treaty had been signed. *Foreign Relations, 1914,* pp. 960, 963.

to the less objectionable program of his predecessor by signing another treaty with Nicaragua which contained essentially the same provisions as had been included in the Taft canal treaty of February 1913. Even this proved unpalatable to some in the Senate and pressure had to be applied in the interval between the signing of the new treaty on August 5, 1914, and its acceptance in amended form by the Senate on February 18, 1916.[156] An analysis of the vote casts some interesting light on the exercise of the treaty-making power. The Republican senators who voted divided almost equally, fifteen for the treaty and fourteen against it. The latter were nearly all Progressives. It was the Democrats who supplied the two-thirds majority, since forty gave their consent and only five voted against the treaty. The shift of the Democrats from hostility to all forms of the policy when proposed by a Republican administration to the support of one application of it when advocated by a Democratic President again makes clear the influence of partisan considerations in the making of treaties.

This episode gave Wilson one of the few opportunities he had before 1919 to supplement from his own experience his scholarly appreciation of the difficulties attending the exercise of the treaty-making power. The experience was not so instructive as it might have been, because the administration had ultimately obtained for a portion of its program the reluctant consent of the Senate and because the President had not made the affair his immediate and personal concern. Indeed, prior to 1919, the Senate's action in only one case might have impressed on Wilson the nature and strength of the forces which could block an important treaty in spite of his utmost efforts. This was the case of the treaty of 1914 with Colombia, which was subsequently accepted by the Senate when Harding was Presi-

[156] The treaty and the vote on it were published in the *Congressional Record* after it was approved. Feb. 18, 1916, p. 2770. Under date of Sept. 31 [sic], 1914, Bryan wrote Wilson requesting a special message or other pressure to overcome senatorial reluctance, and Wilson's reply of the next day said he had written to Senator Stone, the Democratic Chairman of the Committee on Foreign Relations. MSS. Bryan Papers.

dent. For reasons that will be pointed out, the treatment of the Colombian treaty did not serve as an object lesson to Wilson. Nor was he forewarned by the fate of the two treaties of his administration that met with permanent defeat at the hands of the Senate before 1919.

They were two of the thirty treaties for the advancement of peace that Bryan negotiated with so much enthusiasm. The Senate was clearly responsible for the loss of the treaty of September 20, 1913, with Panama and that of February 17, 1914, with the Dominican Republic.[157] No action was ever taken by the Senate on either treaty. Apparently the Senate believed that the relations of the United States with those two countries were of such a nature that it would be unwise to agree not to resort to force until a commission should report on the facts of a dispute. The

[157] All of the thirty Bryan treaties were printed with a long explanatory introduction by the Carnegie Endowment for International Peace. James B. Scott, *Treaties for the Advancement of Peace*. It is possible but not probable that the Senate may have been partially responsible for the loss of four more which the Senate amended and which the other country did not ratify. These four were with Salvador (Aug. 7, 1913), Nicaragua (Dec. 17, 1913), Persia (Feb. 4, 1914), and the Argentine Republic (July 24, 1914). However, there is no evidence that these countries refused to act favorably because of the Senate's amendments which made these treaties conform to the others by the elimination of an article requiring the maintenance of the military and naval *status quo* during the investigation of the dispute. In fact, the contrary seems to have been the case and reasons remote from the action of the Senate seem to have determined the result as they did in the instances of the treaties with Greece and Switzerland, which the Senate had approved without amendments. Another treaty made by Wilson's administration was amended by the Senate and never went into effect. But again the Senate cannot be charged with the responsibility. This was the International Convention Relating to Safety of Life at Sea, signed on Jan. 20, 1914. It was opposed by American labor organizations. *63d Cong., 2 sess., S. Doc.,* No. 463 and No. 476. At one time the British Ambassador believed the convention would be killed by the Senate "at the instance of an organized minority." Gwynn, II, 202. But it was approved with an amendment which had nothing to do with the ultimate failure of the treaty. One other Wilson treaty was amended by the Senate and was not ratified by the other party. This was a convention with Great Britain making the desertion of minor children an extraditable offense. Although it had been signed on Jan. 15, 1917, the Senate did not act until April 27, 1921, after the period covered in this study.

complete contemporary indifference to the fate of these two treaties makes it appear probable that neither politics nor a contest between the President and Senate influenced the Senate. The attention which was given to the Bryan peace treaties naturally centered on the large group that were ratified and even these received far less public notice than they would have if the World War had not begun two weeks before the Senate acted. Ironically the outbreak of the greatest of wars may have saved these treaties for the preservation of peace. When, on August 13, 1914, the Senate ratified the first group of eighteen Bryan treaties difficulty was experienced in obtaining a quorum. Had more senators been present, as they would have been if the treaties had been considered important, a two-thirds majority might have been impossible. As it was, the voting revealed partisan bias, for on the first and decisive test the forty-four votes to approve the treaty were cast by thirty-two Democrats and twelve Republicans, while all five negative votes came from Republican.[158] Certainly inconspicuousness saved the treaties from the experienced and skillful opposition of Senator Lodge who was so little interested in them that he stayed away from Washington that summer.[159]

Although the defeat of these two Bryan treaties could not have acquainted Wilson with the liklihood and paralyzing effects of political opposition to treaties by the Senate, he might have received warning from his experience with the Colombian treaty which was finally ratified during Harding's administration. Thirteen months after Wilson became President, the United States and Colombia signed a treaty in which the former expressed its sincere regret for what had occurred in Panama in 1903, granted Colombia special privileges in the use of the canal and agreed to pay $25,000,000 in exchange for Colombia's recognition of the independence of Panama.[160] A Demo-

[158] The proceedings of Aug. 13, 1914, were first published in the *Congressional Record* during the debate on the Versailles treaty. Mar. 1, 1920, pp. 3693-3696.

[159] In a letter to Roosevelt, Senator Lodge called them "fatuous" and stated he would have resisted them had he been present. Lodge, *Selections,* II, 453.

[160] On Jan. 9, 1909, treaties had been signed with Panama and with Columbia.

cratic admission of national guilt for acts done when the Republican party was in control of the government naturally aroused a determined and vociferous Republican opposition. It was not until March 1917, that the Democratic majority of the Committee on Foreign Relations reported the treaty favorably to the Senate, and the Republican minority submitted a vigorous dissenting report.[161] The attitude of the Republican senators made a two-thirds majority impossible and for that reason more than the pressure of the war business no vote was taken while Wilson remained President.

The subsequent conversion of most of the Republicans from bitter hostility to support can be attributed largely to the fact that a Republican instead of a Democratic administration was sponsoring the treaty. In attempting the unpleasant and arduous task of explaining their shift several senators emphasized the amendment which eliminated the expression of regret by the United States. But that excuse clearly failed to meet their needs, for the payment of $25,000,000 constituted an admission of wrong-doing that, as the Republican spokesmen in the original minority report had insisted, could be concealed by "no combination of words, no niceties of diplomatic language."[162] Much was said then in the debates, and more has

The Senate amended that with Panama, but the amendments were in no way responsible for the failure of the treaties to be ratified. According to their provisions neither was to go into effect without the other and consequently when Colombia rejected the treaty with it, that with Panama was lost too. *Foreign Relations, 1909*, pp. 223-233.

[161] The minority report was signed by Senators Lodge, McCumber, Borah, Brandegee, and Fall. It, the majority report and the treaty can be found in the *Congressional Record,* Mar. 14, 1917, pp. 72-75. When the treaty was approved under the auspices of a Republican administration Borah alone remained loyal to the views expressed when there had been a Democratic administration. Fall, as Secretary of the Interior and as an official concerned with the oil deposits of Colombia, played a leading part in advocating the approval of the treaty. Letters from him were frequently quoted in the debates. The other three Senators spoke and voted for the treaty in 1921.

[162] The emptiness of the contention that the elimination of the expression of regret changed the nature of the treaty was ruthlessly exposed by the Republican

been said since, of the persuasive influence of the rich oil deposits which Colombian resentment withheld from American exploitation. Yet even that factor was by no means solely responsible. At least two Republicans who voted for the treaty admitted frankly that they did so because of the Republican administration.[163] One Republican senator, Norris, asserted that many were voting for it merely because the Republican President so urged, and went on to ask, "Is it a crime to disregard your own convictions and follow the President when he is a Democrat, and a virtue to do the same thing when he is a Republican?"[164]

Illuminating as this sequel was on the extent to which political allegiance can sway the Senate when voting on treaties, it could not, of course, enlighten Wilson. He knew only that the treaty of his administration was being blocked successfully by senators of the opposing party. Unfortunately perhaps for his later and world-fateful treaty no test of the relative strength of the President and Senate was made on the Colombian treaty. If Wilson had not been so distracted by the problems arising from the war and if he had fought for this relatively insignificant treaty with all the various weapons of the Executive, he might have become more fully aware of the decisive and irresistable power that partisan opposition in the Senate could exert. An experience of this kind might easily have changed his entire strategy in the later campaign. As it was, the war did divert his attention, no contest was waged over the Colombian treaty, which met with delays and inaction rather than with positive defeat, and the possible lesson was not given.

On the contrary experience was teaching lessons leading to the opposite conclusion. The ascendency of the Executive over

Senators Kellogg, Johnson, and Kenyon. *Ibid., 67th Cong., 1st sess.*, pp. 191-202, 305-316, 472-474. Several Democratic senators took delight in pressing the point. Since the treaty was considered in open executive session the full proceedings are available in the *Congressional Record.*

[163] Shortridge and McCumber. *Ibid.*, pp. 425, 442.

[164] *Ibid.*, p. 467.

the Legislature which Roosevelt had established had been further extended by Wilson. Roosevelt had encountered a desperate resistance in the Senate, but Wilson, even before the war, had driven through his program with comparative ease. It is true that these presidential successes were not won on issues presented in treaties. Nevertheless the President, the people, and even the Senate accepted as natural the same leadership or domination in the conduct of foreign relations that the President had secured on domestic questions. The war exaggerated the subordination of Congress to the President because it made necessary a great concentration of power in his hands and because it made any opposition to the man conducting the war intolerable and unpatriotic. Never before had a concatenation of events raised any President to such dizzy heights of power from which successful opposition to his major policies must have seemed improbable. Yet inevitably the mastery of the President galled Congress, especially the Senate. Instinctively the first opportunity for challenging the supremacy of the President would be seized. The treaty of peace furnished the occasion.

CHAPTER X

THE VERSAILLES TREATY

At this very moment we have the spectacle, boasted of openly by some, that there are 40 faithful Democrats here who are willing to surrender their own convictions and their own judgment, who are waiting to find out what the President of the United States wants done about the reservations in this treaty, and are then willing to vote however he asks them to vote.

SENATOR LENROOT.

It would be just as much justified if I should say that 49 Republicans on the other side are taking the will of the Republican leader on that side. . . . We allow a reasonable suspicion that Senators on the other side are standing by their own opinions and their own will, and I think the Senator from Wisconsin ought to be fair enough and generous enough to Senators upon this side of the aisle to assume that if Senators upon the other side of the aisle can combine to stand for a certain principle, Senators upon this side of the aisle can do it without doing it at the dictation of any man, either the President or anyone else.

SENATOR HITCHCOCK.[1]

In the final movement of the magnificent César Franck symphony the themes of the earlier movements are woven together and further developed until the tension becomes overpowering. The student of the history of the Versailles treaty in the Senate can scarcely fail to observe a similar blending of themes and to experience a similar emotional tension. Throughout the entire proceedings runs the theme of party politics which ultimately decided the action of the Senate. Blended with this are other themes equally alien to the merits of the momentous question at issue. Yet even the most conspicuous of them—the constitutional struggle with the President—merely reenforces and makes more effective the dominant melody.

The extent to which party politics dominated the Senate in its attitude toward the Versailles treaty is not generally realized. The story cannot be told in all its detail because many years

[1] *Congressional Record,* Nov. 8, 1919, pp. 8133-8134.

must still elapse before the private correspondence of the participants will be available. Nevertheless the basic records are clear and make it certain that the revelations of the future will not destroy the existing story but will only amplify it by disclosing the strategy of this or that group or the acts and thoughts of some individual.[2]

War with Germany brought a political truce to the United States. An adjournment of party politics was loudly and frequently proclaimed and as often observed. It was not in the nature of things that politicians could ignore partisan considerations completely. Under the circumstances the party in power can well afford to have open political warfare ended so as to enjoy both the added powers resulting from expanded activities and the benefit of being identified with the government at a time when all the people will give enthusiastic support. For the same reasons the opposition party is under great temptation to seize what opportunities it can to attack the administration. In this instance the temptation was intensified by the fact that the Republican party had, until the split of 1912, been so long and so firmly in control of the government that the presence of a Democrat in the White House during such a crisis assumed the character of a presumptuous usurpation. Consequently the calm produced by the political truce was on the surface and was as deceptive as that customarily prevailing in the daylight along the battle lines in France. The first major offensive in the hidden political warfare was the public attack on the Democratic administration because of the alleged, or perhaps real, collapse of the War Department.

[2] Naturally, contemporary magazines and newspapers contained many accounts of the Senate's action on the treaty. One of the earliest scholarly treatments was that of H. Barrett Learned entitled, "The Attitude of the United States Senate towards the Versailles Treaty," published as Chapter 5 in the sixth volume of *A History of the Peace Conference of Paris,* edited by H. W. V. Temperley. By far the most complete and best account is the book of Denna F. Fleming, *The United States and the League of Nations.* (1932.) In this large volume there is a wealth of material drawn chiefly from the *Congressional Record* and from a large number of newspapers.

Although a Democratic senator sponsored the movement and although many persons sincerely advocated the creation of a coalition government to conduct the war, Republican politicians supplied most of the driving force. The most prominent of them was ex-President Roosevelt, the Republican leader with the largest personal following and the one who would probably have been nominated in 1920 had not death intervened. This attack was rendered abortive by the energetic measures of President Wilson.[3]

The possibility of criticising the administration for military failure was ended by its success in raising and transporting to France an army of several million men and by the accumulating defeats of Germany. The very achievements of the Democratic administration in the war made it certain that Republican politicians would attempt to discredit the Democratic peace negotiations. Partisan attacks on the peace treaty were practically inevitable in any event. It would furnish the first large issue on which the Republican party could openly renew its political opposition and by which the Republican senators might reclaim for the Senate the powers that the emergency of the war had compelled that body to abdicate. Few of the Republican leaders may have formulated the specific words, "if we permit Wilson to triumph in his peace policy as he triumphed in war the Democratic party may remain in power for many years to come," but the thought must have entered the minds of everyone, even of those who tried not to let it influence their action.

That some did use those terms is proved by that small fragment of personal correspondence that has become available. The opposition to the idea of a league of nations expressed

[3] When private records make it possible the story of this campaign will be an interesting one. At present the best account of it is in William E. Dodd, *Woodrow Wilson and His Work,* pp. 250-276. Like most writers from the scholarly world Professor Dodd is strongly Wilsonian in his sympathies, yet he reminds his readers that judgment is not easy and that the politicians who participated in a comparable attack on Lincoln during the Civil War were honored leaders of the people.

by former Senator Beveridge, one of the most politically-minded and politically ambitious men of the period, was not due to party considerations according to his biographer. To support this conclusion the latter submits evidence of Beveridge's hostility to the proposal at a time when it was not associated with Wilson's name and when Senator Lodge was among its leading advocates.[4] Beveridge did not credit other Republican leaders with his own sincerity. In appealing to them to fight the peace policy of the President he stressed political consequences and not principles. To Roosevelt he presented this argument again and again. "Wilson has hoisted the motley flag of internationalism. Thank God that he has. That makes the issue, does it not? Straight Americanism for us," he wrote in July, 1918.[5] Three months later when the imminent defeat of Germany had increased the prestige of the Democratic President he emphasized the necessities of the Republican party in unequivocal terms. "As the matter stands, the people have heard only one side, and that side has been presented dogmatically and superficially. Also, as a matter of practical party politics, if we are to abandon the issue of Nationalism versus Internationalism, as exemplified in Mr. Wilson's League of Nations scheme, what issue have we?" [6] To Will Hays, the Chairman of the Republican National Committee, he wrote, "if Wilson gets this thing through, especially if he gets it through with Republican support, I think that our prospects of winning, which three months ago seemed a certainty, will be gravely diminished." [7] To Lodge he wrote that the future of the party was in his hands "more than in those of any other man" and that its prospects would be "seriously, perhaps fatally, injured by the acceptance of Mr. Wilson's international plan, or any variation of it." [8] As far as can be ascertained from the quoted portions of the answers to these letters Beveridge's correspondents also considered the peace settlement chiefly in terms of its political consequences in the United States.

[4] Claude G. Bowers, *Beveridge and the Progressive Era,* pp. 496-497.

[5] *Ibid.,* p. 498.

[6] *Ibid.,* p. 499.

[7] *Ibid.,* p. 506.

[8] *Ibid.,* p. 502.

Undoubtedly other Republican leaders participated in similar discussions of political plans and prospects as they anticipated the time when the cessation of military operations would lift the ban on open politics. Indeed the political armistice was broken before the military armistice was signed. The approach of the biennial election of members of Congress, which according to the American practice was to occur by calendar without regard to need or pending crisis, precipitated "the return to normalcy." The political appeals arising from the various state conventions in the late summer and fall, and other early maneuvers probably received less than a passing notice from the public, absorbed as it was in the events of the war, but the plea for the election of a Democratic Congress that President Wilson made on October 25 informed the public that the political truce was over.[9]

Immediately the political fires that had been accumulating heat beneath the surface burst into flame. Republican leaders of all shades of opinion joined in criticising Wilson's appeal and appealed in their turn for party support at the polls. Some, ignoring the parallel action of Republican leaders in 1898, insisted that Wilson had insulted every loyal Republican in the land and that he merited a rebuke at the polls.[10] A fre-

[9] The propriety and wisdom of Wilson's act have been debated from the day he made his appeal. In a temperate editorial pointing out the boldness and risk of his appeal the New York *Times* of Oct. 26, 1918, began by saying, "Mr. Roosevelt's ill-advised and most untimely attempt to stir up a partisan strife against the President lends justification," and later asserted, "let the blame rest upon the Republicans who have forced him to take that course." The best contemporary defense of Wilson was made in the Senate by Senator Pittman who not only quoted documents showing the political activities of leading Republicans which caused Wilson's action but also pointed to the similar appeals made in 1898 by President McKinley, Roosevelt, Senator Lodge, and others. *Congressional Record,* Oct. 28, 1918, pp. 11491-11497. Later defenders have employed the same arguments. Fleming, pp. 44-51. In assigning blame for the revival of politics to one or the other group commentators have neglected to consider the weakness of a constitutional system which necessitated a political election during such a crisis and at a time when no issue was, or could be, presented to the voters.

[10] This was the main point in the answer of Will Hays, the Chairman of the

quent complaint was that Wilson wanted to be an autocrat in peace as well as in war. Another argument urged repeatedly by ex-President Roosevelt and by Senators Lodge and Knox, both before and after Wilson's appeal, was that Wilson proposed a negotiated armistice instead of an unconditional surrender for which a Republican victory in the election was essential. As the earlier attacks based on the collapse of the War Department had been ended by military achievements, this later criticism was completely answered after the election by the terms of the armistice which the military and naval authorities dictated and which left Germany no opportunity to renew hostilities. What effect the political appeals of either side had on the public, engrossed as it must have been in the exciting events of the last weeks of the war, cannot be stated, but the certain and momentous result of the election was that the Republicans secured a majority in both houses of Congress. In the Senate of the next Congress there would be forty-nine Republicans and forty-seven Democrats—a narrow margin yet sufficient to insure control of the organization of that body and of its powerful Committee on Foreign Relations. Little, in fact almost nothing, had been said in the campaign of Wilson's plans for reestablishing and preserving peace. That problem was not an issue in the election.[11]

Republican National Committee, *Congressional Record,* Oct. 28, 1918, p. 11494. That of the Senatorial and Congressional Committees is on p. 11503. The newspapers of the period contained statements from Taft, Hughes and Roosevelt and from many minor leaders.

[11] The best account of this election, certainly one of the most important in the history of the country, is the brief chapter in Charles P. Howland, ed., *Survey of American Foreign Relations,* 1928, pp. 239-246. An intensive study is badly needed. It has become the custom to say that Wilson's appeal, however natural, was a serious mistake that helped the Republicans in the election. This is only surmise, and the contrary conclusion might be a truer one. During the entire period the voters of the country were normally Republican and Wilson's appeal may help to explain the closeness of the vote. In a number of states only a few thousand votes separated the senatorial candidates and if membership in the House had been proportional to the votes cast in each state the result would have been, according to C. A. Beard, 231 Democrats and 193 Republicans instead of the reverse. Fleming, p. 51.

Immediately after Congress reassembled in December partisan attacks were launched with a vehemence and an eagerness which bear eloquent testimony to the galling nature of the restraints imposed during the war. Yet many of them, like those denouncing extravagance and corruption in expenditures, or autocracy on the part of Wilson and his subordinates, had no direct connection with the terms to be applied in the approaching negotiations. Much was made of Wilson's decision to attend the peace conference in person. A group of Republican senators supported a resolution declaring that the President's departure would render him unable to discharge his duties so that the office would be vacant and the Vice-President would necessarily succeed to it.[12] These were minor matters, however, and it was quickly apparent that the subject which would dwarf all other issues was the peace settlement. If he meant the adjective to describe the consequences of the debate rather than the intellectual level of it, the writer in the Boston *Transcript* was correct who prophesied, "One of the great debates in the history of popular government is about to begin in the Senate of the United States." [13]

Significantly, these early assaults on the President's program were made by Republican senators. No Democrat, with the conspicuous exception of Senator Reed of Missouri, participated in them. It is true that it was by no means certain that all the Republicans in the Senate would unite in opposition to Wilson's policy. Even some of the Republican senators who spoke did so in such a way as to give the impression that they were engaged in the normal political skirmishing rather than expressing a fundamental hostility to the principles the President had announced as the basis for the peace.[14] It is also

[12] *Congressional Record,* Dec. 3, 1918, pp. 22-28.

[13] Dec. 18, 1918, cited in Fleming, p. 70.

[14] See, for example, the speech of Senator Sterling on Jan. 13, 1919. *Congressional Record,* pp. 1314-1318. Like the Sabine men in Andreyeff's play his arguments progressed by the method of taking two steps forward and one step backward. "I am not here declaring against a league of nations—even a league to enforce peace. But. . . ." P. 1315.

true that there was one Republican—Senator McCumber of North Dakota— who followed the example of Taft and other Republican leaders outside of the Senate in staunchly defending the idea of a league of nations.[15] Yet it is clear to anyone reading the debates of these first two months, at least when read with the knowledge of later events, that the initiative among the Republicans had been seized by Knox, Borah and the others of that small group who advocated resistance to the slightest appearance in the peace treaty of a league of nations. These few attacked aggressively and frequently, while the large majority of Republican senators did not commit themselves on the main issue but either remained silent or engaged in a desultory sniping at the Democratic administration on minor points.

That the determined minority of extreme opponents were the active and energetic element of the party in the Senate became even more evident during the next stage of the debate. From December until the middle of February both sides had to content themselves with general principles or with speculations on what would be done at the peace conference. A new direction was given to the discussion when the first draft of the covenant of the league of nations was published on February 14. After that date the specific applications of the general principles could be debated. It was an important period for the formation of opinion on the concrete commitments proposed, and the tenor of the Republican speeches in the Senate foreshadowed partisan action in the consideration of the treaty. In the brief interval before the sixty-fifth Congress adjourned *sine die* on March 4, ten Republican senators delivered prepared addresses on the subject of the league of nations. Five of them were members of the small group of fourteen irreconcilable Republicans who later voted against the treaty on all occasions.[16] Four of the others were among the thirty-five Re-

[15] McCumber's first speech was delivered on January 7, 1919. *Ibid.,* pp. 1083-1088.

[16] The senators and the dates on which they spoke were as follows: Poindex-

publican senators who later voted for the treaty with reservations.[17] Thus the irreconcilable element was over three times as active in debate as the majority group of the Republicans. At the time no distinction between the two groups could be recognized as the four later reservationists attacked the plan for a league of nations with as much vigor and with the same nationalistic appeals as the irreconcilables. This unanimity could hardly fail to give the impression that the peace treaty was becoming a partisan issue. It was to correct that impression and to prevent his party from being stampeded into such a position that McCumber, the sole Republican who voted for the treaty with and without reservations, spoke on the day before the session ended because, as he said, he "feared that the country, after reading the arguments that have been made upon this side of the chamber against any league of nations, might be misled into the belief that the Republicans of the United States as a party were opposed to any character of a league or agreement between nations to maintain the peace of the world." [18]

Despite Senator McCumber's assurance that there were "a large number of Republicans who favor a league of nations to maintain the peace of the world," it was ominously apparent that those of them who happened to be in the Senate remained inert and silent. The initiative in determining the policy of the party had been readily surrendered to the sena-

ter, Feb. 18; Borah, Feb. 21; Knox, Mar. 1; Sherman, Mar. 3; La Follette, Mar. 4. The speech of La Follette, who was engaged in a filibuster, was not devoted exclusively to the league of nations.

[17] Cummins on Feb. 26; Lodge, Lenroot, and Frelinghuysen on Feb. 28. Despite their reluctance to assist the filibuster against several essential appropriation bills a number of Democrats spoke at length on the league. Lewis, Owen and Hitchcock spoke in favor of the league on Feb. 24, 26, and 27, respectively. The irreconcilable Democrat, Reed, attacked the proposal on Feb. 22. Two Democrats, who had been defeated for reelection largely because of Wilson's opposition to them, made brief statements showing that they would have joined the irreconcilables if their senatorial careers had not been closing. These were Vardaman and Hardwick who spoke on Feb. 15, and Mar. 1.

[18] *Congressional Record,* Mar. 3, 1919, p. 1872.

tors holding the contrary view. This unwillingness of the pro-league Republican senators to fight openly and immediately against their colleagues who were attempting to commit the party to the policy of rejecting the President's program was of the utmost importance. Indeed its importance can scarcely be exaggerated for the crucial contest was the contest within the Republican party in the Senate. Upon it, and not upon the simultaneous public struggle with the Democrats, depended the future of the world's history. The outcome of this contest was to be decided chiefly by one man because of his powers as Republican leader in the Senate and as Chairman of the Committee on Foreign Relations. This man was Senator Lodge.

The difficult task of attempting an estimate of the character and motives of Senator Lodge has been facilitated because he, disregarding the warning of the man who wished his enemy would write a book, published a defense of his actions. This amplified the official records as did the two volumes of his correspondence with Theodore Roosevelt which, though selected by himself, could not fail to reveal the character of the writer. Nothing in the resulting picture is more distinct than the intense partisanship of the man. During the long years of his public career no member of the Republican party was more faithful in service or more ready to sacrifice ideals or anything else to party loyalty. As a youthful reformer in 1884 he had fought the nomination of Blaine on grounds of personal unfitness and had stated he would not follow such a leader, yet he campaigned actively for Blaine. As a member of the House of Representatives his name was associated principally with the partisan measure known as the Force Bill. As a senator from 1893 to his death in 1924 he never departed from strict party regularity nor failed to render active service despite all the shifting issues and conflicting trends of those years. In 1894 he denounced the gold standard as "the great enemy of good business throughout the world" and advocated action "in the interest of silver," yet, two years later, when Bryan captured the Democratic party with the issue of free silver he damned such heresies in no uncertain terms.[19] When President Roosevelt assured him that the Democrat being considered for an appointment to the Supreme Court was really Republican in philosophy and was "right" about labor, about the corporations, on the negro question, and other issues, Lodge demanded the label as well as the substance and wrote back, "I do not see why Republicans cannot be found who hold those opinions as well as Democrats."[20] The perfect loyalty to the party organization which Lodge consistently exhibited could not easily be duplicated.

Fully as conspicuous as his partisanship, yet subordinated to it, was his loyalty to the idea that the Senate should assert to their fullest extent its powers in the conduct of foreign relations. Such an attitude is customary rather than exceptional, especially in senators who have served many years, but Lodge had it in an exaggerated form. He himself stated that "There is no one more jealous of the prerogatives of the Senate than am I," and his record warranted the statement.[21] On occasion he did not hesitate to contend with a President of his own party on behalf of the Senate's powers. In this cause he fought successfully against the arbitration treaty of 1897 sponsored by McKinley and against the arbitration treaties of 1904 negotiated by Roosevelt. Yet in these cases the party had little at stake and the Senate much. When, as in Roosevelt's Dominican policy, the party might suffer seriously Lodge could sacrifice the lesser loyalty for the greater. Thus in this instance he rallied to the defence of Roosevelt's extreme defiance of the Senate and the Constitution saying:

[19] *Ibid.*, April 6, 1894, p. 3497. This and similar episodes in Lodge's career are severely treated in Oswald Garrison Villard, "Henry Cabot Lodge—A Scholar in Politics," *The Nation*, vol. 119, pp. 539-541. (Nov. 19, 1924).

[20] Lodge, *Selections*, II, 228-231. After reading hundreds of Lodge's letters including the manuscript letters to Roosevelt during his presidency, now in the Library of Congress, I do not remember a favorable judgment of a single Democrat alive or dead. If my memory is correct in this, Lodge was more irreconcilable in his opinion of Democrats than the typical frontiersman was reputed to be in judging Indians.

[21] *Congressional Record*, Jan. 31, 1924, p. 1719.

> No one, I think, can doubt the absolute power of the President to initiate and carry on all negotiations. . . . There is no doubt that the Senate can by resolution advise the President to enter upon a negotiation, or advise the President to refrain from a negotiation; but those resolutions have no binding force whatsoever. . . . We have no possible right to break suddenly into the middle of a negotiation and demand from the President what instructions he has given to his representative. That part of treaty making is no concern of ours. . . .
>
> * * * * * * * *
>
> It is a mere invasion of the powers and rights of the President if we are to plunge in at a stage of the negotiations where we have no business whatever and demand from him the instructions which he has given to his properly appointed representatives.[22]

Such a conflict of loyalties was distressing. Naturally those were happier occasions when Senator Lodge could satisfy both his major passions by asserting the powers of the Senate against a Democratic President. The Versailles treaty presented such an opportunity and Lodge seized it. He was, of course, too careful a speaker, too adept in the art of choosing words to make flagrantly incorrect statements as many Republican senators did. Nevertheless, his arguments conveyed an impression of the rights and duties of the Senate and of American tradition completely at variance with that to be got from his speech during the Dominican affair. When a Republican was President the Senate had no right to interrupt a negotiation even to ask for the instructions given, but when a Democrat was President "the right of the Senate to advise as to a treaty [to participate in the negotiations rather than to await the finished document] becomes a solemn, an imperative duty."[23] The extent to which he permitted himself to reverse his earlier statements and to distort the facts was demonstrated in his debate with President Lowell of Harvard. To Lowell's request for the amendments he would make in the proposed draft of a league of nations he replied that the President should submit the draft to the Senate for its advice while the negotiations were still in progress. Then in words which imply that such

[22] *Ibid.*, Jan. 24, 1906, p. 1470. [23] *Ibid.*, Dec. 21, 1918, p. 724.

a procedure was customary and which illustrate the tactics and tenor of most of his speeches he continued, "I am only asking something that has been done by almost all our Presidents who have consulted the Senate about entering into negotiations, about the character of negotiations, about awards, about pending negotiations. . . . The Senate was consulted prior to negotiations by George Washington; it was consulted prior to negotiations by Abraham Lincoln. And in the path that George Washington and Abraham Lincoln have walked there is no man too great to tread." [24]

The abilities which Lodge devoted to the service of his party and the powers of the Senate were of high order. His literary and scholarly achievements won for him the title of "The Scholar in Politics" until the successful entry of Wilson into the political world. His reputation for erudition was supported by his carefully prepared and well polished speeches. But he was never an orator of the type to inflame an audience or to win an enthusiastic following for his cause. What made him so valuable a member of his party was his skill as a political leader and as a party manager. It was his successful management of the gubernatorial campaign in Massachusetts in 1883 that first brought him into political prominence. His skill developed with the experience acquired in service. No one can read extensively in the *Congressional Record* during his career without being impressed by his mastery of parliamentary technique, by his adroit maneuvers to extract his party from a tight situation or to entangle his opponents, and by his knowledge of what to do under all circumstances. No one in 1919 knew better than he the various devices and methods by which a treaty could be killed, nor had anyone had more

[24] New York *Times,* Mar. 20, 1919. It is hardly necessary here to point out that while both Washington and Lincoln did in a few cases consult the Senate prior to the signing of treaties this procedure was highly exceptional. In contrasting Lodge's constitutional views of 1906 with those of 1919 an editorial in the New York *World* suggested that there must be one constitution for Republican Presidents and quite a different constitution for Democratic Presidents. Mar. 21, 1919.

practice in the use of them. That his ability was great in the more delicate task of holding the members of his own party in the Senate to a given course cannot be doubted, although from the nature of the case little direct evidence can be cited. Numerous successes and his election as Republican leader in the Senate furnish the most conclusive proof. Although not a conceited man compared to most who have attained an equal political position, Lodge credited himself with ability of this nature. In explaining to Roosevelt the manner in which the desperate fight over the treaty of peace had been won in 1899, he asserted that the then Chairman of the Committee on Foreign Relations could not make a canvass and was no manager and then continued: "He would ask me every morning how the vote stood, and I think that is about all he knew about it. Aldrich and I, but particularly Aldrich, made the hard fighting, which does not appear on the surface. . . . We were down in the engine room and do not get flowers, but we did make the ship move." [25] There were many other occasions on which he could have truthfully made the same claim.

None of his success as a leader was due to personal popularity. His Republican colleagues accepted his guidance because of their respect for his ability and not because of affection for the man. Cold, cautious and vindictive in his antagonisms he repelled rather than attracted. Toward Wilson he cherished an intense hatred. This he shared with Roosevelt, as their published correspondence amply testifies, and the two men were driven to the point of frantic exasperation by Wilson's contemptuous indifference—a luxury to be afforded only by those in power. In his public addresses on the peace treaty Lodge made studied but not always successful efforts to eliminate evidence of his hostility to the President. Obviously under the circumstances it would have been impolitic for the Republican leader to have indulged in personal attacks on the President, nor were those his customary tactics. But the feeling proved too strong to be suppressed completely and in the

[25] Lodge, *Selections,* I, 391-392.

book Lodge subsequently wrote to vindicate his conduct his hatred for Wilson shines forth in its full intensity.[26]

To expect a man of that character and with such a record to consider Wilson's treaty of peace solely in the light of its merits as a foreign policy for the United States would be to ask the impossible. That Lodge would attempt to frustrate the policy, whatever it might be, of a Democratic President, whose dictatorial position seemed to threaten the powers of the Senate and whom he personally hated, was axiomatic. It is impossible to be dogmatic about the extent to which a sincere belief in the policy of isolation may have combined with his other reasons for opposing the President. His prominence in the movement for a league to enforce peace, which meant a complete abandonment of the isolationist policy, raises a suspicion that he was converted to isolationism after Wilson had embraced the opposite doctrine. More damaging by far to the thesis that he was sincere is the long memorandum which he gave Henry White on the eve of the peace conference and which contained the terms he wished to have incorporated in the treaty of peace. This memorandum had been prepared with care. It was not only for the guidance of Henry White, the sole Republican commissioner, but was also to be shown—at least such was Lodge's request—to the leading allied statesmen in strict confidence so as to strengthen their hands against Wilson and the other representatives of the United States. The significant thing about the settlement Lodge proposed is not its Punic character but the fact that his terms would have entangled the United States in European affairs and would have necessitated the abandonment of isolation. The United States was to guarantee many portions of the settlement; Lithuania, Livonia and Esthonia were to be independent "under the protection of the

[26] *The Senate and the League of Nations*, pp. 212-226. These pages giving Lodge's estimate of Wilson's character are particularly revealing. The whole book is so permeated with his bitter hatred that the guess might be hazarded that it was written not merely for vindication but also for the relief of expressing the sentiment which had been suppressed during the public debate.

Allies and the United States," the independence of Czecho-Slovakia was to be made "secure and sustained by the Allies and the United States in every way." [27] At least this memorandum makes his professed devotion to the policy of Washington's farewell address seem a hollow pretense.

The baffling question of motives and sincerity is the vital one in any attempt to determine what Senator Lodge's true position was. According to the official record and to all his public utterances he desired the United States to enter the League of Nations and the treaty to be ratified with reservations. Some of his personal associates, including a grandson, accept that view.[28] Yet his daughter, who claimed to be in close association with him during the contest, stated that being uncertain whether the treaty could be rejected as the other irreconcilables wanted, his object was to emasculate it with reservations that would make it valueless.[29] In his printed defense Lodge admitted his opinion, expressed to Senator Borah, that the treaty could not be defeated by a direct vote, "even if it were desirable," and that "there was only one thing to do and that was to proceed in the discussion of the treaty by way of amendment and reservation." [30] Other evidence tends to support the conclusion that for him the reservations were primarily a method of killing the treaty. Senator Lodge was interviewed by Mr. James G. MacDonald, then Chairman of the League of Free Nations Association, and Mr. Allen T. Burns, President of the National Conference of Social Work; and the latter reported that the Senator, after referring to the way in which senatorial amendments had led Taft to reject an arbitration treaty in

[27] Allan Nevins, *Henry White,* pp. 353-354. For an official of the United States to attempt to disclose secretly to foreign governments information to be used against the representatives of the United States in negotiations may seem extraordinary, yet there was precedent for such action. Hamilton, whom Lodge greatly admired and whose biography he had written, did the same thing during Jay's negotiations with Great Britain in 1794.

[28] Fleming, pp. 475-476.

[29] New York *Herald Tribune,* Mar. 25, 1930, cited in Fleming, p. 476.

[30] *The Senate and the League of Nations,* p. 147.

1911, said, "We shall deal with the Versailles treaty in the same way. If President Wilson does not see fit to return it to our allies that is his responsibility." [31] To Henry White, Lodge wrote, "The treaty will be sent to him with reservations, and then it will be up to him to hold it back." [32] Indeed there is nothing in the record to contradict and there is some evidence to support the idea that Lodge preferred killing the treaty with reservations unacceptable to Wilson so that responsibility might fall on the latter. The most damaging evidence against the hypothesis that Lodge was sincere is his action at the Republican convention several months after the treaty had been rejected. When, in a conference over the platform, some Republican leaders urged that the party declare for the league with the Lodge reservations, Lodge stated that he would leave the chair and fight against the proposal from the convention floor.[33] Either he had never been sincere or, fearing the threatened secession of the irreconcilables, he preferred party unity to the policy he had advocated.

If Lodge honestly wanted the ratification of the treaty with reservations he failed as a leader. He was not able to hold the irreconcilable Republicans to the program adopted by the Republican majority under his leadership. Had he done so the treaty would have received the approval of the Senate on the second vote. On the other hand, if he really wished to defeat the treaty, if he did not join the irreconcilables in open opposition because he realized that only the indirect method of

[31] Fleming, p. 481, citing the Springfield *Republican* of Oct. 31, 1920.

[32] Nevins, *Henry White,* p. 455.

[33] New York *Times,* June 11, 1920, quoted in Fleming, p. 452. Lodge's eagerness to have history blame Wilson was frankly expressed in his book. "There was another object which I had very much at heart, and that was that if we were successful in putting on reservations we should create a situation where, if the acceptance of the treaty was defeated, the Democratic party, and especially Mr. Wilson's friends, should be responsible for its defeat, and not the opponents of the treaty who were trying to pass it in a form safe for the United States." *The Senate and the League of Nations,* pp. 164, 214-216. Nevins, *Henry White,* p. 486.

dissimulation could succeed, the result entitles him to the highest possible tribute as a political manager. Although the evidence warrants the latter conclusion it is by no means certain that he entered into a conspiracy with the irreconcilables and that they knew he was fighting for them in the other camp. He may have given private assurances to some of the irreconcilables. Certainly his association with them was exceedingly close and, as will be noted, practically every important decision was made in consultation with them. To ex-Senator Beveridge's repeated pleas for a more aggressive policy Lodge always replied in terms indicating his entire agreement as to the end to be sought while differing as to the method necessary. Thus he wrote that " if we seem to you . . . to be not as effective as you desire, I am sure you will make allowances for the difficulties which confront us "; that he " could not agree that we are against any League " since that position " would drive away support "; and that " the votes to defeat the treaty squarely are not there. . . . I am not arguing the right or wrong of it, but telling you what the situation is. My business was to unite the Republicans so far as I could, and they are united now on strong and effective reservations." [34]

Finding a program to unite the diverse elements composing the Republican membership of the Senate had indeed appeared impossible no matter how ingenious the party leader. Yet Lodge in the first test succeeded in doing that very thing. Just before midnight on March 3, 1919, the day before the session of Congress was to end, he introduced a resolution which, after reciting in the preamble that " it is a function of the Senate to advise and consent to, or dissent from, the ratification of any treaty of the United States, and no such treaty can become operative without the consent of the Senate ex-

[34] Bowers, *Beveridge,* pp. 502, 503-504, 507. Nevertheless, Beveridge did not feel sure of Lodge. Apparently neither did all of the irreconcilables in the Senate, for Lodge was reported as saying they addressed him in language which " no man of my age should be obliged to hear." Mark Sullivan, " America and the League of Nations," *World's Work,* vol. 51, p. 291, cited in Fleming, p. 485.

pressed by the affirmative vote of two-thirds of the Senators present," stated that

> it is the sense of the Senate that while it is their sincere desire that the nations of the world should unite to promote peace and general disarmament, the constitution of the league of nations in the form now proposed to the peace conference should not be accepted by the United States; and . . . that it is the sense of the Senate that the negotiations on the part of the United States should immediately be directed to the utmost expedition of the urgent business of negotiating peace terms with Germany satisfactory to the United States and the nations with whom the United States is associated in the war against the German Government, and that the proposal for a league of nations to insure the permanent peace of the world should then be taken up for careful and serious consideration.[35]

Under the rules of the Senate the resolution could be considered only by unanimous consent and when a Democratic senator objected, as Lodge had anticipated would be done, he read a statement signed by thirty-seven Republican senators and senators-elect of the next Congress to the effect that if they had had an opportnuity they would have voted for the resolution. On the following day two other Republican senators added their names by telegraph.

The significance of this famous round-robin cannot be easily exaggerated. As a public warning from more than one-third of the members of the Senate that the President and the world must take that body into their calculations the maneuver was neither of outstanding importance nor successful. Its true significance lay in its relation to the contest within the Republican party in the Senate over the policy to be applied to the peace negotiations. Before March 3, some Republican senators had disclosed their individual views on the pending negotiations and the league, but no vote or other step had been taken which revealed the position of the large majority. Nor had it been certain even that partisan action would be attempted. The round-robin ended any doubts on that point. It proved that the Republican leader had been able to hold his party

[35] *Congressional Record,* Mar. 3, 1919, p. 4974.

together. It committed the Republican senators, or at least so large a proportion of them as to constitute more than one-third of the total membership of the Senate, to the policy of united, partisan action on the treaty.

Of equal significance was the fact that the policy which Senator Lodge successfully urged on his Republican colleagues represented a victory for the irreconcilable group within the party. How many of the signers of the round-robin sincerely believed that a league of nations to insure permanent peace would result from the "careful and serious consideration" to be given that proposal after the peace terms should have been settled cannot be stated, human credulity being what it is. Certainly the irreconcilables did not, for they supported the round-robin eagerly. Indeed it could accurately be called the first great success of that aggressive minority in aligning the apathetic majority of their party associates against Wilson's peace terms. The irreconcilable Senator Brandegee first suggested the round-robin to Lodge on Sunday morning, March 2. Together they went to the irreconcilable Senator Knox who drafted the document.[36] Four of the first six signatures after Lodge's were those of irreconcilables, and all of the Republican irreconcilables signed the round-robin except La Follette and Norris whose status as Republicans was irregular. If Lodge was sincere in his advocacy of a league of nations with safeguards, his innocence was extraordinary in not being suspicious of the policy of the round-robin coming from the sources it did. As a matter of fact, it committed the Republican members of the Senate to the plan of opposing the inclusion of a league in the treaty of peace. Having taken this stand the Republican majority were more easily induced to a stern resistance when the

[36] Lodge, *The Senate and the League of Nations,* pp. 118-120. By some mistake Lodge in printing the list of signatures to the round-robin omitted the name of Brandegee whose idea it was. On Monday morning the Knox draft was submitted to Senator Cummins at whose suggestion several changes were made. The document was then circulated and since Lodge read it into the *Record* that same night it is evident the signers of it could not have spent much time in deliberation.

treaty of peace did provide for a league of nations. The irreconcilables could, and did, appeal to them to be true to this first statement of party policy. Thus Senator Brandegee on the day of the vote on the resolution of ratification read the round-robin into the *Record* again and informed his colleagues that he was going to redeem his promise.[37]

Victory though it was, the round-robin did not constitute a complete surrender to the irreconcilables. An important qualifying phrase had been necessary to gain the adhesion of some Republican senators. The document expressed the determination of the signers not to accept the constitution of the league "in the form now proposed." If changes should be made many of the signers of the round-robin might accept the league. For that matter, it was not improbable that some of them might do so anyway if confronted with a *fait accompli.* There was nothing in the nature of the round-robin to make it a binding obligation upon its subscribers; certainly none of the irreconcilables considered that it pledged him to encourage or support an attempt to establish any league of nations after peace with Germany had been made.

It was soon evident that the determination of the Republican senators to stand by the policy of the round-robin was to be tested. The challenge had hardly been issued before it was accepted by President Wilson. On the evening of March 4, just before his return to Europe, the President spoke in New York from the same platform with ex-President Taft. To an enthusiastic audience Wilson asserted that senators would find not only the covenant of the league in the treaty he would bring back but "so many threads of the treaty tied to the covenant that you cannot dissect the covenant from the treaty without destroying the whole vital structure."[38]

There was reason for the confidence which Wilson displayed. The period between the announcement of the round-robin and the next meeting of the Senate on May 19, was a depressing

[37] *Congressional Record,* Nov. 19, 1919, pp. 8774-8775.

[38] New York *Times,* Mar. 5, 1919.

one for his opponents and a black one for the irreconcilables. Obviously the Democratic senators with only a few exceptions would vote for his treaty. Obviously also the public was approving his program. There was no doubt of the course desired by public opinion even in the minds of those senators whose wish would have produced a different thought had the evidence permitted. When Lodge was discussing plans with Senator Borah—again it is significant that the first conference of this nature after the adjournment of Congress was with an irreconcilable—he gave his interpretation of the state of public opinion. The " great mass of the people," he believed, did not understand the treaty and wanted peace, while " the vocal classes of the community, most of the clergymen, the preachers of sermons, a large element in the teaching force of the universities, a large proportion of the newspaper editors, and finally the men and women who were in the habit of writing and speaking for publication, although by no means thoroughly informed, were friendly to the League as it stood and were advocating it." [39] A month later he made a more unpleasant admission to Henry White, for he then included the great mass of the people with the intelligent minority and said " a majority of the people of the country " favored the proposal although they would insist on amendments covering the Monroe doctrine and the question of immigration.[40] Not only were the Democrats and the general public of this opinion but some of the most prominent Republican party leaders outside of the Senate were actively campaigning for the league of nations idea. The most conspicuous of them, former President Taft, mingled with his arguments on the merits of the question an occasional warning to any who might be moved by other considerations. " The Re-

[39] *The Senate and the League of Nations,* pp. 146-147. Senator Borah is reported as agreeing " entirely with my description of the situation."

[40] April 8, 1919. Nevins, *Henry White,* p. 413. Senator Cummins gave his similar view publicly. *Congressional Record,* Feb. 26, 1919, p. 4311. In private Knox, Brandegee and others of the irreconcilable group were dejected by the same belief. George Harvey, *Henry Clay Frick, The Man,* p. 325.

publican members of the Senate," he wrote in the Philadelphia *Public Ledger* of December 1, 1918, " will do well to consider whether it would be wise for them to furnish to Mr. Wilson and the Democratic party an issue upon which the Administration would be most likely to win." [41]

The gloom of the irreconcilables during this period deepened when the covenant of the league was changed to meet the principal objections that had been made in America. These made it possible for the signers of the round-robin to accept the league and were, in fact, pressed by the United States commission in order to win support for the treaty in the Senate. Immediately after the Republicans in the Senate had agreed upon a policy and had announced it to the world by means of the round-robin, Senator Hitchcock, the acting Democratic leader and therefore in a position to know the sentiment of that body, had written to Wilson urging amendments. " A number of Republican Senators," he wrote, " who signed Lodge's manifesto on the league of nations will, in my opinion, vote for it nevertheless if it is a part of the peace treaty. A still larger number will give it support if certain amendments are made." [42] The amendments he suggested were substantially the same as those recommended in the well-known cablegram sent by Taft.

If you bring back the treaty with the League of Nations in it, make more specific reservations of the Monroe Doctrine, fix a term for the duration of the League, and the limit of armament, require expressly unanimity of action in the Executive Council and Body of Delegates, and add to Article 15 a provision that where the Executive of the Body of Delegates finds the difference to grow out of an exclusively domestic policy, it shall recommend no settlement, the ground will be completely cut from under the opponents of the League in the Senate. . . . Monroe Doctrine reservation alone would probably carry the treaty, but others would make it certain.[43]

A few weeks later when it appeared unlikely that a change to

[41] *Taft Papers on League of Nations*, p. 156.

[42] David Hunter Miller, *My Diary at the Conference of Paris*, VI, 398. *Document* No. 511.

[43] Ray Stannard Baker, *Woodrow Wilson and World Settlement*, I, 328.

safeguard the Monroe doctrine would be made, Taft and Lowell sent a message to Wilson expressing alarm over the prospect but adding that with such an amendment the "treaty will be promptly ratified." [44]

Heeding advice of this nature the American delegation in Paris secured the consent of the other nations to changes in the covenant on these points. However, negotiating with the Senate on one side and foreign diplomats on the other proved an embarrassing process and a price had to be paid. Wilson only reluctantly requested these changes for the United States because he feared they would induce other parties to the bargain to present demands which might jeopardize his whole plan and because he, unlike most of his advisers, felt that concessions to the Senate would only cause the opposition there to advance its ground.[45] Nevertheless, the risk was taken and the covenant was revised to make certain of success in the Senate.

Wilson clearly believed that the opposition in the Senate would be overcome with ease. The tremendous demonstrations of enthusiasm which had greeted him on his trip to the United States, his earlier successes, the public support given his policies during the war, and the reports received from other leaders all confirmed this belief. "The people of the United States," he cabled House on the eve of his return to Europe, "are undoubtedly in favor of the League of Nations by an overwhelming majority. I can say this with perfect confidence, but there are many forces, particularly those prejudiced against Great Britain, which are exercising a considerable influence against it, and you ought to have that constantly in mind in everything you do." [46]

Looking back it is easy to see that Wilson and the American delegation did not concern themselves sufficiently about the

[44] *Ibid.*, p. 325.

[45] *Ibid.*, p. 321. Charles Seymour, *The Intimate Papers of Colonel House,* IV, 411. The course of the negotiations and the language of the revisions made to reassure American fears can be found in these two books, or perhaps more clearly in David Hunter Miller, *The Drafting of the Covenant,* pp. 276-302.

[46] Seymour, IV, 353.

danger of hostile action by the Senate. Viewed solely in the light of the existing situation their confidence was entirely warranted. No adequate warning reached them from America. Political leaders like the Democrat Hitchcock and the Republican Taft agreed that with the safeguards inserted in the treaty ratification was assured. When no one in the United States correctly estimated the danger Wilson and his associates, overwhelmed as they were with the problems of settling a world war and of creating a new international system, can be excused for making the same mistake. Still it is noticeable that politically-minded men were conspicuously absent from the American delegation. House, like Wilson, had earlier shown himself to be a keen judge of the trend of political currents in the United States, but his published letters prove he grossly misinterpreted the situation in the Senate, at least until his return to the United States in October, 1919. Henry White, the one Republican member of the American commission, had been a diplomat all his life and never a professional politician. He, too, misread the future. When the peace conference began he "thought the Republicans would support the general principle of a League of Nations, as he had talked with Mr. Roosevelt about it before he left."[47] Later he knew from his constant private correspondence with Lodge of the Senator's personal opposition, but there is no record that he either suspected the danger or warned Wilson of it.

Nothing could illuminate more clearly both White's misconception and Lodge's general attitude than an incident in their correspondence. Throughout the entire conference White tried valiantly to overcome the Senator's objections and when he learned, with a shock, of the round-robin he wrote a long letter defending the league idea and asking for the precise changes needed to make the covenant acceptable. Then wishing to avoid delay he cabled Lodge requesting him to cable through the State Department the "exact phraseology of amendments modifying League of Nations Covenant which Senate considers

[47] Miller, *Diary,* I, 49.

important. Our desire is to meet Senate's views as closely as it is possible to obtain acquiescence therein of other nations anxious for recognition of their own special interests which they will immediately insist upon in the Covenant if we demand exceptions in favor of ours." [48] To White, who had consulted with no one, this action seemed natural and obvious. Lodge was an intimate friend of many years standing who had advised him confidentially before he had started for Paris and who maintained the United States should enter a league with safeguards not in the pending covenant. Other Republican leaders who favored entering the league voluntarily suggested changes in the covenant to improve it or to make it more acceptable to critics in the United States. To Lodge, however, the White cablegram was a political trap. In his printed account Lodge expressed confidence in White's good faith yet insisted that if Wilson did not instigate the trick the President would know through control of the cables the contents of the message and Lodge would be committed to propositions he might not want to accept. Disturbed by these suspicions Lodge sought the advice of others. Significantly the people he consulted were not senators who favored entering the league with reservations but the irreconcilables Brandegee and Knox and Elihu Root. They shared his belief and he refused then, as always while the covenant was being drafted, to specify on what terms he would support it. Lodge was thinking in terms of political traps and political warfare; Henry White was as yet hardly aware that this political war had been declared.[49]

It was not only the leading members of the American mission in Paris who failed to realize the deadly nature of the weapons in the senatorial armory. Among the minor delegates none played a larger part in drafting the covenant or was consulted more frequently concerning it than David Hunter Miller.

[48] Lodge, *The Senate and the League of Nations,* p. 123.

[49] *Ibid.,* pp. 123-128. Nevins, *Henry White,* pp. 394-402. The reader of White's letters to Lodge on this and other occasions cannot fail to be impressed with the rugged integrity of this mild gentleman whose experience had not been such as to enable him to realize the effect his cablegram would produce.

A memorandum on the relative strength of the President and the Senate in a possible contest over the treaty, which he prepared for Colonel House, contained the generally accepted view. The President had the upper hand, the memorandum said, because he could refuse amendments proposed by the Senate and the Senate would be compelled to accept the treaty as it stood, or to insist upon a new and separate treaty with Germany to end the war. The latter alternative was highly improbable if the leading powers of the world should have already ratified the treaty.

> In other words, if the whole world is at war waiting for the United States Senate to abandon its position of obstruction in order to get to peace, the President's position will be impregnable and the Senate will be compelled by force of public opinion to do what he likes.
>
> Subsequently, the Senate can doubtless pass such resolutions as it pleases, which will have no legal effect whatsoever so far as the Treaty is concerned.[50]

Whether or not President Wilson saw this memorandum there can be no doubt it expressed his views exactly. Not only was his policy based on this belief but in a book written many years before personal participation could bias his judgment he had reached the same conclusion. "The initiative in foreign affairs, which the President possesses without any restriction whatever," he had written, "is virtually the power to control them absolutely. . . . He need disclose no step of negotiation until it is complete, and when in any critical matter it is completed the government is virtually committed. Whatever its disinclination, the Senate may feel itself committed also."[51]

There were few who did not then agree that the Wilsonian estimate of the situation was correct. The most flattering compliment paid to it was the dejection of the irreconcilables. George Harvey, who regularly participated in the private

[50] Miller, *Diary,* IX, 311-312. Document No. 944.

[51] *Constitutional Government in the United States,* pp. 77-78. This passage was quoted as proof of Wilson's intention to disregard the Senate and defy its powers. *Congressional Record,* Dec. 21, 1918, p. 724.

deliberations of the Republican irreconcilables, has told of the despondency of the group when they met at Senator Brandegee's house in May 1919. The outlook was "lamentably gloomy." [52] Little had been accomplished since the round-robin. The one notable achievement was the maintenance of party solidarity when the revised covenant of the league had been published. There was danger that some of the Republican senators scattered throughout the country might take the position that the amendments made the treaty acceptable to them. To avert any break in the party ranks a telegram signed by Lodge and Curtis, the Republican whip, was sent to all Republican senators, urging them to reserve "final expression of opinion respecting the amended league covenant until the latest draft has been carefully studied and until there has been an opportunity for conference." [53] Although all the Republican members of the Senate except six agreed to avoid making commitments until after a party conference, Lodge himself on the very day of this telegram issued a statement saying further amendments would be required.[54]

Except for this indication that the party in the Senate was still able to act together, the Republican senators of all shades of opinion had done little but wait for the new Congress to assemble. Plans had been discussed. Lodge and the irreconcilables Borah and McCormick had wanted Beveridge to undertake a continental speaking tour to counterbalance that which Taft was making for the league. That idea was dropped lest it serve

[52] Harvey, *Henry Clay Frick, The Man,* pp. 325-326. Harvey tells how he successfully solicited funds from Frick for the support of the irreconcilable propaganda campaign. Frick and Andrew W. Mellon, who had been approached by Senator Knox, supplied most of the money used. Many of the furious editorials appearing in *Harvey's Weekly* are quoted by Fleming. Further information of the part played by Harvey can be found in the biography of him by Willis Fletcher Johnson entitled *George Harvey, a Passionate Patriot.*

[53] New York *Times,* April 30, 1919.

[54] *Congressional Record,* May 28, 1919, p. 329. In the course of his speech Senator Robinson inserted a number of newspaper comments on this telegram and other attempts to secure party action on the treaty. Fleming, pp. 196-198.

to "advertise Taft." [55] Lodge had decided, as he told Borah and Beveridge, "there was only one thing to do and that was to proceed in the discussion of the treaty by way of amendment and reservation." [56]

As soon as the new Congress met in special session on May 19, 1919, the contest between the various elements within the Republican party was resumed. At the very outset the irreconcilable Republicans secured a great advantage. The election in November had given the Republicans a majority of two in the Senate, there being forty-nine of them and forty-seven Democrats. This small margin, which included the vote of Senator Newberry whose election was contested and who was later forced to resign, was of the utmost importance. It meant that the Republicans would organize the Senate and would have a majority on each committee. It meant that through their control of the Committee on Foreign Relations they could delay indefinitely or hasten the final action of the Senate according to the trend of public opinion and the needs of their policy. It meant that all the weapons of that powerful committee could readily be used. The important question was which element among the Republicans would represent the party on the Committee on Foreign Relations. The announcement of the composition of the committee made it known that once again the irreconcilables had won a victory within the party. Of the ten Republican members six were openly irreconcilable. Constituting less than one-third of the Republicans in the Senate they could outvote the majority group in the proceedings of the committee. With them on the committee were the chairman Lodge, really an irreconcilable, McCumber, the most outspoken advocate of the league among the Republican senators, and two staunch party regulars who could be trusted to follow the party leaders.

This victory of the irreconcilables resulted in part from senatorial custom. Lodge, McCumber and four of the irreconci-

[55] Bowers, *Beveridge*, p. 505.

[56] *The Senate and the League of Nations*, p. 147. Bowers, *Beveridge*, p. 507.

lables had been members of the committee in the preceding Congress and following the usual practice continued to serve. It was the appointment of the four new Republican members that constituted the success of the extreme opponents. These new members were the irreconcilables Moses of New Hampshire and Johnson of California, and Senators Harding and New, two loyal partisans then known only for their strict regularity. The extraordinary composition of the committee drew forth some bitter comments from both Democrats and Republicans. Senator Hitchcock, in appealing to the Republicans who favored the league, pointed to the membership of the committee as evidence that there was a settled purpose to make a political issue out of the treaty. That, he said, was the purpose of the aggressive minority of the

> controlling interests over on the Republican side which filled the Committee on Foreign Relations with Senators practically pledged to oppose the league of nations and practically pledged to bring an amendment out of the Foreign Relations Committee.
>
> Do Senators think I have not talked with Republicans? I know Republicans on the other side of this Chamber who feel just as I feel, indignant that agreement with the leaders on the treaty should have been made a test to decide whether a Senator should go on the Foreign Relations Committee or not. I am not the only indignant one. There are Republican Senators on the other side of this Chamber, and a number of them, indignant that their personal views on the league of nations should have been inquired into, and it should have been made necessary for them to pledge themselves on an issue which should be decided upon its merits and not on political considerations.[57]

Ex-President Taft, making the same effort as the Democrat Hitchcock to rally the majority of Republican senators against the group that was endeavoring to make the treaty a partisan issue, used more specific language. The Republican leaders, he said, had proved their purpose by fixing the Committee on Foreign Relations so they

> should have Republicans enough to give them a majority without the vote of Mr. McCumber, known to be favorable to the treaty, and by a

[57] *Congressional Record,* June 9, 1919, p. 791.

careful selection of Republicans for that majority whose opposition to the treaty has been pronounced. Senator Kellogg would naturally have been taken before Senator Moses, a new Senator, and one whose term expires in two years. Senator Kellogg, however, ventured to make a speech in favor of a league of nations even before the covenant was agreed upon, and declined to sign the 'round-robin.' [58]

No explanation was offered by any Republican leader in the Senate. The sole comment of Lodge in his *apologia* was, "It will be seen at once that this was a strong committee and such as the existing conditions demanded." [59]

With the Committee on Foreign Relations safely under their control the irreconcilables faced the future with greater confidence than ever before. They were, however, still far from ultimate victory and their immediate program met with failure. Senator Knox introduced a resolution demanding that the Senate be given an opportunity to ratify the treaty of peace without the covenant which was to be left for future consideration.[60] This was the policy of the round-robin, but, as Wilson had correctly judged, the Republican senators could not be held to it when confronted with the fact of the peace terms and the covenant of the league fused into one settlement. Enough opposition developed to prevent the Knox resolution from being pushed to a vote.[61]

Nevertheless, it became increasingly clear during the debates in May and June, when the irreconcilables continued to display more activity than the others, that the Republicans in the Senate were going to make the treaty an issue for party action. The best evidence of this can be found in the desperate protests and the growing alarm of those Republicans who favored the league and who knew that partisan consideration would endanger the treaty.[62] In promoting this unity and in suggest-

[58] *Congressional Record,* June 20, 1919, p. 1430.

[59] *The Senate and the League of Nations,* p. 152.

[60] *Congressional Record,* June 10, 1919, p. 894.

[61] New York *Times,* June 22, 1919. Fleming, pp. 221-227.

[62] McCumber in the Senate, *Congressional Record,* June 18, 1919, pp. 1264-1276. Taft in public addresses, *Ibid.,* June 10, 1919, pp. 898-899; June 20,

ing the terms on which it could be achieved Elihu Root played a noteworthy part. A former Secretary of State and a former senator, he had a large following among the conservatives of the country and enjoyed a reputation for statesmanship hardly justified by his actions during this crisis, for he either valued party solidarity higher than the league of nations or ingenuously played into the hands of the irreconcilables. At the psychological moment when Republican senators were still undecided Root made public a letter to Lodge in which he praised much in the covenant but said the Senate should insist on reservations to eliminate article 10, to make more certain the right of withdrawal from the league, and to protect further domestic questions and the Monroe doctrine.[63] The effect of Root's letter was momentous. Lodge wrote in a private letter that it " has consolidated feeling in the Senate " and " is producing immense effect upon public opinion throughout the country." [64]

According to a newspaper account it was Root's advice and action that had persuaded the irreconcilables to drop the Knox resolution for the separation of the covenant from the league and to concentrate on the opposition to be expressed after the treaty should reach the Senate.[65] Certainly the irreconcilables were well satisfied. On the day before the letter was made public Knox wrote to Beveridge that he had " spent six or seven hours with Root yesterday " and that Beveridge would be pleased with the news he would find in the paper on the next day.[66] There was reason for this satisfaction. The response to Root's letter indicated that the party in the Senate could be held together on a policy which might kill the treaty. The majority

1919, pp. 1430-1431. For a protest by twenty-eight prominent Republicans see the New York *Times,* June 21, 1919.

[63] New York *Times,* June 22, 1919. *Congressional Record,* June 23, 1919, p. 1549. In a public statement Taft criticised Root's advice and contrasted his opposition to Article 10 with his former approval of it in a letter to Will Hays. *Ibid.,* p. 1550.

[64] Nevins, *Henry White,* p. 449, n. 1.

[65] New York *Times,* June 22, 1919.

[66] Bowers, *Beveridge,* p. 506.

of Republican senators were being maneuvered into the position of insisting on drastic changes in the treaty while the irreconcilables were not being bound to accept the treaty when changed. Of course the unity of the Republicans in the Senate was by no means certain. It was after Root's letter that the Chairman of the Republican National Committee, replying to a warning that if Wilson got the treaty ratified the next election would be lost, stated that he knew of no way to commit the party "when the party is divided as it is." [67] Much would depend on the course of public opinion, on what Wilson and the Democrats would do, and on the ability of the Republican leaders in the Senate to hold their followers together.

Such was the situation when Wilson returned with the peace treaty—more accurately treaties, for the settlement was embodied in several separate documents. On July 10, the day after his return from Europe, the President submitted the peace treaty to the Senate and delivered an address in person. On July 29, he sent to the Senate the treaty by which Great Britain and the United States guaranteed France against attack.[68] No final action was ever taken by the Senate on the treaty of guarantee so that it shared the fate of the peace treaty to which it was supplementary.

With the treaty of peace in the hands of the Senate the powers of the Committee on Foreign Relations were brought into play by the opponents of the league. Their control of the committee enabled them to keep the treaty from the Senate for

[67] *Ibid.*

[68] In addition to these two treaties three protocols had been signed on June 28, 1919, as a part of the general settlement. They were sent to the Senate on Aug. 1 and Aug. 29. No action was ever taken on them nor was any necessary after the rejection of the basic agreement. A characteristically bitter attack made by Senator Brandegee on the President because the treaty of guarantee was not submitted on the same day as the peace treaty can be found in the *Congressional Record* of July 24, 1919. According to a newspaper account there was a conference of Republican leaders in the cloak room immediately after the President's address on July 10. Significantly, those named as participants were Lodge and the irreconcilables Borah, Brandegee, Fall and McCormick. New York *Tribune,* July 11, 1919, quoted in Fleming, p. 238.

two months. Delay was essential to their cause, for the state of public and senatorial opinion was such that prompt action would be fatal. Several years later one of them, Senator Moses, asserted that if the rules of the Senate had permitted a quick decision "the Versailles treaty would have been ratified without reservation." [69] Time was needed to arouse a hostile public opinion, to wait for a public reaction against the ideals of the war period, and to work further on the majority of their Republican colleagues in the Senate. Devices to gain time proved readily available. First, the long treaty of several hundred printed pages was read aloud line by line. The emptiness of this formality is shown by the fact that on one occasion, at least, Senator Lodge found himself reading only to the clerk of the committee and even the clerk absented himself from the room.[70] The reading consumed two weeks. Then the committee held public hearings which lasted for six weeks more. Naturally the proponents of the league complained of these dilatory tactics, but they lacked the votes necessary to take the treaty out of the hands of the committee. With the tide of opinion running against them it was futile for the minority members of the committee to protest that the majority recommendations were "a foregone conclusion" and that "they could have been made in July as well as in September and would have been the same." [71]

The hearings served another purpose in addition to delaying the action of the Senate. The treaty was to be considered in open executive session. As on the former occasions when the galleries were opened during the consideration of a treaty the opponents of the treaty took the lead in demanding that procedure.[72] Now, however, for the first time in the history of the United States hearings on a treaty were to be open to the public. The character of the hearings amply demonstrated their pur-

[69] Washington *Post,* April 29, 1925.

[70] New York *Tribune,* July 29, 1919, quoted in Fleming, p. 295.

[71] *Congressional Record,* Sept. 11, 1919, p. 5213.

[72] Senator Borah. *Congressional Record,* Dec. 4, 1918, p. 71.

pose, which was decidedly not to enlighten the majority of the committee who had already expressed their unwavering hostility. Various members of the American delegation to the peace conference gave testimony, but no one else appeared before the committee except representatives of national groups that felt their countries had received less than justice at Paris. There were many such. Self-appointed spokesmen pled the causes of Ireland, China, India, Albania, Sweden, Czecho-Slovakia, Egypt, Hungary, Italy, Jugo-Slavia, Esthonia, Latvia, Lithuania, Persia and Ukrainia.[73] Even a group of American negroes were permitted to state their case and to offer amendments to protect their minority rights in the United States. As one writer shrewdly observes, " the record does not include what the Committee would have said if the Peace Conference had attempted to legislate in behalf of the American Negro." [74] Stirring up opposition to the treaty among the foreign elements in the United States was a natural policy for the irreconcilables.

The majority report of the Committee on Foreign Relations, that reached the Senate on September 10, made several things certain.[75] The irreconcilables no longer entertained any hope of persuading the Republicans in the Senate to unite on a policy of complete rejection. Not one of the six Republicans on the committee who openly desired rejection signed a report to that effect. Following the advice of Lodge they proceeded " by way of amendment and reservation," and with Lodge, Harding and New recommended forty-five amendments, many covering the same point, and four reservations. There was no pretence in

[73] The hearings, filling a volume of 1300 pages, were published as *S. Doc.* No. 106, *66th Cong., 1st sess.*

[74] Fleming, p. 329.

[75] The report can be found in the *Congressional Record* of the same date and the Democratic minority report and that of McCumber under the dates of Sept. 11, and 15, 1919. They are also printed in *S. Rep.* No. 176, *66th Cong., 1st sess.* Curiously, in neither of these official printings are the names of the signers of the majority report listed. Yet it is clear that nine Republicans did so. The names of six Democrats signing their minority report are given. Apparently one Democrat, Shields of Tennessee, signed no report.

the report of the majority that these changes would make them want to ratify the treaty. On the contrary the report exhibited a bitter hostility that brought a scathing rebuke from the tenth Republican member of the committee. Participants in events seldom express the matured judgment of posterity, yet the passage of time will probably confirm, rather than modify, the criticism made by Senator McCumber in his minority report.

> It has always been understood that the purpose of a report from any Senate committee was to briefly explain the object of a bill or treaty reported and the reasons for any amendments thereto. And this has been the general rule adopted by all committees in reporting any matter to the Senate. The majority of the Committee on Foreign Relations have deviated from this rule in reporting this treaty. The great purpose of the covenant upon which 27 nations, the great and small of the world, studied and labored for six months in an attempt to formulate a plan that would tend to insure good fellowship among the nations of the world and prevent another such catastrophe as we have just passed through have not been even alluded to. Not one word is said, not a single allusion made, concerning either the great purpose of the league of nations or the methods by which those purposes are to be accomplished.
>
> Irony and sarcasm have been substituted for argument, and positions taken by the press or individuals outside the Senate seem to command more attention than the treaty itself. . . . It is regrettable that the consideration of a matter so foreign to any kind of partisanship should be influenced in the country as well as on the floor of this Senate by hostility toward or subserviency to the President of the United States. No matter how just may be any antagonisms against President Wilson, the aspirations and hopes of a wounded and bleeding world ought not to be denied because, under our Constitution, the treaty must first be formulated by him.[76]

With nine of the ten Republican members of the Committee on Foreign Relations demanding serious changes in the treaty, while six of the seven Democratic members signed a report urging its acceptance with no changes, no doubt of the influence of political allegiance could have existed. But the committee did not accurately represent the Senate. Though the enemies of the league who controlled the committee did not propose the

[76] *Congressional Record,* Sept. 15, 1919, p. 5356.

direct rejection of the treaty, their report was not one on which the Republicans in the Senate could be held together. That Republican unity was not attainable on those terms had been made clear even before the report reached the Senate. All during July and August, when the treaty was still in committee, the debate in the Senate had continued and for the first time the expression of Republican senatorial opinion was not left chiefly to the irreconcilables. The speeches of these previously silent Republican senators and their numerous press statements proclaimed the defeat of the irreconcilables who had struggled to commit the party to a rejection of the treaty. The campaign of the irreconcilables may have driven them to the policy of insisting on reservations to the treaty, but with some reservations the Republican majority in the Senate was going to vote for the entry of the United States into the league of nations. Some desired strong reservations, others would be satisfied with mild reservations. Seven of the latter, disregarding their Republican leaders, began to hold conferences to decide on a program of interpretative reservations. According to newspaper accounts they expected that about twenty Republicans would join their movement and hoped that the results of it would be accepted by the Democrats, for they were seeking an agreement with the Democrats as much or even more than with the Republican leaders.[77]

The contest had so far produced only one final and definite result. The irreconcilables had failed in their attempt to commit the Republican senators to an outright rejection of the treaty, and they themselves had admitted their defeat in the majority report of the Committe on Foreign Relations. Three other possibilities remained. The Republicans might be held together on a program of reservations that could be supported by all of them, even by the mild reservationists. Or by offering

[77] New York *Times*, Aug. 1, 1919. The seven senators mentioned were McCumber, Cummins, Kellogg, Lenroot, Spencer, McNary and Colt. Only when the private papers of these senators become available will it be possible to know the details of what happened. The contemporary newspaper accounts enable the reader to follow the main course of events.

to accept less severe reservations, Wilson and the Democrats might reach an understanding with the mild reservationists that would detach them from the other Republicans. With them—and their numbers were likely to be augmented once party lines were definitely broken—the necessary two-thirds vote might easily be secured. Or by resolutely refusing any concessions, the Democrats might yet win completely through the votes of some Republican senators who would be willing to sacrifice their desires for mild reservations, rather than have the treaty rejected and the league of nations crippled at birth by the absence of the United States.

This last alternative was the one which the Democratic leaders publicly insisted could and would be attained. In a newspaper interview Senator Hitchcock traced the retreat of the Republicans and confidently predicted complete victory for his side. First, he said, the Republicans in the Senate had advocated the separation of the league from the treaty, then there was talk of rejecting the treaty, then of direct amendments, still later of reservations, now of mild reservations and finally the treaty would be ratified exactly as submitted to the Senate.[78] Publicly, Wilson gave no hint that he contemplated the slightest concession. Privately, he gave to Senator Hitchcock, even before starting his speaking tour, an outline of the interpretative reservations he would accept if necessary.[79] But, either because he hoped that it would not be necessary to accept any reservations, or because he feared that concessions by him so early in the proceedings would lead to further demands, the President took no steps to meet the advances of the mild reservationist group among the Republicans. No bid was made for their support until after they had come to terms with the other Republican senators.

Wilson had begun to fight for his treaty immediately after his return to the country. He invited many of the Republican

[78] New York *Times,* Aug. 1, 1919.

[79] H. Maurice Darling, "Who Kept the United States Out of the League of Nations?" *Canadian Historical Review,* X, 197-198.

senators to the White House for individual conversations.[80] He placed his chief reliance, however, on an appeal to the people, the weapon in the presidential armory which he preferred to all others. Bringing the force of public opinion to bear on an unruly Congress was, of course, nothing new, but none of Wilson's predecessors had turned to the public for support more consistently or more successfully than he. Inevitably in this crisis he appealed to the people once again. The speaking tour, begun early in September, ended three weeks later in his collapse. The burden of the presidency during the war, during the peace conference and now during this new contest at home had finally exhausted his strength and he returned to the White House where he remained broken and paralyzed. The most powerful defender of the treaty could fight no more. The strongest weapon that could be used in behalf of the treaty was useless, for no one but the President could wield it.[81]

Under normal circumstances, only the President is in a position to arouse and organize public sentiment in a contest with the Senate. In the fall of 1919 peculiar circumstances deprived the fight for the treaty of all leadership. Although Wilson was too sick to participate, the doubts concerning the duration of his illness and even his presence rendered it difficult for any other Democrat to assume full command and responsibility.

[80] Lodge printed a list of the senators invited to the White House and wrote that all of them assured the President some reservations would be essential if the treaty were to be approved. *The Senate and the League of Nations,* pp. 157-158.

[81] Naturally many have speculated on what would have happened if Wilson's strength could have endured the strain for several months more. Naturally, also, the conclusions reached are apt to depend on the speculator's premises. Lodge and other opponents of the league say the trip had been a failure, the audiences cold and public opinion hostile. Wilson's friends assert the contrary. No answer can be given with any assurance of truth. Although the newspapers are supposed to have become far more objective in reporting events than they were in the days of the Lincoln-Douglas debates, the facts here were imponderable and the reports highly colored by prejudice. On the other hand, there are substantial reasons for believing that if Wilson's collapse had been immediately fatal the treaty would have been ratified with reservations.

As a matter of fact, there was no dominant figure in the Democratic party to act as leader. Senator Hitchcock, who acted during the crucial months as Democratic leader in the Senate because of the protracted fatal illness of the titular leader, struggled valiantly but neither commanded a national following nor displayed outstanding parliamentary skill. Indeed all the Democrats seemed to be palsied by a consciousness of certain defeat in the approaching national election. In the nature of things no prominent Republican was in a position to supply the necessary leadership.

The serious consequences of this lack of leadership became apparent in the two months following Wilson's collapse. Public opinion, which according to common agreement had been decidedly in favor of joining the league, and upon which Wilson had counted for success, had become confused and drifted away from its earlier position.[82] In the United States, as throughout Europe, there was occurring that shift in opinion which one writer has labelled a "slump in idealism," but which might more accurately be described as a substitution of near-sighted nationalism for international cooperation and the general good. The people of Europe and America showed themselves less willing than during the war to sacrifice any immediate national interest for the sake of future international peace. The changing attitude of the American public toward the new international system Wilson proposed paralleled the changes taking place on solely domestic questions. During the

[82] Throughout the entire debate on the league quantities of material illustrating the views of the public were inserted in the *Congressional Record.* Petitions and memorials appeared daily, editorials from the newspapers of the country almost as often, and straw votes or polls of various business associations, women's clubs, college faculties and religious groups were also recorded. The above statement regarding public opinion is based on these data, on a reading of the files of several newspapers, on seminar reports of more than a dozen students each of whom examined the newspapers of a different state, and on the few secondary studies available. Of these last, the most valuable are Fleming and the *Survey of American Foreign Relations,* 1928, edited by Howland.

war, despite profiteering and human selfishness, there was a widespread willingness to subordinate personal economic interests to those of the country. After the armistice that sentiment quickly evaporated and there arose a general demand for the economic *sauve qui peut* which characterized the post-war period. The people who believed they would prosper individually under that policy inclined to the belief that the United States could safely trust itself to an international system based on the same doctrine.

There is as yet no evidence that the opponents of Wilson's treaty anticipated this reaction in public opinion. They did sense the process in its early stages and took full advantage of it. Indeed by beating the tom toms of nationalism they inflamed the public and contributed to the process. The fragmentary studies which have been made indicate that the newspapers which shifted from a complete endorsement of the league to a demand for reservations or to outright opposition generally lagged behind the irreconcilables in the Senate, taking arguments from their speeches rather than supplying them. It was the knowledge that the tide of opinion was running their way that made the irreconcilables use their powers to delay action. When Senator Johnson of California was called back to Washington from his speaking tour to lead the fight for an amendment he had proposed, he pled with his irreconcilable associates for more time. "If we could just get sixty days before the final vote," a newspaper reported him as saying, "the American people would make their desires known in such unmistakable terms that nothing would be left of this treaty." [83]

Although the delay of sixty days which Johnson requested was secured, his prediction was not fulfilled by the means he had contemplated. Public opinion in the United States had not expressed itself against the league when the Senate voted. On

[83] New York *Tribune,* Sept. 24, 1919, cited by Fleming, p. 341. According to the calculations of Hitchcock the opponents of the treaty consumed two and a half times as much time as its supporters during September and October. *Congressional Record,* Nov. 13, 1919, p. 8426.

the contrary there is every reason to believe that, despite the reaction and despite the confusion, the public was accurately represented by the Senate in which over eighty per cent of the votes were cast for the treaty with and without reservations. Newspaper editorials and all other indices to public opinion support that conclusion. So also does the judgment of Wilson's coldest and most calculating opponent. Writing to Harvey about the Republican platform of 1920, which he wanted " so broad that those of us who have fought the treaty for a year in the Senate can all stand upon it without any difficulty, and that we can use every argument, from Borah's down to McCumber's," he said, " I think the bulk of the Convention and the mass of the people at the present moment are in favor of the treaty with the reservations which bear my name. But I do not want to make any pledge as to the future." [84] If the Republican party in the Senate had joined the irreconcilables, public opinion might have operated as Wilson had expected, but the majority of the Republicans insisted they wanted to enter the league with a few reservations to protect American interests. Hence no clear issue was presented and public opinion could not be mobilized for the treaty.

While the public and the majority in the Senate groped toward some decision the debate in the Senate continued with increasing tension. The intellectual level of it, even when judged by the better speeches on either side, gave no cause for national pride. It was decidedly inferior in this respect to the debate in the constitutional convention of 1787. However, on that occasion the speakers addressed themselves solely to the mental capacity of the other members, whereas in 1919, the debate being in open session, the senators necessarily appealed to the public. Many of the speeches did not compliment the public mind, for there was much demagoguery. Most of this came from the opponents of the treaty, since the circumstances of the case restricted to them the opportunities to curry favor by pandering to popular and nationalistic prejudices.

[84] Johnson, *George Harvey*, p. 274.

The hatred of the Irish in America for Great Britain was exploited, as so often in the past. The British Ambassador informed Henry White that two "prominent Republicans" had explained to him that in using the Irish question to defeat the Democrats they would attack England without mercy and had wished him to inform his government that there was no real animosity.[85] The identity of the Republicans in question was not revealed. Lodge was keenly aware of the possibilities in the Irish question. "You know what the Irish vote is in this country," he wrote Henry White, "As far as I can make out, they are bitterly opposed to the League, and the fate of the Democratic party in the Northern States is in their hands." [86] Other groups besides the Irish received attention. One irreconcilable, Sherman, gave a perfect example of the demagogue in a speech devoted to the thesis that the majority of countries in the league would be Catholic in religion, that the Papacy had never abandoned its claim to temporal power, and that the league would be under the domination of the Pope.[87] The Democratic irreconcilable Reed, who generally warned the public that the six votes of the British empire would mean English domination of the league, devoted one speech to proving for the benefit of the South that the league would be ruled by colored peoples.[88] Next to the "injustices" of the Irish the

[85] Nevins, *Henry White,* p. 456.

[86] *Ibid.,* p. 455.

[87] *Congressional Record,* June 20, 1919, pp. 1435-1438. The nature of his appeal can be judged by this extract. "Shall the United States commit itself to the mercy of a power from which our ancestors delivered us? Shall we risk entangling ourselves and our posterity in the toils we have escaped through their wisdom and the warnings they left to guide us on the duties and perils of our generation? The covenant of the league of nations bears within its folds a reactionary power more fatal and insidious than a Prussian helmet, more dangerous than future war!"

[88] *Ibid.,* May 26, 1919, pp. 235-246. In the course of this speech he submitted "statistics" showing that the 17 dark countries among the original signatories of the league had a population of over 800 million while the 15 white countries numbered fewer than 300 million people. His description of

most frequent subject for this type of attack were the wrongs done the Chinese in Shantung. The treaty was vulnerable on this point and probably the speakers were not unaware of the effects of their speeches on anti-Japanese feeling along the Pacific coast. Even the Koreans had their day in court, although little sympathy had been extended before 1919.[89] The irony of the situation was that the treaty was being opposed not because of the real or alleged injustices in it, but because of the machinery provided to correct international wrongs.

When the voting began in October, no steps had been taken by the Democrats to reach an understanding with the Republicans wanting mild reservations and the latter were drifting toward a politically natural alliance with their fellow Republicans on terms more hostile to the treaty than those they would have preferred. In the votes on the amendments proposed both by the Committee on Foreign Relations and by individual senators the mild reservationists joined with the almost solid Democratic membership and all the amendments were lost. On November 7, the voting began on the reservations and then the mild reservationists united with the balance of the Republicans. Belated efforts by the Democrats to detach the mild reservationists by offering to accept interpretative reservations failed completely. Equally futile were the frantic last minute appeals to the mild reservationists not to assist the Republicans who had always wanted to kill the treaty by voting for reservations they had earlier condemned as being equivalent to rejection.[90] The Republican ranks held firmly together. The final position of the mild reservationists was described by one of them in these

conditions in the dark countries was worthy of a stump speech in South Carolina in the 1890's.

[89] *Ibid.,* Oct. 13, 1919, pp. 6812-6826.

[90] Among these appeals none was more powerful than that of Senator Pittman on the day of the final vote. In it he recapitulated from the *Record* the various attempts made by the Democrats to compromise with the mild reservationists. *Congressional Record,* Nov. 19, 1919, pp. 8793-8796. The reservations proposed by Hitchcock as a substitute for the Lodge or Republican reservations were presented on Nov. 13, and are printed in the *Record* of that date, p. 8433.

terms. When the administration forces declined to listen to any efforts at agreement the " middle ground Senators found themselves obliged to commit themselves to the Lodge program after concessions were made by the radicals, and they now are unable to break away." [91]

As reservation after reservation was added to the treaty by the unbroken Republican majority, some friends of the league in alarm pled with the Democrats to accept what could be gotten rather than lose everything. Senator McCumber made such a plea immediately before the vote was taken. Other sincere advocates of the league who were not members of the Senate urged the same course. On the day of the final vote a mild reservationist read into the *Record* a statement by the executive committee of the League to Enforce Peace condemning some of the reservations, yet advising their acceptance since the league could still accomplish its purpose. These pleas, too, fell on deaf ears. At a conference of Democratic senators held before the final vote Senator Hitchcock read a letter from the White House in which the President called upon the friends and supporters of the treaty to vote against the Lodge resolution of ratification because the reservations in it nullified the treaty.[92]

Consequently when the Senate voted on the treaty it failed to

[91] New York *Times,* Nov. 17, 1919.

[92] *Congressional Record,* Nov. 19, 1919, p. 8768. Wilson went on to say—" I understand that the door will probably then be open for a genuine resolution of ratification." Others beside Wilson thought the same. Theodore Marburg, a prominent Republican who had been one of the founders of the League to Enforce Peace and whose published correspondence shows that he was generally correct in estimating the situation, supported Wilson's tactics at this time. On Nov. 13, he wrote in a letter to Lord Bryce, " Making concessions to the opponents of the treaty only serves to whet their appetites. . . . Personally I feel that if the friends of the treaty in the Senate refuse to ratify it with the objectionable reservations we will get the treaty unimpaired because the alternative of going back to Germany to negotiate a new treaty is too absurd." He signed the appeal of the League to Enforce Peace to the Democrats, solely because he thought the minority in that organization should loyally support the policy of the majority. *Development of the League of Nations Idea,* II, 657-658, 673.

receive a two-thirds vote both with and without reservations. With the fourteen reservations it was rejected by a vote of 39 to 55.[93] Without the reservations it was rejected by a vote of 38 to 53. An analysis of the final votes and the decisive vote on each reservation (Table 1) reveals the controlling influence of party politics. The reservations were added by practically solid Republican votes. Three times, on the preamble and on reservations 6 and 14, Senator McCumber left his party, as did Senator Sherman on reservation 13. With those rare exceptions the Republicans were unanimous on the reservations every one of which needed only the Republican votes it received to be adopted. The Democrats were practically, although not absolutely, as united as the Republicans on the reservations. There was a handful of Democrats who voted for all the reservations and on the less important reservations several others deserted the party ranks. On the final votes the Democrats voted 42 to 4 against ratification with the reservations, and 37 to 7 in favor of ratification without reservations. The Republicans preserved their unity in voting against ratification without reservations, the vote being 46 to 1. Only McCumber left the party ranks. But on the vote for ratification with the reservations a decided break occurred. Thirteen Republicans, all irreconcilables, refused to go with the party majority. Nevertheless, the Republicans cast more than two-thirds of their votes for the treaty with reservations, the numbers being 35 for and 13 against. The refusal of the thirteen irreconcilable Republicans to remain with their party did not affect the result because the nearly solid Democratic vote would have prevented the ratification of the treaty with reservations.

When the same votes are analyzed by groups rather than by party affiliation, the importance of the irreconcilables in decid-

[93] There was one vacancy in the Senate when the vote was taken. Senator Fall was absent but was recorded as being opposed to the treaty either with or without reservations.

TABLE I

Votes on the Versailles Treaty by Parties.

		November, 1919		March, 1920	
		Yea	Nay	Yea	Nay
Preamble	Democrats	3	39		
	Republicans	45	1		
Reservation No. 1 (Withdrawal)	Democrats	5	35	10	20
	Republicans	45	0	35	0
Reservation No. 2 (Article 10)	Democrats	4	33	14	26
	Republicans	42	0	42	0
Reservation No. 3 (Mandates)	Democrats	9	31	30	4
	Republicans	41	0	38	0
Reservation No. 4 (Domestic questions)	Democrats	10	36	14	25
	Republicans	49	0	42	0
Reservation No. 5 (Monroe Doctrine)	Democrats	9	34	17	22
	Republicans	46	0	41	0
Reservation No. 6 (Shantung)	Democrats	5	40	10	21
	Republicans	48	1	38	0
Reservation No. 7 (Appointment of representatives)	Democrats	5	40	17	14
	Republicans	48	0	38	0
Reservation No. 8 (Reparations commission)	Democrats	5	40	6	22
	Republicans	49	0	35	0
Reservation No. 9 (Expenses of League)	Democrats	7	39	8	25
	Republicans	49	0	38	0
Reservation No. 10 (Armaments)	Democrats	7	39	9	26
	Republicans	49	0	40	0
Reservation No. 11 (Covenant-breaking states)	Democrats	5	41	5	28
	Republicans	48	0	39	0
Reservation No. 12 (Illegal acts)	Democrats	4	41	8	26
	Republicans	48	0	37	1
Reservation No. 13 (International labor)	Democrats	8	34	6	27
	Republicans	46	1	38	0
Reservation No. 14 (Dominion votes)	Democrats	8	37	17	20
	Republicans	47	1	40	0
Reservation No. 15 (Irish self-determination)	Democrats			21	16
	Republicans			17	20
Ratification With Reservations	Democrats	4	42	21	23
	Republicans	35	13	28	12
Ratification Without Reservations	Democrats	37	7		
	Republicans	1	46		

ing the issue becomes more apparent. (Table 2).[94] The irreconcilables occupied a strong position because of the peculiar rule of the Senate which, since 1868, permitted amendments to be inserted or reservations added by an ordinary majority although a two-thirds majority was necessary on the final vote of ratification.[95] There were 39 Democrats who voted against the treaty with reservations. There were 39 senators, 35 Republicans and 4 Democrats, who wanted the treaty with reservations. Since the reservationists did not constitute a majority no reservations could have been added without the votes of the 17 irreconcilables.[96] As a matter of fact the Democrats did not always muster their full strength against the reservations, but

[94] A similar table published in an article by George A. Finch, "The Treaty of Peace with Germany in the United States Senate," in the *American Journal of International Law,* XIV, 155-206, is inaccurate because of mistakes in allocating senators to the three groups. For one thing it is evident from a check that Senator Thomas was not included among the irreconcilables.

[95] See page 120. The Vice-President during the crisis seized an opportunity to express to the Senate his views on this rule and denounced it as being "in derogation if not in violation of the Constitution of the United States." *Congressional Record,* Nov. 19, 1919, p. 8788.

[96] There has been much confusion and inaccuracy regarding the number of irreconcilables, or senators against the treaty either with or without reservations. This is due in part to the fact that one was absent on the final vote and in part to the fact that the membership of the group changed between the vote in November and the vote in March. In November there were 14 Republicans in the group: Borah, Brandegee, Fernald, France, Gronna, Johnson, Knox, LaFollette, McCormick, Moses, Norris, Poindexter, Sherman and Fall. Fall was absent on the final vote but had voted with the irreconcilables on reservations and was paired against the treaty without reservations. His opposition to the treaty in any form was announced and he must properly be included with the irreconcilables. There were 3 Democratic irreconcilables in November, Reed, Thomas and Trammel. The case of the last named was peculiar. He several times stated publicly he was for the treaty. New York *Times,* Sept. 28, 1919; *Congressional Record,* Nov. 18, 1919, p. 8738. Nevertheless he voted against it in both forms. In March, however, he voted for it with reservations. He was the only one who left the irreconcilable group in March while Shields, a Democrat, and Penrose, a Republican, who had both voted for the treaty with reservations went against it in March, making 18 irreconcilables on the second test.

TABLE II

Votes on the Versailles Treaty by Groups.

		November, 1919		March, 1920	
		Yea	Nay	Yea	Nay
Preamble	Advocates	0	36		
	Reservationists	33	2		
	Irreconcilables	15	2		
Reservation No. 1 (Withdrawal)	Advocates	1	33	6	19
	Reservationists	34	0	28	0
	Irreconcilables	15	2	12	1
Reservation No. 2 (Article 10)	Advocates	0	31	9	25
	Reservationists	33	0	33	1
	Irreconcilables	13	2	14	0
Reservation No. 3 (Mandates)	Advocates	3	30	24	4
	Reservationists	34	0	33	0
	Irreconcilables	15	1	11	0
Reservation No. 4 (Domestic questions)	Advocates	3	36	8	25
	Reservationists	39	0	34	0
	Irreconcilables	17	0	14	0
Reservation No. 5 (Monroe Doctrine)	Advocates	3	33	11	22
	Reservationists	38	1	34	0
	Irreconcilables	14	0	13	0
Reservation No. 6 (Shantung)	Advocates	0	38	5	20
	Reservationists	37	2	30	1
	Irreconcilables	16	1	13	0
Reservation No. 7 (Appointment of representatives)	Advocates	0	38	11	14
	Reservationists	39	0	31	0
	Irreconcilables	14	2	13	0
Reservation No. 8 (Reparations commission)	Advocates	0	38	2	20
	Reservationists	39	0	29	1
	Irreconcilables	15	2	10	1
Reservation No. 9 (Expenses of League)	Advocates	1	38	3	24
	Reservationists	39	0	29	1
	Irreconcilables	16	1	14	0
Reservation No. 10 (Armaments)	Advocates	1	38	5	25
	Reservationists	39	0	31	1
	Irreconcilables	16	1	13	0
Reservation No. 11 Covenant-breaking states)	Advocates	0	39	2	27
	Reservationists	38	0	30	1
	Irreconcilables	15	2	12	0
Reservation No. 12 (Illegal acts)	Advocates	0	38	5	26
	Reservationists	37	1	28	1
	Irreconcilables	15	2	12	0
Reservation No. 13 (International labor)	Advocates	2	33	2	26
	Reservationists	38	0	29	1
	Irreconcilables	14	2	13	0

		November, 1919		March, 1920	
		Yea	Nay	Yea	Nay
Reservation No. 14	Advocates	2	36	11	20
(Dominion votes)	Reservationists	38	1	33	0
	Irreconcilables	15	1	13	0
Reservation No. 15	Advocates			17	13
(Irish self-determination)	Reservationists			11	22
	Irreconcilables			10	1
Ratification With Reservations	Advocates	0	39	17	20
	Reservationists	39	0	32	0
	Irreconcilables	0	16	0	15
Ratification Without Reservations	Advocates	37	0		
	Reservationists	1	37		
	Irreconcilables	0	16		

their leaders would have gotten out the votes had not the affirmative votes of the irreconcilables removed any doubts as to the outcome. So the irreconcilables first joined one group in putting reservations into the resolution of ratification and then voted against the resolution with the third group whose opposition was caused by those reservations.

The rejection of the treaty caused great amazement and immediately a widespread demand arose for renewed efforts to effect a compromise. It seemed absurd that the national policy adopted should be the one advocated by only 17 senators. Common sense revolted at seeing the votes of 78 senators to enter the league nullified because they could not agree among themselves on the terms of entry. Many Republican newspapers and Republican leaders outside the Senate joined with the Democrats in refusing to accept the decision reached by such means. Spurred on by this pressure the mild reservationists began to seek a basis for common action with the Democrats.[97]

[97] The best account of these compromise negotiations is in the article of H. Maurice Darling, entitled "Who Kept the United States Out of the League of Nations?" in the *Canadian Historical Review,* X, 196-211. It is based in part on newspaper reports and in part on statements furnished him by some of the senators participating in the conferences. Senator Colt, a Republican from Rhode Island, and Senator McKellar, a Democrat from Tennessee, initiated the movement according to an account written by the latter. *Ibid.,* pp. 199-200. Lodge's version reads as if he had been responsible for the affair, although he frankly asserts he entered it not to reach a compromise but to make plain to the

After a number had agreed upon tentative terms the leaders of the two parties were added to the group which became known as the " Bi-partisan Conference." Notwithstanding the presence of Lodge such progress was made in the discussions, which were kept secret, that newspapers of all persuasions stated that the deadlock was nearly broken and the prospects for passing the treaty were bright. This situation called forth storms of protest from the irreconcilables as well as threats of leaving the party. There is a dramatic story that on January 23, 1920, they called Lodge from what was to be the crucial meeting of the Bi-Partisan Conference and harangued him for three hours in Senator Johnson's office during which time the conference got tired of waiting and adjourned.[98] However, in view of the record, it is doubtful that Lodge would have accepted any significant reductions in his reservations so long as the mild reservationists did not threaten to leave the party on that issue. The danger of a secession by them proved to be easily averted. Lodge kept them with him even when the Democrats offered to accept the Taft reservation to Article 10, " the heart of the covenant,"—a reservation which expressly disavowed any obligation and which, therefore, conceded all that the Republicans wanted, according to Lodge's statement of two days earlier.[99]

In spite of the failure of the Bi-partisan Conference to reach an agreement the treaty again came before the Senate. On February 9 the Senate reconsidered its vote of November 19 and sent the treaty back to committee, on the next day it was reported to the Senate from committee, and on February 16 the debate was resumed. This second vote, taken in deference to public opinion, constituted a test of the loyalty of the Democrats to Wilson and of their determination to adhere to their former course. Everyone realized that the Republican

world that a compromise could not be reached. *The Senate and the League of Nations,* p. 193.

[98] New York *Times,* Jan. 22, 23, 24, 1920. Darling, pp. 205-206. Fleming, pp. 407-410. Lodge, *The Senate and the League of Nations,* p. 194.

[99] Darling, p. 208.

senators would preserve their unity in passing the Lodge reservations without essential changes. Everyone knew how the irreconcilables would then vote on the resolution of ratification. The only question open was whether enough Democrats would consider there was no other alternative and would prefer the Lodge reservations to a complete rejection. Again many undoubtedly sincere advocates of the league pled with the Democrats to take what was possible. But again Wilson wrote a letter from his sick-bed in the White House urging his Democratic followers to stand firm against nullifying reservations. The Lodge reservation to Article 10, he wrote, "cuts at the very heart and life of the covenant itself." After explaining the reasons for this statement, he gave his conclusion that "either we should enter the league fearlessly, accepting the responsibility and not fearing the rôle of leadership which we now enjoy, . . . or we should retire as gracefully as possible from the great concert of powers by which the world was saved." [100] Wilson still hoped that public opinion would compel the ratification of the treaty with no more than interpretative reservations and his faith in the people made him willing to wait for the approaching national election.[101]

The final vote in the Senate took place on March 19, 1920. Before then the fourteen Lodge reservations had again been made a part of the resolution of ratification with a few immaterial verbal changes, and to them was added a new reservation expressing sympathy with the "aspirations of the Irish people for a government of their own choice." With these fifteen

[100] *Congressional Record,* Mar. 9, 1920, p. 4052.

[101] Senator Hitchcock shared Wilson's hopes and perhaps contributed to them since he was one of the very few persons admitted to the isolated sick-room. Henry White, who expressed irritation at Hitchcock's management, wrote to his son that "Hitchcock has a light and airy way of treating the subject every time I talk to him about it, the last occasion being two or three evenings ago, when he said he thought it would be rejected and then lie fallow for four or five weeks, and then the pressure on the Republicans would be so great to get it out of the way that they would have to make concessions to the President and that then it might be got through." Nevins, *Henry White,* p. 482.

reservations the resolution of ratification received a majority of the votes cast but not the requisite two-thirds majority, 49 votes being in favor of it and 35 being opposed.[102]

The analysis of the voting during this second struggle over the treaty discloses some significant similarities and contrasts with the voting in November. As before, the Republican senators cast a practically solid party vote for the Lodge reservations. The only exception was the vote of Senator Nelson against the twelfth reservation. In contrast with this Republican unity the Democrats split decidedly and many more of them than on the former occasion voted for the Lodge reservations. The fifteenth reservation concerning Irish independence was a Democratic contribution. It was introduced by a Democrat and it alone of the reservations was put in by Democratic votes since more than half of the Republicans who voted opposed it. There were Democrats who, like Lodge, appreciated the importance of the Irish vote to their party. On the final vote of ratification the Republican ranks broke as they had in November. Twenty-eight of the Republican senators, or more than two-thirds of the number voting, favored the ratification of the treaty with the reservations. Twelve Republicans again deserted their party and voted against ratification with reservations. The Democrats voting divided almost equally, 21 for ratification and 23 against.

Of the 21 Democrats voting for the treaty, 4 were reservationists who had refused to vote for the treaty without reservations in November. The other 17, and the 2 Democrats paired in favor of the treaty refused for the first time to support the policy of their party leaders. They too had wanted the treaty without any reservations, but preferred to take what was offered rather than to risk losing all.[103] Of the 23 Democrats who op-

[102] Eight senators were paired in favor of the treaty against four who would have voted in the negative had they not been paired. Six of the eight were Republicans, and three of the four recorded in the negative were Republicans. Hence of the total membership of the Senate 57 were recorded in favor of the resolution of ratification and 39 against it.

[103] In one of the few notable speeches of the entire debate Senator Walsh of Montana eloquently stated the position of these Democrats, *Congressional Record,* Mar. 19, 1920, pp. 4581-4585.

posed the treaty, 3 were irreconcilables and 20 were senators who had voted for the treaty without reservations in November and against it with the Lodge reservations. These 20, and the one Democrat paired in the negative, followed Wilson's advice and leadership. All of them were from Southern states except Hitchcock of Nebraska and Johnson of South Dakota. Had Wilson not used his influence on the Democrats the resolution of ratification would certainly have passed, since a two-thirds majority would have been obtained if only seven of this loyal band of 21 had transferred their votes.[104]

Wilson's success in commanding the support of some of the Democratic senators shared responsibility for the rejection of the treaty with Lodge's failure as a leader. If Lodge had been able to hold all the Republican senators to the program of his party, the treaty would have received the approval of the Senate by an ample margin. But the irreconcilable Republicans, increased to the number of 15 by the addition of Penrose, repeated their desertion of November. After voting solidly with their party in favor of the reservations that made 21 Democrats oppose the treaty, they left their fellow-Republicans and joined the 21 Democrats in opposition. Twelve of them voted in the negative on the resolution of ratification, the other three being paired on the same side. Thus the policy of the Republican party was defeated by this break in its ranks. As the party leader Lodge had failed. As a true irreconcilable himself, he could view his management with satisfaction although it meant the conquest of the majority he led by the minority of his party.[105]

[104] According to Lodge, Wilson "was obliged to exert all his power to prevent its acceptance with the reservations, and two of his Cabinet officers were on the floor of the Senate on that last day using every possible effort to keep enough Democrats in line to assure the defeat of the Treaty." *The Senate and the League of Nations,* p. 214.

[105] Although the treaty was defeated, the irreconcilables did not commit the Republican party to that policy until later. During the presidential campaign they gained much ground but the issue was confused. It was not until after the election that they finally won and the party adopted their policy. The result

Notwithstanding the deceptive division of both parties on the final vote, politics had killed another treaty—the most distinguished on its long list of victims. There were, however, other considerations that helped determine the action of the Senate. None of these minor factors had as much weight as the senatorial desire to assert the Senate's powers in making treaties. The Senate was the equal partner of the President in making treaties. The Senate must protect its powers from an autocratic President by insisting upon altering the treaty he had signed. That refrain was constantly present throughout the entire controversy, accentuating and supplementing the dominant theme of politics. It was on appeals to the Senate's jealousy of its powers that the irreconcilables chiefly depended in their early efforts to rally the Republican majority to an attack on Wilson's program. Scarcely a speech was made by the opposition in which some variation of this idea was not included.

To have the Senate alter or reject a treaty merely as a means of asserting its powers against the President was nothing new. As Viscount Grey explained to a bewildered British public, "The American Constitution not only makes possible, but under certain conditions renders inevitable, a conflict between the Executive and the Legislature." [106] In 1919 conditions were such that the conflict was not only inevitable but was certain to be ruthless. The war had made Wilson a dictator and had reduced Congress to negligible proportions both in power and in public attention. The crisis had compelled Congress to do what the President wanted or to sanction what he had already done. Once the war was ended the Senate, as the stronger branch of Congress, attempted to restore the balance of power in the government. Consequently the treaty of peace containing the outstanding issue of the period was certain to serve as a battle-

was due to continued hard fighting by the irreconcilables and a humiliating surrender by those Republican leaders like Hoover, Hughes and Stimson, who had assured the country they and the Republican party wanted the United States to join the league but who permitted the irreconcilable policy to be imposed without a struggle.

[106] From his letter to the London *Times* of Jan. 31, 1920.

ground, and one where the Senate was in an advantageous position because of the constitutional provision requiring a two-thirds majority. Moreover, the Senate received more public support in its contest than under ordinary circumstances. The dictatorship had irritated many, even of those who had wanted it. They and all who had been forced to suppress their hostility to Wilson's policies now applauded the senators opposing the President with the cry of " no autocracy."

Probably there were few in or out of the Senate who honestly believed it would have been proper for the Senate to execute the plan suggested by Senator Cummins. Before the peace conference opened, that defender of the Senate's prerogatives introduced a resolution into the Senate providing that eight senators should proceed to the conference and acquaint themselves with everything that transpired.[107] The mere suggestion of such a plan for the first time in the history of the United States was significant. The same claim that the Senate should participate in the negotiations was made by others. Senator Lodge, as has already been noted, demanded that procedure on a number of occasions, notably in his speech of December 21, 1918. With an amazing disregard of both his former statements and precedent he tried to make it appear that the President departed from American tradition by not consulting the Senate during the negotiations.[108] The senators who signed the round-robin expressed the same theory and were attempting to act on it.

Although these efforts to extend the powers of the Senate to the extent of participating in the making of the treaty failed, they did create an atmosphere favorable to the re-making of the treaty when the Senate had its opportunity. The impression spread that the President had invaded the rights of the Senate.

[107] *Congressional Record,* Dec. 2, 1918, pp. 3-5.

[108] His extreme sensitiveness on this subject was illustrated by a statement in his *apologia.* When the President, he wrote, directly or by implication advanced the proposition that the Senate was bound to accept the Versailles treaty he was attempting " to overthrow the powers of the Senate and thus indirectly to violate and set aside the provisions of the Constitution." *The Senate and the League of Nations,* p. 121.

Time after time this note was struck. A typical example occurred in a speech by Senator Spencer. "The President," he asserted, "alone pursued his course, without any conference with the country he represented and with special disregard of the Senate, which, by the Constitution of the United States is made his legal adviser, particularly in connection with treaties." [109] The results of this attitude can be seen not only in the insistence of senators on changes merely as a method of vindicating their powers but also in the changes made. A number of the reservations defined the way in which the United States should reach a decision in certain cases and each time the powers of Congress were specifically protected. The most glaring instance of this was in the first reservation which stated that a notice of withdrawal from the league might be given by a concurrent resolution of the Congress of the United States. A concurrent resolution requires a majority of both houses of Congress but not the signature of the President so the latter was not to participate in the making of that important decision. Indeed the hostility of the Senate toward the Executive was so strong and so disastrous for the treaty that two Republican mild reservationists made the statement—astounding in the American Congress—that they favored a parliamentary system in which such friction was impossible.[110] The victory of the Senate over the President ushered in a period during which the Senate dictated foreign policy as it had never done before.

Yet the constitutional struggle of the Senate against the President was subordinated to politics. Only Republicans entered the battle in defense of the Senate's prerogatives. The Democrats, with the exception of the very few who fought Wilson, saw no invasion of the rights of the Senate. This division proved the supremacy of political considerations. A Republican senator gave evidence to the same effect. In speaking of the first reservation McCumber said, "I am satisfied that if we had a Republican President today we would not be insisting

[109] *Congressional Record,* Mar. 5, 1920, p. 3896.
[110] *Ibid.,* Nov. 8, 1919, pp. 8135, 8136.

that he should be eliminated from any voice in the matter of any future action that we might take in respect to staying in or getting out of this league of nations." [111]

Politics and the contest over the treaty-making power were not the only forces in the Senate operating against the Versailles treaty. A third, although relatively minor, factor was the personal hatred of Wilson which other senators besides Lodge felt. Wilson aroused more hatred than any President since the days of Lincoln and Johnson. Naturally no senator publicly admitted either the sentiment or its influence. Nevertheless it was reflected in many speeches, and other senators believed it swayed some individuals. Senator Walsh of Montana, who did not indulge in intemperate statements, evidently believed it a factor of importance. "I undertake to say," he asserted, "that nine out of ten letters I get in protest against this treaty breathe a spirit of intense hatred of Woodrow Wilson . . . , and I am led to believe that that feeling forms a very large element in the opposition to this treaty; but I am astounded that Senators of the United States should allow considerations of that character to influence their judgment." [112]

Combined with these three unworthy causes of opposition was a fourth which was entirely proper. This was the desire to return to the traditional policy of isolation. Some persons must have believed sincerely in the superior wisdom of that policy and must have reached that conclusion through a judgment on the merits of the two policies and not through political or other irrelevant prejudices. The public which with no discernible exceptions had approved the new policy began to swing back in the other direction. Undoubtedly the recrudescence

[111] *Ibid.,* Nov. 7, 1919, p. 8077.

[112] *Ibid.,* Nov. 8, 1919, p. 8131. Senator Robinson had just made the same accusation. "I am not asserting that any Senator is consciously or unconsciously moved to support the measure by a purpose to humiliate the present Chief Executive. I merely declare that such motives are unworthy of Senators, and that the subject must be decided on a higher plane, and I inquire what is the motive behind the provision." *Ibid.,* p. 8126. See also the opinion of Senator McCumber, *Ibid.,* Nov. 7, 1919, p. 8077.

of isolationism was also felt in the Senate. The extent to which it influenced individual senators cannot be measured. But it can be asserted with as much certainty as is possible in human affairs that a sincere belief based on the merits of the issue was not the dominant cause of the Senate's action. It was the reservations that killed the treaty. And in adopting them the Senate divided on party lines, all the Republicans for them and practically all the Democrats against them. Such a division eliminates all doubts.

The fate of the treaty of Versailles turned the attention of thoughtful people to the treaty-making power of the United States. They saw that the exercise of that power had produced such bitter conflicts between the President and the Senate and had so increased the opportunities for political warfare unconnected with the merits of the question that many treaties had been lost. They knew that the ratification of nearly every important treaty had been endangered by a constitutional system which, instead of permitting a decision solely on the merits of the question, produces impotence and friction. They realized that if no disaster had resulted it was due partly to good fortune and chiefly to the relative unimportance of foreign relations in the history of the United States so that few treaties had contained vital issues. They also realized that, if the United States was to play the part in world affairs demanded by its interests and its strength, a deadlock between the President and the Senate over a treaty involving a really critical foreign problem may end in ruin.

BIBLIOGRAPHY

THE MOTIVES OF THE SENATE

In seeking the reasons or influences that caused senators to vote as they did it is necessary to rely on (A) deductions from the official record of what happened, (B) the testimony of senators, Presidents, members of the Cabinet and diplomatists who participated in the proceedings or had an official relation to the affair, and (C) the opinions of contemporary observers who enjoyed no official connection.

A. Since nearly all the treaties have been considered in secret or executive session the official record of the Senate's action in each case is to be found in the *Journal of the Executive Proceedings of the Senate of the United States.* None of the arguments used or speeches made are published in this *Journal* which contains only the recorded votes on amendments, resolutions of ratification or any other action taken. So far 32 volumes of the *Executive Journal,* covering the period from 1789 to March 9, 1901, have been issued. The first order for printing the *Journal* was given on April 4, 1828, and resulted in the publication of the first 3 volumes, in an edition of 700 copies, covering the first 20 Congresses. It was 58 years later before another order for printing was given. Then, on June 28, 1886, the *Journal* from the 20th to the close of the 40th Congress was ordered to be published and volumes 4 to 16 were issued. The edition was only 125 copies, 76 of which were immediately distributed to members of the Senate. The next order for printing was given on January 21, 1901, when it was provided that the *Journal* should be published to the end of the 51st Congress, or March, 1891. This edition, including volumes 17 to 27, was 250 copies. The last order provided for the printing of the *Journal* through the 58th Congress, March, 1905, but only volumes 28 to 32 have been issued. The injunction of secrecy has not yet been removed from the other volumes then printed, and no further orders for printing have been given. This edition was also 250 copies.

The official record next in importance to the *Executive Journal* is that which contains the verbatim debates of Congress and which has been published under the titles *Annals of the Congress of the United States, Register of Debates in Congress, Congressional Globe,* and finally under the present title *Congressional Record.* This publication contains the full proceedings, including everything said as well as done, on the fisheries treaty of 1888, the Taft arbitration treaties of 1911, and the Versailles treaty. These, and these alone before 1920, were considered by the Senate in open executive session. Nevertheless the *Congressional Record* and its predecessors are of value in connection with other treaties. There have been numerous occasions when references have been made in debates in both Houses of Congress which throw light on the attitude of members of the Senate toward a treaty.

A third official record, but one of far less value than the two already mentioned, is the *Compilation of Reports of Committee on Foreign Relations, United States Senate, 1789-1901.* These 8 volumes, compiled by the clerk of the committee, are very unsatisfactory. Only a fraction of the reports mentioned in the *Journal* are included here. Many of those printed are the very ones printed in full in the *Journal.* There was no Committee on Foreign Relations prior to 1816 yet reports for that period are included. Many of the reports, of course, have nothing to do with the defeated treaties. These were printed as *56th Cong., 2d sess., S. Doc.* No. 231.

B. The best direct evidence of the motives influencing members of the Senate can be found in the private letters and diaries of senators, Presidents and members of the Cabinet who were interested in the fate of a treaty. Practically nothing can be found in the official diplomatic correspondence of the Secretary of State. Explanations of the motives of the Senate have almost never been offered to foreign governments through official channels. Olney, for example, wanted the British government to understand what caused the rejection of the arbitration treaty of 1897, but used a private letter to convey his explanation. The official despatches of foreign governments, especially those from diplomatic representatives to their home governments, are of inestimable value. Naturally a diplomat watches the course through the Senate of a treaty his government has signed with the United States. He is almost certain to discover everything he can regarding the reasons for senatorial opposition and to send reports on that subject. Occasionally a statement of this kind has been published by the government concerned, as in the *British Parliamentary Papers,* but such cases are rare. Unfortunately, also, defeated treaties have been more numerous since the Civil War—or so recently that the archives of most foreign governments are relatively inaccessible. If the photostat collection of such material now being gathered by the Library of Congress is continued, it will add greatly to our knowledge on this as well as on other subjects.

In listing the books or sources containing the private correspondence of this nature which I have used, I have deliberately mingled printed and manucsript material because the historical value of the evidence does not depend on whether or not it happens to be in print. The biographies included have been used only as sources from which to quote letters.

Adams, Charles F., editor, *Memoirs of John Quincy Adams.* 12 vol. Philadelphia, 1874-1877.

Adams, Ephraim D., editor, *British Diplomatic Correspondence concerning the Republic of Texas, 1833-1846.* Austin, 1918.

Ambler, Charles H., editor, *Correspondence of Robert M. T. Hunter.* Washington, 1918. Published as vol. ii of the *Annual Report of the American Historical Association for 1916.*

Baker, George E., editor, *The Works of William H. Seward.* 5 vol. Boston, 1884.

Baker, Ray Stannard, *Woodrow Wilson, Life and Letters.* 4 vol. New York, 1927-1931.

Bancroft, Frederic, *The Life of William H. Seward.* 2 vol. New York, 1900.

————, editor, *Speeches, Correspondence and Political Papers of Carl Schurz.* 6 vol. New York, 1913.

Benton, Thomas H., *Thirty Years View.* 2 vol. New York, 1863.

Bigelow, John, *Retrospections of an Active Life.* 5 vol. New York, 1913.

Bishop, Joseph Bucklin, *Theodore Roosevelt and His Time.* 2 vol. New York, 1920.

Blaine, James G., *Twenty Years of Congress.* 2 vol. Norwich, Conn., 1886.

Bonaparte. Charles J. Bonaparte Papers, Library of Congress.

Bowers, Claude G., *Beveridge and the Progressive Era.* Boston, 1932.

Brown, Everett S., editor, *William Plumer's Memorandum of Proceedings in the United States Senate, 1803-1807.* New York, 1923.

Bryan. William Jennings Bryan Papers, Library of Congress.

Carnegie, Andrew, *Autobiography of Andrew Carnegie.* Boston, 1920.

Chandler. William E. Chandler Papers, Library of Congress.

Coolidge, Louis A., *An Old Fashioned Senator, Orville H. Platt.* New York, 1910.

Cortissoz, Royal, *The Life of Whitelaw Reid.* 2 vol. New York, 1921.

Cox, Jacob D., "How Judge Hoar Ceased To Be Attorney-General" in *Atlantic Monthly,* vol. lxxvi, No. 454.

Cullom, Shelby M., *Fifty Years of Public Service.* Chicago, 1911.

Curtis, George T., *Life of Daniel Webster.* 2 vol. New York, 1870

Doolittle. James R. Doolittle Papers, Library of Congress.

Fitzpatrick, John C., editor, *The Autobiography of Martin Van Buren.* Washington, 1920. Published as vol. ii of *Annual Report of the American Historical Association for 1918.*

Foster, John W., *Diplomatic Memoirs.* 2 vol. New York, 1909.

Foulke, William D., *Life of Oliver P. Morton.* 2 vol. Indianapolis, 1899.

Garrison, George P., editor, *Diplomatic Correspondence of the Republic of Texas.* Published as vol. ii of the *Annual Report of the American Historical Association for 1907.*

Gresham, Matilda, *Life of Walter Quintin Gresham.* 2 vol. Chicago, 1919.

readily available in the usual sources, resort has been had to biographies, local histories, or contemporaneous newspapers. The greatest difficulties are presented in those periods when political parties are in a state of transition and a senator, elected on one ticket, runs on a different one at the next election. What to call him in between elections or at what point he changed parties is a problem. Another difficulty is presented by the senators elected by a coalition in the state legislature, such as the frequent combinations in the free silver-populist movement. Such men, like the independents, usually drifted to one party or the other before the next election, but in the interim their status is often doubtful. The principal sources used to determine the party affiliations of senators are, (A) the various Congressional directories and (B) some secondary studies.

A. The Congressional directories are of two kinds, one listing the members of a particular Congress and the second containing the names of all members of Congress since the beginning. The early directories for each Congress did not give the party to which each member belonged, but since the 40th Congress, 1867-1869, the small biographical sketches of the members regularly included furnish that information. Because the sketches are written by the members themselves the statements regarding their party affiliations are the most authentic possible. The first composite directory to include the members of all preceding Congresses was compiled by Charles Lanman in the 1860s. Subsequently six later editions of it were issued as government documents but each compiler did little but add the data to be found in the later annual directories. A new compilation made by Ansel Wold, clerk of the Joint Committee on Printing, was published in 1928 with the title, *Biographical Directory of the American Congress, 1774-1927*. It was issued as *H. Doc.* No. 783, *66 Cong., 2d sess.*

B. The secondary studies dealing with political affiliations which have been cited are:

Bancroft, Frederic, and Dunning, William A., "Sketch of Carl Schurz's Political Career, 1869-1901" in *The Reminiscences of Carl Schurz,* vol. iii.

Beard, Charles A., *Economic Origins of Jeffersonian Democracy.* New York, 1915.

Bowers, Claude G., *Jefferson and Hamilton.* New York, 1925.

———, *The Party Battles of the Jackson Period.* New York, 1924.

Dunning, William A., "The Second Birth of the Republican Party" in *American Historical Review,* vol. xvi.

Libby, Orin G., "A Plea for the Study of Votes in Congress," in the *Annual Report of the American Historical Association for 1896.* Washington, 1897.

Lowell, A. Lawrence, "The Influence of Party upon Legislation in England and America," in the *Annual Report of the American Historical Association, 1901,* vol. i.

Phillips, Ulrich B., "The South Carolina Federalists" in the *American Historical Review,* vol. xiv.

Ross, Earle D., *The Liberal Republican Movement.* New York, 1919.

Stanwood, Edward, *A History of the Presidency from 1788 to 1897.* New York, 1898.

The Treaties and Their Diplomatic Setting

Until 1932, the task of discovering the defeated treaties was a severe one, and only possible by turning the pages of the *Executive Journal of the Senate.* In 1932, however, an official list of the unperfected treaties was published by the Department of State as Publication No. 382, under the title, *List of Treaties Submitted to the Senate, 1789-1931, Which Have Not Gone Into Force.* This includes all the treaties that failed of ratification and supplies the further information showing which were rejected, amended, withdrawn, accepted by the Senate, or on which no final action was taken.

The treaties that were ratified can be found in Malloy, William M., compiler, *Treaties, Conventions, International Acts, Protocols and Agreements between the United States and Other Powers. 1776-1923.* 3 volumes. The first two volumes were published as *61st Cong., 2d sess., S. Doc.* No. 357. The third volume, covering the years 1910-1923, was printed as *67th Cong., 4th sess., S. Doc.* No. 348. It includes a chronological list of all treaties perfected.

To understand the foreign policies presented in the defeated treaties and their diplomatic setting I have relied on the official diplomatic correspondence and on secondary studies. In only one case did I find it necessary for my purposes to consult the official correspondence in manuscript in the archives of the Department of State. Not being primarily interested in the diplomatic negotiations the published correspondence sufficed. Extracts of this correspondence for the period before 1828 were published in 6 volumes as *American State Papers, Foreign Relations, 1789-1828.* The familiar annual volume first published by the State Department in 1861 bore the title *Diplomatic Correspondence* until 1869 and has since been known as *Foreign Relations.* Some of the diplomatic correspondence between 1828 and 1861 was printed in Senate or House Documents. The burden of locating the material in this form has been lightened by the *Index to United States Documents Relating to Foreign Affairs,* 1828-1861, prepared in 3 volumes by Adelaide R. Hasse and published by the Carnegie Institution of Washington. It would serve no useful purpose to list the many Senate Documents cited in the footnotes.

The secondary works cited are as follows:

Adams, Charles F., *Lee at Appomattox and Other Papers.* Boston, 1902.

Adams, Ephraim D., *British Interests and Activities in Texas, 1838-1846.* Baltimore, 1910.

———, "Lord Ashburton and the Treaty of Washington" in *American Historical Review,* vol. xvii.

Adams, Henry, "The Session" in *North American Review,* vol. cviii.

———, "The Session" in *North American Review,* vol. cxiii.

Baker, Ray Stannard, *Woodrow Wilson and World Settlement.* 3 vol. New York, 1922.

Bemis, Samuel F., editor, *The American Secretaries of State and Their Diplomacy.* 10 vol. New York, 1928.

———, *Jay's Treaty.* New York, 1924.

———, *Pinckney's Treaty.* Baltimore, 1926.

Callahan, James M., *American Relations in the Pacific and the Far East.* Baltimore, 1901.

———, "The Mexican Policy of Southern Leaders under Buchanan's Administration" in the *Annual Report of the American Historical Association for 1910,* pp. 135-151.

Dana, Charles S., "Theodore Roosevelt and Tiberius Gracchus", *North American Review,* vol. clxxx.

Darling, H. Maurice, "Who Kept the United States Out of the League of Nations?", *Canadian Historical Review,* vol. x.

Dennis, Alfred L. P., *Adventures in American Diplomacy, 1896-1906.* New York, 1928.

Dodd, William E., *Woodrow Wilson and His Work.* Garden City, N. Y., 1920.

Du Bois, W. E. Burghardt, *The Suppression of the African Slave Trade to the United States of America, 1638-1870.* Harvard Historical Studies, vol. i. New York, 1896.

Dunbar, Edward E., *The Mexican Papers.* New York, 1860-1861.

Dunning, William A., *The British Empire and the United States.* New York, 1914.

———, "Paying for Alaska" in *Political Science Quarterly,* vol. xxvii.

Finch, George A., "The Treaty of Peace with Germany in the United States Senate" in *American Journal of International Law,* vol. xiv.

Fish, Andrew, "The Last Phase of the Oregon Boundary Question" in *Quarterly of the Oregon Historical Society,* vol. xxi.

Fisk, George M., *Die handelspolitischen und sonstigen volkerrechtlichen Beziehungen zwischen Deutschland und den Vereinigten Staaten von Amerika.* Stuttgart, 1897.

Fleming, Denna F., *The United States and the League of Nations, 1918-1920.* New York, 1932.

Fogdall, Soren J. M. P., "Danish American Diplomacy," in *University of Iowa Studies,* vol. viii, No. 2.
Foster, John W., *American Diplomacy in the Orient.* New York, 1903.
Garber, Paul N., *The Gadsden Treaty.* Philadelphia, 1923.
Golder, Frank A., "The Purchase of Alaska" in *American Historical Review,* vol. xxv.
———, "The Russian Fleet and the Civil War" in *American Historical Review,* vol. xx.
Gordon, Leland J., *American Relations with Turkey, 1830-1930.* Philadelphia, 1932.
Hayden, Ralston, *The Senate and Treaties, 1789-1817.* New York, 1920.
———, "The States' Rights Doctrine and the Treaty-Making Power" in *American Historical Review,* vol. xxii.
Henderson, John B., Jr., *American Diplomatic Questions.* New York, 1901.
Hill, Howard C., *Roosevelt and the Caribbean.* Chicago, 1927.
Howland, Charles P., editor, *Survey of American Foreign Relations, 1928.* New Haven, 1928.
Johnson, Willis F., *America's Foreign Relations.* 2 vol. New York, 1916.
———, *George Harvey, a Passionate Patriot.* Boston, 1929.
———, "The Story of the Danish Islands" in *North American Review,* vol. cciv.
Latané, John H., *America As a World Power.* New York, 1907.
———, editor, *Development of the League of Nations Idea. Documents and Correspondence of Theodore Marburg.* 2 vol. New York, 1932.
Laughlin, J. Lawrence and Willis, H. Parker, *Reciprocity.* New York, 1903.
Manning, William R., *Early Diplomatic Relations between the United States and Mexico.* Baltimore, 1916.
Marburg, Theodore, and Flack, H. C., editors, *Taft Papers on the League Of Nations.* New York, 1920.
Miller, David Hunter, *The Drafting of the Covenant.* New York, 1928.
Moore, John Bassett, *History and Digest of the International Arbitrations to Which the United States Has Been a Party.* 6 vol. Washington, 1898.
———, *A Treatise on Extradition and Interstate Rendition.* 2 vol. Boston, 1891.
Newlands, Francis G., "The San Domingo Question," *North American Review,* vol. clxxx.
Parton, James, *The Danish Islands.* Boston, 1869.
Paullin, Charles O., *Diplomatic Negotiations of American Naval Officers, 1778-1883.* Baltimore, 1912.
———, "The Opening of Korea by Commodore Shufeldt" in *Political Science Quarterly,* vol. xxv.
Putnam, George H., *The Question of Copyright.* New York, 1891.
Reeves, Jesse S., *American Diplomacy under Tyler and Polk.* Baltimore, 1907.
Rippy, J. Fred., *The United States and Mexico.* New York, 1926.

Rivas, Raimundo, *Relaciones Internacionales entre Colombia y los Estados Unidos.* Bogota, 1915.
Robinson, Chalfant, *A History of Two Reciprocity Treaties.* New Haven, 1904.
Scott, James Brown, *Treaties for the Advancement of Peace.* New York, 1920.
Smith, Justin H., *The Annexation of Texas.* New York, 1911.
———, *The War with Mexico.* 2 vol. New York, 1919.
Smith, Theodore C., " Expansion after the Civil War " in *Political Science Quarterly,* vol. xvi.
Tansill, Charles C., " The Canadian Reciprocity Treaty of 1854 " in *Johns Hopkins University Studies,* vol. xv, No. 2.
———, *The Purchase of the Danish West Indies.* Baltimore, 1932.
Temperley, Harold W. V., editor, *A History of the Peace Conference of Paris.* 6 vol. London, 1920-1924.
Travis, Ira D., *The History of the Clayton-Bulwer Treaty.* Ann Arbor, Michigan, 1900.
Updyke, Frank A., *The Diplomacy of the War of 1812.* Baltimore, 1914.
Villard, Oswald Garrison, " Henry Cabot Lodge—A Scholar in Politics," *The Nation,* vol. cxix.
Whitaker, Arthur P., *The Spanish-American Frontier; 1783-1795.* Boston, 1927.
Williams, Mary W., *Anglo-American Isthmian Diplomacy, 1815-1915.* Washington, 1916.
Wilson, Beckles, *America's Ambassadors To England.* New York, 1929.
Wilson, Howard L., " President Buchanan's Proposed Intervention in Mexico " in *American Historical Review,* vol. v.
Zimmermann, Alfred, *Geschichte der preussisch-deutschen Handelspolitik.* Leipzig, 1892.

Miscellaneous Works

Some of these general works are cited as authorities for the story, but others are used as illustrations of what historians have said. Others are non-historical studies of the Senate and especially of its participation in the treaty-making power. The books cited are:

Adams, Henry, *The Education of Henry Adams.* New York, 1918.
———, *History of the United States of America.* 9 vol. New York, 1889-1891.
Bancroft, Hubert H., *History of Mexico.* 6 vol. San Francisco, 1890.
Broglie, Achille C. L. U., duc de, *Vues sur le Gouvernement de la France.* Paris, 1872.
Butler, Charles H., *The Treaty-Making Power of the United States.* 2 vol. New York, 1902.
Channing, Edward, *A History of the United States.* 6 vol. New York, 1905-1925.

Corwin, Edward S., *The President's Control of Foreign Relations.* Princeton, 1917.

Crandall, Samuel B., *Treaties, Their Making and Enforcement.* Second edition. Washington, 1916.

Dawes, Anna L., *Charles Sumner.* New York, 1892.

Elliot, Jonathan, editor, *The Debates in the Several State Conventions on the Adoption of the Federal Constitution.* 5 vol. 1836-1845.

Farrand, Max, *The Framing of the Constitution of the United States.* New Haven, 1913.

———, editor, *The Records of the Federal Convention of 1787.* 3 vol. New Haven, 1911.

Fleming, Denna, F., *The Treaty Veto of the American Senate.* New York, 1930.

Hogarth, D. G., *Accidents of an Antiquary's Life.* London, 1910.

Hudson, Manley O., "The 'Injunction of Secrecy' with Respect to American Treaties," *American Journal of International Law,* vol. xxiii.

Lodge, Henry C., editor, *The Federalist.* New York, 1888.

———, *The Senate of the United States.* New York, 1921.

———, "The Treaty-making Power of the Senate" in *A Fighting Frigate and Other Essays and Addresses.* New York, 1902.

Low, A. Maurice, "The Usurped Powers of the Senate," *American Political Science Review,* vol. i.

———, "The Oligarchy of the Senate" in *North American Review,* vol. clxxiv.

McCall, Samuel W., "The Power of the Senate," *Atlantic Monthly,* vol. xcii.

McMaster, John B., *A History of the People of the United States.* 8 vol. New York, 1883-1913.

McMaster, John B., and Stone, Frederick D., editors, *Pennsylvania and the Federal Constitution.* Philadelphia, 1888.

Mathews, John M., *The Conduct of American Foreign Relations.* New York, 1922.

Moore, John Bassett, *International Law and Some Current Illusions.* New York, 1924.

Nelson, Henry Loomis, "The Overshadowing Senate," *Century Magazine,* vol. lxv.

Peck, Harry T., *Twenty Years of the Republic, 1885-1905.* New York, 1907.

Rhodes, James F., *History of the United States from the Compromise of 1850.* 8 vol. New York, 1910-1919.

Sullivan, Mark, *Our Times: The United States, 1900-1925.* 4 vols., New York, 1927-1930.

Thach, Charles C., "The Creation of the Presidency, 1775-1789" in *Johns Hopkins University Studies,* Series XL, No. 4. Baltimore, 1922.

Vexler, Paul, *De L'Obligation de Ratifier les Traits.* Paris, 1924.

von Holst, Hermann E., *The Constitutional and Political History of the United States.* 8 vol. Chicago, 1889-1892.

Wheaton, Henry, *Elements of International Law.* Sixth edition. Boston, 1855.
Wilson, Henry, *History of the Rise and Fall of the Slave Power in America.* 3 vol. Boston, 1872-1877.
Wilson, Woodrow, *Congressional Government.* New York, 1885.
———, *Constitutional Government in the United States.* New York, 1908.
Wright, Quincy, *The Control of American Foreign Relations.* New York, 1922.
Wriston, Henry M., *Executive Agents in American Foreign Relations.* Baltimore, 1929.

INDEX